ARCO

Everything you need to score high

Words for Smart Test-Takers

SAT · ACT · GRE · GMAT · LSAT

Mark Alan Stewart

D1367174

Macmillan • USA

Macmillan Reference USA
A Simon & Schuster Macmillan Company
1633 Broadway
New York, NY 10019-6785

An ARCO Book

ARCO is a registered trademark of Simon & Schuster Inc.
MACMILLAN is a registered trademark of Macmillan, Inc.

Manufactured in th United States of America

10 9 8 7 6 5 4 3 2 1

Library of Congress Number: 97-80923

ISBN: 0-02-862188-3

Contents

5   Academic Challenge

33 Fields—from Anatomy to Zoology 119

1

The Smart Way
to Learn Words

By opening this book, you've made an important first step toward mastering those difficult vocabulary words that appear on the SAT, GRE, ACT, and MAT. This book was designed from the ground up to target the tests. It's packed with 100% "testworthy" words—those that only students with an educated vocabulary are likely to know. These are the words that the test-makers love to include on standardized exams—especially in exam questions involving analogies and antonyms, which test vocabulary directly.

This book targets the tests more directly than any other vocabulary book. Here you'll learn as many of the "right" words (words you don't already know but that are likely to appear on future exams) as efficiently as possible. You won't waste time reading about how to use a dictionary (you no doubt already know how). You won't wade through the finer points of etymology (word origins). And you won't learn definitions that, while acceptable, are not in common use today. That's what a good dictionary is for.

Before we get started learning words, let's first answer some frequently asked questions about learning words for standardized exams. Then we'll also take a look at alternative strategies for using this book to your best advantage.

Questions and Answers about Learning New Words

Q: *How is vocabulary measured on standardized exams?*

A: The SAT, GRE, and MAT all test your vocabulary head-on through the use of *analogy* questions, in which your task is to determine the relationship between words in pairs. The GRE also includes *antonym* questions, in which your task is to choose which word among five choices is most contrary (opposite) in meaning to a particular word. Analogy and antonym questions are essentially vocabulary questions. If you know the meaning of every word in the question, you'll probably get the question right. And the more words you know, the better your chances of narrowing down the choices to the correct one. The SAT also includes "vocabulary-in-context" questions, in which your task is to determine the meaning of words as used in particular sentences.

Many standardized tests, including the SAT, ACT, GRE, LSAT, GMAT, and MCAT, gauge your vocabulary *indirectly*, through the use of Reading Comprehension passages and questions. Test-takers with a strong vocabulary no doubt hold a slight advantage when it comes to these questions.

Q: *How do the test-makers choose words for the exams?*

A: The test-makers want to determine whether you possess a well-rounded, "educated" vocabulary—the kind of vocabulary you need to read, write, and speak effectively in college and beyond. Testworthy words include those that *any* educated person might use in speaking or writing, as well as those that are quite specific to particular academic fields. (On your test, there's a good chance you'll encounter at least one word from each of the 33 academic fields included in Chapter 5 of this book.) Consider, for example, these three words:

> *bib*
>
> *bibliophile*
>
> *bibelot*

The test-makers would not be interested in *bib* (a cloth hung around the neck) for the purpose of gauging your vocabulary, since it is a common word with which most people, even those without an educated vocabulary, are familiar.

The word *bibliophile* (a person who collects and/or appreciates books) is more testworthy. You may have heard it, but you might be unsure of its precise meaning. A person with a highly developed vocabulary will probably know the word's meaning. If not, he or she may be able to take an "educated guess" as to its meaning, since it is derived from the Greek words *biblio* (which means "book") and *philo* (which means "love").

The word *bibelot* (a small relic or artifact) is a good example of a testworthy word from a specific academic filed: anthropology. Only a small minority of test-takers would be familiar with this word; nevertheless, its meaning is readily understood by any educated person. So it's a good candidate for a more challenging exam question.

Q: *What kind of words won't I find on my exam and in this book?*

A: Here are the types of words excluded from this book—because they're not worthy (*test*worthy, that is):

- relatively common words that most high-school students already know

- highly technical words understood only by specialists or experts in certain academic fields and professions

- non-English words that are not widely used among English speakers, and non-English words with accent marks or other symbols

- informal jargon, slang, or colloquialisms

- archaic English words, which are no longer in common use

- phrases (two or more words)

Q: *Does this book include all the words I need to know for my exam?*

A: Of course not. The English language includes many thousands of testworthy words. Be forewarned: you *will* encounter new and unfamiliar words on your exam, no matter how thoroughly you've prepared. If you believe otherwise, either you're kidding yourself or you've committed to memory *Webster's Unabridged Dictionary* (in which case you certainly don't need this book).

Q: *How many of the words in this book will appear on my exam?*

A: Rest assured that *some* of the words in this book will appear on your exam. How many? Maybe two; maybe twenty; but probably somewhere between two and twenty. It's impossible to predict, since the test-makers continually change exam questions. If you don't think these odds make it worth your effort to learn new words for your exam, think again. Standardized testing is a "game of inches" in which just one additional correct answer can significantly enhance your scaled score and percentile ranking. So even if this book helps you get two or three questions correct that you otherwise would have missed, it's well worth the effort.

Q: *Why not save time and just study a short list of words appearing "most frequently" on my exam?*

A: This strategy would be a big mistake! Do you really think these words will continue to appear "most frequently" on future exams? If, so I've got swampland in Florida I'd like to sell to you. Sure, words from "top 100" or "hit parade" vocabulary lists will show up from time to time on future exams, so by all means learn them. (In fact, Chapter 3 of this book includes three such lists.) Be assured, however, that these words are *not* more likely than a host of other testworthy words (such as those in Chapters 4 through 7) to appear on your actual exam.

Q: *Can't I learn the words I need to know by taking simulated practice tests?*

A: No. You'll learn a few new words this way, but not nearly enough. Simulated testing is more useful for learning test-taking "skills"—analyzing questions and developing strategies for responding to them—than for improving vocabulary.

How to Get the Most out of this Book

Each of the following chapters in this book attacks vocabulary from a different angle, and many of the words appearing in one chapter will also appear in others, although usually in different contexts. This feature, along with the quizzes provided throughout each chapter, serve as a valuable review to help you fix new words in your memory.

You *could* read this book straight through from cover to cover, but consider alternative strategies. Focus first on certain chapters, or start with the "Quiz Time" quizzes, depending on how you prefer to learn new words and on how much time you have. Here's a brief description of each chapter, along with some suggestions for using your study time most effectively.

Chapter 2—Test Your Word Smarts. Start here to gauge your vocabulary in a testing format. This 44-word diagnostic quiz will help you become familiar with the kinds of words that appear throughout this book and on the exams.

Chapter 3—Words to the Wise. Start here for the most insightful analysis of specific words and to impress others in conversation. These are high-frequency

SAT and GRE words that are also useful in understanding and communicating with educated people. Illustrative sentences provide insight (and entertainment) as well as incorporating words that appear elsewhere in the book. Related words are also defined and distinguished. This is a good place to begin if you are *not* pressed for time.

Chapter 4—Confounding and Confusing Words. Start here to master many of the most confusing words the English language dishes up (words that look and/or sound "foreign" or similar to other words). This is a good place to start if you already have a powerful vocabulary but just need to fine-tune it or "brush up" for your exam.

Chapter 5—Academic Challenge. Start here for a focused approach toward specific academic areas. Thirty-three different fields—from Anatomy to Zoology—are represented. This chapter includes only the most testworthy words from each discipline, avoiding highly technical terms that only specialists in their fields understand.

Chapter 6—Flexibility Training (Prefixes and Roots). Start here if your time is limited and you need to take a flexible approach to improving your vocabulary. The most common roots, stems, and prefixes (most from either Latin or Greek) are listed here, along with testworthy words (and brief definitions) for each one.

Chapter 7—The A-to-Z List of Testworthy Words. Start here to cover many words as quickly as possible, without bothering with sample sentences. For each entry (headword), words that are similar and contrary in meaning are provided. Most of these words also appear elsewhere in the book, so you can review them later in different contexts.

Chapter 8—Word Games for Smart Test-takers. Start here for a highly interactive approach to learning new words by association. Each game deals with closely related words. Your job is to distinguish among them in either a grouping game or a matching game. Most of the words in Chapter 8 also appear elsewhere in the book. Thus, these games can also serve as a final review or test.

The "Quiz Time" Quizzes. Start here for a test-centered approach to learning new words. Quizzes are interspersed throughout the book. To find them quickly, check the Table of Contents. After taking a quiz and checking the answers, use the index to look up the words that stumped you.

Tips for Learning (and Remembering) New Words

If learning all of the words in this book seems an overwhelming task, remember that you can prioritize your study by starting with any chapter or with the quizzes. Here are seven tips that will help you build a smart vocabulary and boost your verbal test scores.

Tip #1: Break up the task into bite-size pieces. Don't try to learn hundreds of words in one session. You'll overload your mental circuits. Try tackling perhaps 20–30 words at a time. The words in this book are divided up this way to help you.

Tip #2: Take meaningful breaks between sessions. Limit yourself to three or four sessions per day (20–30 words per session), depending on how much time you have to prepare for your exam. Take meaningful breaks—at least a few hours—between study sessions.

Tip #3: Sleep on it. Study a new batch of words just before bedtime. Your mind is more likely to retain information received just prior to sleep. Don't be surprised if you hear a few of these words in your dreams!

Tip #4: Vocalize as you learn. Saying words aloud or hearing somebody else say them helps you to recall them later. Try reading sample sentences and definitions aloud as well.

Tip #5: Learn words in the context of a story. You remember new words more easily if you learn them in the context of a brief "story"—an interesting and instructive sentence or short paragraph. All of the words in Chapter 3 are presented this way. For the other words, make up your own stories. Try to include at least two or three "testworthy" words in each story.

Tip #6: Incorporate new words into everyday conversation. This may seem like hackneyed advice, but it's nevertheless good advice. Use new words as you converse with friends. As you do so, pause to explain what the word means, and ask your friend if he or she knows any similar or contrary words. You're bound to discover even more testworthy words this way!

Tip #7: Review, review, review. It's not enough to "learn" a word once. Unless you review it, the word will soon vanish from your memory banks. This book is packed with quizzes and word games to help refresh your memory.

About the Definitions and Phonetic Spellings in this Book

Every "headword" (main entry in bold capital letters) in this book is followed by its

phonetic spelling (which shows you how to pronounce the word)

part of speech [either noun (*n*), verb (*v*), or adjective (*adj*)]

definition (If a word includes more than one definition, the definitions are separated by semi-colons.)

Here's an example:

CHURLISH (CHER lish) *adj* peasantlike or rustic; crude, crass, or vulgar

The phonetic spelling "spells out" a word just the way it sounds when spoken, without those funny-looking marks you find in dictionaries. The syllable receiving primary emphasis is spelled with capital letters. Phonetic spellings for some spoken sounds, especially vowel sounds, can be a bit confusing—at least until you become accustomed to them. Here's a guide to help you properly interpret the phonetic spellings used in this book:

phonetic spelling	sample word	word spelled phonetically
a	cat	KAT
ah	otter	AH ter
ay	state	STAYT
	airplane	AYR playn
aw	awesome	AW sum
ee	neat	NEET
e *or* eh	necklace	NEK lis
	espouse	eh SPOWZ
i *or* ih	indicate	IN dih kayt
y	kite	KYT

oh	**o**pen	OH pin
oo	b**eau**tiful	BYOO tih ful
ow	c**ou**ch	KOWCH
u *or* uh	st**u**ck	STUK
	appreciate	uh PREE shee ayt
	b**u**lly	BUL ee
zh	excur**s**ion	eks KER zhun

Why bother with phonetic spellings, since standardized exams don't test on pronunciation? Well, if you're learning a new word, you might as well learn how to pronounce it correctly. Then you can incorporate it into your permanent *spoken* vocabulary. Imagine the impression you'll make when you use your new educated vocabulary in talking with your job interviewer, boss, teacher, colleagues, or classmates!

Words on the Web

If you are interested in learning even more words after completing this book, the World Wide Web offers lots of different ways to do it. Here are some vocabulary-building Web sites you may want to explore.

Dictionary.com
http://www.dictionary.com

Search for any headword (the word being defined) contained in *Webster's Revised Unabridged Dictionary* or *Roget's Thesaurus* directly from this Web page. Just type in a word and click! This site also includes links to an on-line version of *Bartlett's Familiar Quotations* (1901 Edition) as well as to a few on-line dictionaries of computer terminology. The thesaurus is also available at *http://www.thesaurus.com.*

Webster's Dictionary
http://humanities.uchicago.edu/forms_unrest/webster.form.html

An on-line version of *Webster's Revised Unabridged Dictionary* (1913 Edition); includes 109,562 entries. Perform simple "headword" searches or search the entire dictionary text. You can also perform floating (wild card) searches for words that contain strings of letters (e.g., prefixes or roots).

Roget's Thesaurus
http://www.thesaurus.com

Search the headwords or full text of Roget's Thesaurus (as supplemented, July 1991). Internal cross references are represented as clickable hyper-text links.

Webster's Dictionary—a hypertext interface
http://gs213.sp.cs.cmu.edu/prog/webster

This on-line search tool accesses on-line Webster's dictionaries and incorporates a hypertext interface; that is, it links headwords as well as key words in definitions to related words (and definitions). Very cool! A project of a former computer science student at Carnegie Mellon University.

2

Test Your
Word Smarts
With This 44-Word Warm-up Quiz

Before embarking on our journey into the vast sea of vocabulary, let's first "test the waters" with the 44-word warm-up quiz that begins on the next page. Be forewarned: these are tough words—just the kind you'll need to learn for your exam. Also, keep in mind that the format of this quiz does not conform to that of any specific standardized exam. The same is true for the other quizzes in this book.

Directions: For each word in bold letters, circle the answer choice—(a), (b), or (c)—that most closely suggests the meaning of the word. The answer choices are of the same part of speech (noun, verb, or adjective) as the original word. After completing the quiz, check the answers and definitions on pages 14 and 15.

The 44-Word Warm-up Quiz

1. **agape**
   (a) sentimental (b) gruesome (c) open

2. **artifice**
   (a) deception (b) argument (c) sculpture

3. **aver**
   (a) avert (b) assert (c) avoid

4. **baleful**
   (a) complete (b) sinister (c) loud

5. **belabor**
   (a) enslave (b) volunteer (c) repeat

6. **broach**
   (a) disappear (b) decorate (c) propose

7. **castigate**
   (a) investigate (b) punish (c) remove

8. **commodious**
   (a) capable (b) helpful (c) spacious

9. **crepuscular**
   (a) dim (b) shriveled (c) supervisory

10. **cupidity**
    (a) beauty (b) greed (c) fickleness

11. **depraved**
    (a) wicked (b) hungry (c) poor

12. **disoblige**
    (a) insult (b) pardon (c) sharpen

13. **escheat**
    (a) thief (b) transfer (c) escape

14. **exude**
    (a) perspire (b) separate (c) calculate

15. **florid**
    (a) clean (b) colorful (c) liquid

16. **fracas**
    (a) split (b) appetizer (c) disturbance

17. **functionary**
    (a) rule (b) official (c) organization

18. **gainsay**
    (a) fasten (b) deny (c) acquire

19. **imbroglio**
    (a) imprecation (b) dilemma (c) novel

20. **inchoate**
    (a) new (b) chalky (c) underground

21. **incubus**
    (a) creativity (b) miniature (c) nightmare

22. **indefatigable**
    (a) energetic (b) hazy (c) difficult

23. **legerdemain**
    (a) roof (b) magic (c) territory

24. **libertine**
    (a) advocate (b) rake (c) liaison

25. **limpid**
    (a) sad (b) transparent (c) sluggish

26. **littoral**
    (a) coastal (b) intellectual (c) legal

27. **machination**
    (a) vehicle (b) alienation (c) scheme

28. **nefarious**
    (a) indigent (b) negligent (c) wicked

29. **obsequies**
    (a) antiques (b) difficulties (c) rites

30. **pique**
    (a) discover (b) solve (c) irritate

31. **prevaricate**
    (a) prevail (b) lie (c) diversify

32. **prurient**
    (a) careful (b) lustful (c) generous

33. **pulchritude**
    (a) beauty (b) selfishness (c) power

34. **purview**
    (a) scope (b) purpose (c) pursuit

35. **quixotic**
    (a) confused (b) idealistic (c) undecided

36. **rebuff**
    (a) respond (b) massage (c) reject

37. **recreant**
    (a) fearful (b) young (c) casual

38. **recriminate**
    (a) recoil (b) accuse (c) review

39. **rend**
    (a) tear (b) oppress (c) provide

40. **reprove**
    (a) denounce (b) contradict (c) convince

41. **serendipity**
    (a) luck (b) favoritism (c) balance

42. **symbiotic**
    (a) pitiful (b) interdependent (c) typical

43. **truant**
    (a) lazy (b) angry (c) straight

44. **verisimilitude**
    (a) truth (b) appearance (c) vestige

STOP.

(Answers and definitions begin on the next page.)

Answers and Definitions (Warm-up Quiz)

1. **AGAPE** (uh GAYP) *adj* open-mouthed **(c)**

2. **ARTIFICE** (AR tuh fis) *n* a clever and deceptive trick; cunning or craftiness **(a)**

3. **AVER** (uh VER) *v* to assert or affirm confidently; declare; claim; posit; maintain **(b)**

4. **BALEFUL** (BAYL ful) *adj* evil; destructive; sorrowful **(b)**

5. **BELABOR** (buh LAY ber) *v* to repeat, reiterate, or go over again and again, to the point of being tiresome **(b)**

6. **BROACH** (BROHCH) *v* to open up; to mention a subject; propose; introduce **(c)**

7. **CASTIGATE** (KAS tuh gayt) *v* to punish, chastise, or criticize severely **(b)**

8. **COMMODIOUS** (kuh MOH dee us) *adj* spacious; roomy; capacious **(c)**

9. **CREPUSCULAR** (kreh PUS kyoo ler) *adj* pertaining to twilight; slightly wicked **(a)**

10. **CUPIDITY** (kyoo PID ih tee) *n* greed; avarice **(b)**

11. **DEPRAVED** (dee PRAYVD) *adj* corrupted; wicked **(a)**

12. **DISOBLIGE** (dis uh BLYJ) *v* to offend, insult, or slight; to refuse or act contrary to **(a)**

13. **ESCHEAT** (ih SHEET) *n* transfer of property ownership to the government by default **(b)**

14. **EXUDE** (eg ZOOD) *v* to ooze out or emit, as through pores **(a)**

15. **FLORID** (FLOR id) *adj* highly ornate, colorful, or flowery **(b)**

16. **FRACAS** (FRAY kus) *n* a loud disturbance; melee **(c)**

17. **FUNCTIONARY** (FUNK shun ayr ee) *n* an official; a person holding an office or position of authority **(b)**

18. **GAINSAY** (GAYN say) *v* to deny; refute; contradict; impugn; repudiate **(b)**

19. **IMBROGLIO** (im BROH lee oh) *n* a perplexing situation; entanglement; dilemma **(b)**

20. **INCHOATE** (in KOH ayt) *adj* just begun; incipient; elementary; rudimentary **(a)**

21. **INCUBUS** (ING kyoo bis) *n* a nightmare; something that burdens or oppresses like a nightmare or demon **(c)**

22. **INDEFATIGABLE** (in dih FAT ih guh bul) *adj* tireless; inexhaustible; unflagging **(a)**

23. **LEGERDEMAIN** (lezh uh duh MAYN) *n* sleight of hand; prestidigitation **(b)**

24. **LIBERTINE** (LIB er teen) *n* an amoral or sexually unrestrained person **(b)**

25. **LIMPID** (LIM pid) *adj* transparent; crystal-clear **(b)**

26. **LITTORAL** (LIH ter ul) *adj* pertaining to a coastal region (shore) **(a)**

27. **MACHINATION** (mak uh NAY shin) *n* a plot or scheme, especially a wily or deceptive one; ploy; ruse; sham; chicanery **(c)**

28. **NEFARIOUS** (neh FAYR ee us) *adj* stingy; parsimonious **(c)**

29. **OBSEQUIES** (AHB suh kweez) *n* funeral rites **(c)**

30. **PIQUE** (PEEK) *v* to irritate; annoy **(c)**

31. **PREVARICATE** (pruh VAYR uh kayt) *v* to lie; fabricate; distort **(b)**

32. **PRURIENT** (PROO ree unt) *adj* having or causing lascivious or lustful thoughts **(b)**

33. **PULCHRITUDE** (PUL krih tood) *n* beauty; attractiveness; comeliness **(a)**

34. **PURVIEW** (PER vyoo) *n* scope or range (of operation or understanding) **(a)**

35. **QUIXOTIC** (kwik ZAH tik) *adj* idealistic but impractical **(b)**

36. **REBUFF** (rih BUF) *v* to refuse bluntly; to snub or repulse **(c)**

37. **RECREANT** (REK ree unt) *adj* cowardly; faint-hearted; craven **(a)**

38. **RECRIMINATE** (ree KRIM ih nayt) *v* to accuse; charge; indict **(b)**

39. **REND** (REND) *v* to tear, pull apart, or rip up **(a)**

40. **REPROVE** (rih PROOV) *v* to express disapproval; censure; reprobate **(a)**

41. SERENDIPITY (sayr en DIP uh tee) *n* accidental good fortune or luck **(a)**

42. SYMBIOTIC (sim bee AH tik) *adj* characterized by a mutually beneficial relationship; interdependent **(b)**

43. TRUANT (TROO unt) *adj* shirking one's duty; habitually absent from school or one's job; idle; lazy **(a)**

44. VERISIMILITUDE (vayr ih SIM ih lih tood) *n* the appearance of truth **(a)**

3

Words to the Wise

This book includes 100% testworthy words—just the type of words you can expect to encounter on the SAT, GRE, and other standardized tests that target vocabulary directly. So what makes the 264 *headwords* (main entries, in upper-case letters) in Chapter 3 *extra* special? Well, each word in Chapter 3 has either appeared with particular frequency on the exams or is closely related to several high-frequency words. The words in the first list (66 Words Wise People Know) have been hand-picked for their widespread use today among educated people.

Keep in mind that a high-frequency word may nevertheless be excluded from the three lists in this chapter—

if it is particularly odd in appearance or easily confused with other words (you'll find words of these types in Chapter 4) or

if it is specific to a particular academic field or profession (you'll find words of this type in Chapter 5).

Many of the words in Chapter 3 are related to one another. This feature is quite intentional. It provides a built-in means of reviewing words you have already en-countered. As you read the **illustrative sentences**, each of which is indicated by a pencil icon (✎), you'll notice that many of them include more than one testworthy word. When you encounter an unfamiliar word, guess its meaning based on its context, then either check the index and look up the word right away or wait until you come across it later. Also sprinkled throughout this chapter are a variety of interesting **quotations**, each one indicated by an open-quotation icon (❝), as well as matching-type **quizzes.** These features are designed to help fix each new word firmly in your memory.

66 Words Wise People Know

ACQUIESCE (ak wee ES) *v.* to comply with or assent to passively, by one's lack of objection or opposition

> The word is properly accompanied by the preposition *in*, not *with* or *to*.

> 66 ...I had to *acquiesce* in the situation and accept the fact that no major reorganization, reform, or voluntary fiscal restraint would come from Congress during my first term." —Richard Nixon, *R.N.*

> The noun form is *aquiescence*.

> ✎ Our next-door neighbors have tacitly sanctioned our use of their driveway by their *acquiescence* in our using it during the past several months.

> A *timorous*, *reticent*, or *taciturn* person (one who is shy or reluctant to speak) might *acquiesce* in a situation which he actually finds repugnant.
> A closely related word is *accede*: to agree or surrender to.

ALACRITY (uh LAK rih tee) *n.* cheerful readiness or willingness; briskness or liveliness

> ✎ With ardent *alacrity* the volunteers help the earthquake victims salvage their belongings.

> 66 I have not that *alacrity* of spirit, Nor cheer of mind that I was wont to have." —Shakespeare

> The adjective form is *alacritous*.
> An alacritous person might also be described as *ardent* (hopeful, confident) or *zealous* (fervent or ardent, especially in devotion or activity).

ANOMALY (uh NAH muh lee) *n.* deviation from the norm; abnormality; peculiar or unusual event or phenomenon

> *Anomaly* is a favorite word among *Star Trek* screenwriters:

> 66 I've completed my analysis of the *anomaly*. It appears to be a multiphasic temporal convergence in the space-time continuum....It is, in essence, an eruption of anti-time." —Data, *Star Trek: The Next Generation* (final episode)

> The adjective form is *anomalous*.

> 66 Poverty is an *anomaly* to rich people. It is very difficult to make out why people who want dinner do not ring the bell." —Walter Bagehot

> A closely related word is *aberration*: a deviation from what is normal, common, or morally right.

APPEASE (uh PEEZ) *v.* to pacify or make content; to concede to a beligerant demand in order to bring about peace

> 66 An *appeaser* is one who feeds a crocodile—hoping it will eat him last."
> —Sir Winston Churchill

Similar words include *mollify*, *placate*, *addle*, and *conciliate*.
An implacable person is not capable of being appeased, placated, or pacified.
Appease is closely related to *please*; appeasing others will also please them.

ASCETIC (uh SEH tik) *n.* one who denies oneself life's material satisfactions and normal pleasures, usually as part of religious belief or discipline

> ✎ The *ascetic* and unpretentious life style of the Hollywood movie mogul seemed an anomaly among his flamboyant industry colleagues and associates.

> 66 *Asceticism* is the secret mother of many a secret sin. God...did not give us fibre too much nor a passion too many." —Theodore Parker

A closely related word is *anchorite*: a person who has retired to a religious life of solitude and seclusion.

BANAL (BAY nul) *adj.* commonplace; trite; hackneyed; unoriginal

> ✎ New jazz music today seems *banal* and uninspired compared to the music of the bebop era.

The noun form is *banality*, as in the following sentence:

> 66 ...he despised the aggressive young men of the electronic media....They just flitted from flower to flower, intoning resonant *banalities*." —Spiro T. Agnew, *The Caufield Decision*

A similar word is *insipid*.

BANE (BAYN) *n.* any cause of ruin or destruction, lasting harm or injury, or woe

> ✎ The woman grew to abhor her vituperative husband; among friends she would refer to him hyperbolically as "the *bane* of my existence."

> 66 Money, thou *bane* of bliss, and source of woe." —Herbert

The adjective form is *baneful*. A synonym of *baneful* is *pernicious*.
Do not confuse *bane* with *banal*: trite; hackneyed. The two words are unrelated.

CENSURE (SEN sher) *n.* severe criticism, scolding, or fault-finding.

> ❝ All *censure* of a man's self is oblique praise. It is in order to show how much he can spare. It has all the invidiousness of self-praise and all the reproach of falsehood." —Dr. Samuel Johnson

Aside from criticism, *censure* does not involve punishment.

The word is also used as a verb, but there is no adjective form of the word.

Similar words include *reproach*, *reproof*, *stricture*, and *pan*.

Another closely related word is *censor*: to criticize, object to, and possibly delete (from a broadcast or publication), especially on moral grounds. However, censure involves vehement disapproval and thus is a slightly stronger word than censor.

CHAGRIN (shuh GRIN) *n.* irritation marked by disappointment or humiliation

> ✎ His favorite team lost the big game, much to his *chagrin* since he had bet a large sum of money that his team would win.

The word is often improperly used to refer simply to sadness; while disappointment does tend to suggest sadness, chagrin requires humiliation, irritation, or annoyance.

A closely related word is *vexation* (irritation, annoyance, or provocation), as illustrated in this sentence:

> ✎ The winner's facetious and *vexing* remark after the spelling bee comparing the loser's performance to Dan Quayle's misspelling of "potato" exacerbated the loser's *chagrin*.

CHICANERY (shih KAY nuh ree) *n.* trickery or deception, usually used to gain an advantage or to evade

The verb form is *chicane*.

Similar words include *guile*, *knavery*, *disingenuousness*, and *artifice*.

> ✎ Some unscrupulous knaves would resort to any sort of *chicanery* in order to fleece an unwitting dupe of his last dollar.

CHOLERIC (kuh LAYR ik) *adj.* tempermental; hotheaded; irascible

> ✎ Just beneath his affable and disarming veneer lay a *choleric*, jilted ex-husband.

Although *choleric* is unrelated to *caloric*, both words involve the notion of heat (a calorie is a unit of measure for heat).

Similar words include *mercurial*, *peevish*, and *acrimonious*.

CHURLISH (CHER lish) *adj.* peasantlike or rustic; crude, crass, or vulgar

> The noun form is *churl*.
>
> The word has two related but distinct meanings, as illustrated by these two sentences:
>
> ✎ The Dark Ages were a *churlish* and difficult time to live.
>
> ✎ His *churlish* and uncivilized demeanor seems more befitting the Dark Ages than this age; I want nothing to do with the *churl*.
>
> Similar words include *boorish*, *impudent*, and *insolent*.

CIPHER (SY fer) *n.* nothing, zero, or null; a worthless person or thing; a secret code (of numbers or letters); a distinctive emblem, monogram, or colophon; *v.* to use numbers arithmetically

> As suggested above, *cipher* is a very flexible word. In terms of the first meaning, similar words include *naught*, *null*, *nihil*, *nonentity*, *void*, and *vacuum*.
>
> To *decipher* a secret code is to determine or "crack" the code.
>
> The word's flexibility is illustrated in this anecdote:
>
> ✎ The jilted husband's incipient autonomy was precipitated by his wife's "Dear John" letter, which she scribbled on her company's letterhead (with the company's *cipher* printed at the top). Although he had trouble *deciphering* her writing, he could discern that she referred to him throughout the letter as a "*cipher*."
>
> Do not confuse *cipher* with *siphon*: to withdraw liquid by suction.

CIRCUMSPECT (SER kum spekt) *adj.* cautious; wary; watchful; leery

> The word's literal meaning is "to look around"—derived from the Latin words *circ* (round) and *spec* (see).
>
> ✎ Wild animals should be *circumspect* about drinking alone at their favorite watering hole; if they do so, it behooves them to constantly look around for predators.
>
> 66 Be very *circumspect* in the choice of thy company...To be the best in the company is the way to grow worse; the best means to grow better is to be the worst there." —Francis Quarles
>
> A related word is *qualms*: doubts; misgivings.
>
> A circumspect person might have qualms about engaging in a capricious course of action.

COUNTERVAIL (KOWN ter vayl) *v.* to use equal force against

> ✎ At the car dealership, I was especially enamored with the Ferrari. As prepossessing as it was, *countervailing* considerations, not the least of which was the price tag, dissuaded me from purchasing it and saved me from a potential credit debacle.

> ❝ A good conscience...more than *countervails* all the calamities and afflictions which can befall us without." —Joseph Addison

Here are two similar words:
antagonistic: directly opposed to
counterpoise: a weight that influences or offsets another

CREDULOUS (KREH jyoo lus) *adj.* believing easily; gullible; ingenuous

The noun form is *credulity.*
A credulous person could be described as a *dupe.*

> ✎ The unctuous real estate agent duped the gullible vacationers into buying a condominium time share without bothering to see the property beforehand; their *credulity* bought them one week a year in a run-down hovel in the most perilous part of town. A more circumspect attitude would have helped them avoid the chagrin they now feel.

> ❝ When people are bewildered they tend to become *credulous.*"
> —Calvin Coolidge

The opposite of credulous is *incredulous* (skeptical).
Do not confuse credulous with *credible*: worthy of acceptance; having integrity; believable.

CURMUDGEON (ker MUH jun) *n.* a person with a rude, irascible attitude

> ✎ The character of Scrooge from Dicken's *A Christmas Carol* is perhaps the archetypal *curmudgeon*, and a veritable paragon of parsimony. As the story went, though, he turned out not so incorrigibly penurious after all.

A curmudgeon might be described as a *churl* or *boor.*
By the way, Scrooge was not only curmudgeonly, but miserly as well. As the sentence above suggests, synonyms of *miserly* include *penurious* and *parsimonious.*

DEMAGOGUE (DEM uh gahg) *n.* a political agitator and charismatic orator who appeals to emotions and prejudice

> ✎ Hitler was the epitome of *demagoguery*; this quintessential *demagogue* ingratiated himself with the masses by inciting passions, quashing and quelling reason, and rewarding jingoism and chauvinism.

> ❝ The secret of the *demagogue* is to make himself as stupid as his audience so that they believe they are as clever as he." —Karl Kraus

A demagogue engages in *demagogy* or *demagoguery*.

The adjective form is *demagogic*.

Demagogue is sometimes confused with *demigod* (a deified mortal), understandably since an effective demagogue might be viewed almost as a god by his or her followers.

Do not confuse *demagogue* with *pedagogue*: a teacher.

A similar word is *proselytizer*.

DEPRECATE (DEP ruh kayt) *v.* to express disapproval of

> ❝ The friends of humanity will *deprecate* war, wheresoever it may appear." —George Washington

The noun form is *deprecation*.

The adjective form is *deprecatory*.

Similar words include *reprove*, *reprimand*, *rebuke*, and *reprobate*.

Synonyms of deprecation include *disapprobation* and *reprobation*.

Deprecation does not necessarily involve blame, criticism, or punishment. Here are similar words which do carry one or more of these meanings:

castigate: to punish in order to correct or reform

censure: to strongly disapprove, criticize, or blame

reproach: to find fault with; blame; criticize

DUBIOUS (DOO bee us) *adj.* questionable; of doubtful quality or propreity

The word is usually used to refer to a misrepresentation as to the qualitative characteristics of something or someone, where the actual quality is worse than what is represented.

A dubious distinction is one that is not deserved or fitting.

> ✎ The label on the nutrition supplement package makes numerous *dubious* claims about the product—that it drastically impedes the aging process and helps to burn body fat without exercise.

A closely related adverb is *indubitably*: beyond a doubt.

ENIGMA (eh NIG muh) *n.* a mystery or puzzle; a perlexing or baffling situation, occurrence, or person

> The adjective form is *enigmatic*.
> The word is often used to describe a person with a self-contradictory character.
> It might be redundant to describe a person as an "enigmatic conundrum" or an "anomalous enigma."
> The word is also used more particularly to describe a fable or other brief story that contains a hidden meaning or that poses a riddle.

EPHEMERAL (ih FEM uh rul) *adj.* lasting only a short time; short-lived

> 66 ...an author may find his, or her, lifework reduced to a handful of paperbacks, as *ephemeral* as yesterday's snowflakes." —Pearl S. Buck, *Journey In Dialogue*

> Similar words include *fleeting, evanescent*, and *transitory*
> In botany and zoology, the word is used more narrowly to refer to a plant or animal living less than one day. In fact, *ephemerid* refers to a particular order of insects that includes certain flies.
> The noun form is *ephemera*.

EPITAPH (EP ih taf) *n.* an inscription on a monument in memory of a dead person

> 66 A joke is an *epitaph* on an emotion." —Nietzsche

> The Latin prefix *epi-* means "upon." (You are at the *epicenter* of an earthquake if you are up on top of its center.)
> Do not confuse *epitaph* with these words:
> *epithet:* a word or phrase describing a person used instead of or added to the person's name; an insulting or derogatory characterization
> *epigram:* a clever, pithy saying

ERUDITE (AYR yoo dyt) *adj.* scholarly; learned

> The word does not refer to intelligence but rather to knowledge learned

> 66 ... he sat formally and talked to her in his stiff, pedantic way on cold and *erudite* subjects for two hours." —William Faulkner, *Sartoris*

> As suggested by the sentence above, a related word is *pedantic*: showing off one's learning or overemphasizing trivial rules or knowledge
> Do not confuse *erudite* with *arrogant*. An erudite professor might seem arrogant in his her knowledge, but the two words are unrelated in meaning.

ESCHEW (eh SHYOO) *v.* to avoid or abstain from

✎ I *eschew* officious, overbearing people in favor of affable, complaisant folks like myself.

❝ From taking an occasional glass of beer as an excuse to gorge on free lunch,...he drank quite a few glasses in a row and *eschewed* the food." —Robert Lewis Taylor, *W.C. Fields*

A similar word is *shun*: to avoid or spurn.

EXPEDIENT (ek SPEE dee unt) *adj.* suitable for a particular purpose; practicable; fitting for one's advantage or interest

✎ If you want to succeed financially in life, investing your money in your own education is actually more *expedient* than investing it in the stock market.

❝ No man is justified in doing evil on the ground of *expediency*." —Theodore Roosevelt

The verb form is *expedite*. To expedite a process is to make it more feasible, practicable, and "do-able."

EXTRICATE (EK strih kayt) *v.* to free or release from entanglement or engagement

✎ As their relationship waned, the two lovebirds found it difficult to *extricate* themselves from each other. She felt beholden to him for taking care of her. He coveted her pulchritude and her compact disc collection.

The adjective form is *extricable*, as this sentence suggests:

❝ [W]ith the conduct of business human happiness or misery is *inextricably* interwoven." —Louis Brandeis

The word is used commonly in chemistry to refer to the separating out of a chemical substance from others—for example, by centrifuge or by heat.

FACETIOUS (fuh SEE shus) *adj.* frivolously comical; funny; witty; amusing

✎ In a eulogy at a funeral, *facetious* remarks about the decedent might be considered indecorous or even insolent.

The word is often misused to refer to a sarcastic remark in which the speaker says one thing but means the opposite. A facetious remark might be sarcastic, but is not necessarily so.

Two synonyms of facetious are *droll* and *jocular*.

HALCYON (HAL see un) *adj.* calm; peaceful; serene

✎ The lake's quiescent waters and the *halcyon* summer air seemed propitious for only two activities: flyfishing and truancy.

The word is derived from the mythical bird *halcyon*, known for its power to calm the wind and sea.

Halcyon also means "carefree," as illustrated in this sentence:

✎ The *halcyon* days of summer were, alas, ephemeral, succumbing as always to the encumbrances of autumn.

HARANGUE (huh RANG) *n.* a lengthy speech, especially a vehement, bombastic, or chastising one

The term "halcyon harangue" is an oxymoron.

✎ Our drill sergeant was quite a martinet; any contumacious behavior, even the slightest peccadillo, was followed by a *harangue* and a hundred pushups.

HARBINGER (HAR bin jer) *n.* anything that foreshadows a future event; omen

✎ The recent merger of two multinational banks is a *harbinger* of what's to come in the financial services industry.

✎ I view the proliferation of nuclear weapons as a *harbinger* of doom. This trend does not bode well for humanity's future; indeed, it portends our impending demise.

A similar word is *presage*.

Do not confuse *harbinger* or *presage* with these two related words:

prophecy: a prediction (*v* prophesy)

prescience: foreknowledge of future events based on firsthand experience

HIATUS (hy AY tus) *n.* a pause or break in a sequence; opening; aperture; gap; chasm

The word is usually used to refer to an extended break from one's job or regular schedule.

✎ Always trying to engender a work ethic at the office, the boss announced to his staff that he was "going on *hiatus*" to do some "uninterrupted work." He realized that his attempt to beguile his underlings had failed when they responded, "Have a great vacation!"

HYPERBOLE (hy PER buh lee) *n.* an obvious exaggeration, intentionally used for emphasis and not to be taken literally

> ✎ A facetious example of hyperbole: "If I've told you once, I've told you a thousand times: don't ever use hyperbolic language with me!"

> ❝ The speaking in perpetual *hyperbole* is comely in nothing but in love." —Francis Bacon

The opposite of hyperbole is *litotes*: an understatement made for emphasis.

IDYLLIC (y DIL ik) *adj.* charmingly simple and carefree

The word is usually used to describe a lifestyle or culture rather than a personal disposition.

The word is derived from *idyll*: a poem describing pastoral scenes or simple carefree episodes.

> ❝ ...life in these rural towns was never as *idyllic* as our poets remember it." —Bill Moyers, *Listening to America*

A charmingly simple and carefree life might seem ideal (perfect). Nevertheless, do not confuse *idyllic* with *ideal*.

IMPERTINENT (im PER tuh nent) *adj.* inappropriate under the circumstances; ill-mannered; rude; insolent

> ✎ His off-color jokes, sexist remarks, and other *impertinent* utterances in the presence of the company's president cost him a job promotion.

> ❝ Do not love your neighbor as yourself. If you are on good terms with yourself, it is an *impertinence*; if on bad, an injury." —George Bernard Shaw

Do not treat *impertinent* and *pertinent* as antonyms. *Impertinent* is used to describe a person's behavior, while *pertinent* is used to describe an idea or statement as relevant or to the point.

INDIGENT (IN dih junt) *adj.* poor; destitute; impoverished

An indigent person is sometimes referred to as a pauper.

A synonym of indigent is *impecunious* (*pecuniary*: pertaining to money).

The noun form is *indigence* (poverty; destitution; impoverishment; penury).

A closely related but distinct word is *mendicity*: begging or living off alms (charity) of another. Some would view mendicity merely as feigned indigence.

Do not confuse *indigent* with these words:

  indigenous: native to or characterizing a particular region

  indulgent: permissive; tolerating

INEXORABLE (in EK sor uh bul) *adj.* relentless; unyielding; merciless

> ✎ No B-rated science fiction "epic" is complete without the *inexorable* attack of the grotesque monster, impervious to bullets and bombs but capitulating to the charms of a pretty girl.

> ❝ What other dungeon is so dark as one's own heart! What jailer so *inexorable* as one's self!" —Nathaniel Hawthorne

A similar word is *implacable*: incapable of being pacified or appeased; stubbornly unyielding (*placate*: to appease or pacify).

Do not confuse *inexorable* with *inevitable*: unavoidable; certain.

INTERLOPER (IN ter lohp er) *n.* intuder or trespasser; one who intrudes into the private affairs of others

An interloper might be accustomed to hearing the phrase, "That's none of your business!"

An interloper might be considered impertinent, meddling, and indecorous.

> ✎ The *interloping* dormitory resident suffered from numerous vexing habits: he would rummage through others' desk drawers, saunter into rooms without knocking first, and, worst of all, rifle through others' refrigerators foraging for free snacks!

IRRESOLUTE (ih REZ uh loot) *adj.* unable to decide (make up one's mind)

> ✎ Every year I make the same New Year's resolution: to be less *irresolute* and more decisive. And every year I violate my covenant. It seems the only thing I am resolute about is what my New Year's resolution will be.

> ❝ One never can achieve anything lasting in this world by being *irresolute*." —Ghandi

A similar word is *vacillating*: wavering or moving back and forth.

A person might be irresolute as a result of being in a *quandary* or *imbroglio*, both of which refer to perplexing situations or predicaments in which the best course of action is uncertain.

LAUDABLE (LOWD uh bul) *adj.* praiseworthy; commendable

> ✎ According to theater critics, the leading actress gave a *laudable* performance as the recalcitrant and incorrigible Kate in the repertory's recent production of *The Taming of the Shrew*. The critics' reviews of the overall production have also been *laudatory*.

The verb form is *laud*.

The noun form is *laudation*, as illustrated in this sentence:

> ❝ Self-*laudation* abounds among the unpolished, but nothing can stamp a man more sharply as ill-bred." —Charles Buxton

The word is unrelated to loud (volume).

LOQUACIOUS (loh KWAY shus) *adj.* talkative; chatty

A loquacious but vacuous person might exude inanity and fatuousness.
Synonyms of loquacious include *garrulous*, *verbose*, and *voluble*.
The noun form is *loquacity*.
Related *loqu-* and *loc-* words include:
  eloquent: fluent in speech or writing
  elocution: the art of public speaking
  grandiloquent: pompous or bombastic in speech or language
  circumlocution: talk that is not to the point

MAGNANIMOUS (mag NAN uh mus) *adj.* noble or elevated in mind; generous

A magnanimous person typically puts the needs of others before his or her own needs.
The noun form is *magnanimity*.
A magnanimous person may be generous with his or her time, money, or talents.
A similar word is *munificent*, which describes a generous person, but not necessarily a noble person, as illustrated in this sentence:

> ❝ Everyone, even the richest and most *munificent* of men, pays much by check more lightheartedly than he pays little in specie." —Sir Max Beerbohm

Similar words include *altruistic*, *benevolent*, *philanthropic*, and *beneficent*.

MISANTHROPE (MIS in throhp) *n.* a person who hates or distrusts humankind

> ✎ The neighbors came to know her as "Cat Woman"; some saw her as an enigma, while others viewed her as a *misanthrope*—morose and aloof around other people, yet jocund and carefree around her menagerie of felines.

The word is derived from the Greek word *anthro* (mankind).
A misanthrope (or *misanthropist*) engages in *misanthropy*.

> ❝ [M]isanthropes...are so sure that the world is going to ruin that they resent every attempt to comfort them as an insult to their sagacity." —Edwin Percy Whipple

MUNDANE (mun DAYN) *adj.* of or pertaining to the world or to earthly (as opposed to spiritual) concerns

> 66 To medieval man the world was itself the ultra*mundane* and the supernatural."
> —Ortega y Gasset

Similar words include *temporal* and *secular*.

The word is now used somewhat imprecisely to describe the commonplace and ordinary, as illustrated in this sentence:

> ✎ Among household tasks, vacuuming floors is far more mundane than cooking, since cooking at least allows for some creativity.

Synonyms of mundane, as used (imprecisely) immediately above, include *banal*, *prosaic*, and *quotidian*.

NEBULOUS (NEB yoo lus) *adj.* vague and indistinct, without definite form; cloudy or hazy

> The word is often used to describe ideas or expressions, as in this sentence:

> ✎ The written manual for the computer program was so *nebulous* and confusing that I had to call for help to perform the most basic tasks.

The noun form is *nebula*: a cloudlike, gaseous mass (a word often overheard on the bridge of *Star Trek's* Enterprise).

Related words include:

turbid and *muddled*, both of which essentially mean "cloudy or muddy"

fuliginous: smoky; sooty

OBFUSCATE (AHB fyoo skayt) *v.* to confuse, muddle, or bewilder

> The word is commonly used in referring to the persuasive and often evasive rhetoric of lawyers, politicians, and pundits.

> ✎ When the precocious youngster was caught with his hand in the cookie jar, rather than admitting guilt, he *obfuscated* by averring that the cookies were stale and therefore nobody would have wanted them, anyway.

The noun form is *obfuscation*.

PANACEA (pan uh SEE uh) *n.* a universal remedy for all ills; cure-all

> The word is used in relation to health problems as well as to other problems or difficulties, as illustrated in this sentence:

> 66 [George Washington] advocated no sure cure for all the sorrows of the world, and doubted that such a *panacea* existed." —H.L. Mencken, *Pater Patriae*

The meaning of the word comes from *Panacea*, the Greek goddess of healing.

Do not confuse *panacea* with the unrelated word *panoply*: a complete array (from the Greek word *pan*, meaning "flock").

✎ Our local health-food store stocks a *panoply* of *panaceas*.

PANDER (PAN der) *v.* to cater to the base (morally low) desires of others

✎ *Pandering* to the most prurient of interests, the barkers at the peep shows and pornographic theaters of Times Square coax and wheedle passersby twenty-four hours a day.

The word "bears" no relation, of course, to *panda*: a bearlike carnivorous animal indigenous to the Himalayas.

PARADIGM (PAYR uh dym) *n.* a model; standard; pattern; example

✎ The research methodology used to discover a cure for a certain virus might become a *paradigm* for future research of similar diseases.

The adjective form is *paradigmatic*.

A closely related word is *paragon*: a model of perfection; an ideal. The distinction is illustrated in this sentence:

✎ My secretary is a *paragon* of organization and efficiency; her filing system should be *paradigmatic* for our entire office staff.

Another closely related word is *archetype*: anything that serves as a model for (example of) all other similar things.

PARIAH (puh RY uh) *n.* a person or thing generally rejected or despised; outcast

A derelict, vagrant, bum, or other person who has been rejected and cast off by society would properly be referred to as a *pariah*.

✎ Joseph Stalin is perhaps the paradigmatic "posthumous *pariah*." This despot's name and image have been expunged throughout the former Communist Soviet Union. At the same time, he has left an indelible mark in recorded history under the words "opprobrium" and "depravity."

A similar but distinct word is *anathema*: a person or thing condemned, accused, damned, cursed, or generally loathed.

PATRONIZE (PAY truh nyz) *v.* to treat condescendingly; talk down to; look down on

A haughty, consequential, or supercilious person patronizes others.

❝ Cat: a pygmy lion who loves mice, hates dogs, and *patronizes* human beings."
—Oliver Herford

The word is derived from *patron*: father; provider.

A similar word is *deign*: to condescend

The noun form is *patronage*. Be careful, though. *Patronage* is usually used in a different sense— to refer to financial support by a wealthy or powerful person.

PHLEGMATIC (flayg MAT ik) *adj.* indifferent, apathetic, or unemotional; sluggish

> 66 The most *phlegmatic* dispositions often contain the most inflammable spirits, as fire is struck from the hardest flints." —William Hazlitt

Similar words include *insouciant*, *impassive*, and *stolid*.

The word is derived from *phlegm*: a thick mucus secreted by the respiratory system and expelled through the mouth. In ancient and medieval medicine, phlegm was one of the humours (substances) that defined a person's emotional and psychological makeup.

PLETHORA (PLEH ther uh) *n.* overabundance; excess; surplus

> 66 Consumption of the *plethora* of consumer goods churned out by affluent economies is itself a time-absorbing activity." —E.J. Mishan, *The Economic Growth Debate*

The word is often misused to refer merely to a large quantity or an abundance, a meaning properly conveyed by the words *cornucopia*, *copiousness*, *plenitude*, and *bounty*.

Synonyms of the word include *surfeit*, *glut*, and *superfluity*.

Antonyms of the word include *dearth*, *paucity*, and *want*, all of which mean "insufficiency" or "scarcity."

PROPENSITY (proh PEN sih tee) *n.* natural tendency, inclination, or bent

The word has no verb form, and the adjective *propense* is not used today.

> 66 A *propensity* to hope and joy is real riches; one to fear and sorrow is real poverty." —David Hume

Similar words include *penchant*, *proclivity*, and *affinity*.

PROSELYTIZE (PRAH suh luh tyz) *v.* to convert (or attempt to convert) another to a belief system, ideology, or sect

A *proselyte* is a convert—a person who has been proselytized, typically by a demagogue or other persuasive, charismatic person.

> 66 Ambition sufficiently plagues her *proselytes* by keeping them always in show and in public, like a statue in the street." —Dr. Thomas Fuller

Proselytes to religious cults and extreme ideologies are often insular (narrowminded), overzealous, and ardently fervent.

PUNDIT (PUN dit) *n.* an expert or authority.

> The word is also used to describe a person who makes comments or judgments with an air of authority, regardless of actual knowledge or expertise. This type of pundit might come across as *bombastic*, *pompous*, or *consequential*.

> ✎ During election years, candidates try their best to ignore the plethora of political *pundits*—those journalistic "talking heads," each claiming to know the real reason for every development and the true intentions of every candidate.

QUINTESSENCE (quin TES uhns) *n.* the pure and concentrated essence of a substance

> ❝ I have found in Mozart's music the *quintessence* of all that I feel keenly in mind and in emotion." —Marcia Davenport, *Mozart*

> The adjective form is *quintessential*. Leonardo de Vinci was the *quintessential* "Renaissance Man." Bill Clinton is the *quintessential* politician. Alan Alda is the *quintessential* nice guy.

> The word is derived from the Latin term meaning "the fifth essence." In ancient and medieval philosophy, the five elements (essences) included air, fire, earth, water, and ether (the heavens), ether being the fifth element.

> A similar word is *epitome*: a person or thing that is typical of or characterizes a whole class; a summary of a topic or work.

> Other similar words are *paradigm*, *paragon*, and *archetype*.

RECALCITRANT (reh KAL sih trunt) *adj.* unruly; resistant of authority; disobedient; rebellious

> ✎ When the *recalcitrant* mob refused to disperse, the governor ordered the National Guard to restore order by force.

> A recalcitrant person might also be described as *refractory* and *contumacious*.
> The word is also used as a noun.
> The verb form is *recalcitrate*.
> The word bears no relation to either *calculation* or *calcification*.

RENEGE (rih NIG) *v.* to go back on one's promise or word; to deny or renounce

> ✎ The world abounds with *renegers*: spouses *reneging* on their wedding vows, politicians *reneging* on their campaign promises, and dieters *reneging* on their pledge to cut calories.

> ❝ Nations don't literally *renege* on their debts; they either postpone them indefinitely...or else pay them off in depreciated currency." —Roger Bridwell

> A *renegade* (traitor or deserter) is a person who reneges on his or her loyalty.

SALIENT (SAY lee unt) *adj.* prominent or conspicuous; notable or significant

The word is usually used to describe features or characteristics.

Note the two related but distinct meanings of the word, as underscored by these two sentences:

✎ The most *salient* feature of my house is its orange color.

✎ At the end of his sermon, the preacher reiterated what he considered to be the most *salient* points for the congregation to remember.

In this sentence, the word might carry either meaning:

✎ The "Women Seeking Men" personal ads were resplendent with such *salient* words as: "adventurous," "petite," "spiritual," and, perhaps most *salient* of all, "single."

SANCTION (SANK shun) *v.* to authoritatively or officialy approve, authorize, permit, or support

✎ The motor vehicle code *sanctions* stopping on a freeway shoulder only in the event of an emergency.

✎ A parent *sanctions* a child's delinquency by failing to chastise him or her.

The word is also used as a noun (see below).

In law, the word has a slightly different meaning: official (court) reward for obedience or, more commonly, a penalty for disobedience.

✎ A lawyer failing to comply with proper court procedure might be *sanctioned* by fine or imprisonment.

In international politics, the word has yet a different meaning: an action by a nation (or nations) designed to force another nation into compliance with a treaty or other agreement.

✎ Joint *sanctions* against Iraq failed to dissuade Saddam Hussein from his oppressive acts against the Kurdish rebels.

SUPERCILIOUS (soo per SIL ee us) *adj.* disdainful in a haughty and arrogant way

✎ While stopped at the traffic light, the *supercilious* socialite in her brand new luxury car glanced disdainfully to her left at the beat-up old sedan and at the car's driver.

Similar words include *haughty*, *consequential*, and *patronizing*.

Imagining a supercilious person raising his or her eyebrows is helpful in understanding the definitions of these technical words:

superciliary: in zoology, pertaining to the facial eyebrow bone

supercilium: in architecture, a narrow horizontal molding at the top of a cornice

SUPERFLUOUS (soo PER floo us) *adj.* adding nothing necessary or important; excess; unecessary; surplus

> 66 Education is the only cure for certain diseases the modern world has engendered, but if you don't find the disease, the remedy is *superfluous*." —Sir John Buchan

Similar words include *extraneous*, *pleonastic*, and *redundant*.

The phrase "superfluous redundancy" is redundant in that the word "superfluous" is superfluous.

UMBRAGE (UM brij) *n.* anger; resentment; sense of having been maligned or insulted

The word derives from the astronomical term *umbra*, which refers to the darkest shadow formed by an eclipse. Accordingly, a person with *umbrage* is ensconced in a dark shadow of anger and resentment.

> 66 The patient who sees 'SOB' on his chart should not take *umbrage*, as it is usually intended to mean 'short of breath.'" —William Safire, *New York Times Magazine*

Similar words include *vexation*, *animosity*, and *spite*.

VENERATE (VEN er ayt) *adj.* to treat reverantly; revere; respect and admire greatly

The noun form is *veneration*.

The adjective (and most commonly used) form is *venerable*:

> 66 Corruption...takes away every shadow of authority and credit from the most *venerable* parts of our [nation's] constitution." —Edmund Burke

An outward demonstration of one's veneration is referred to as *obeisance*: bowing or other physical gesture of honor or respect

A similar word is *esteem*: to consider as having worth or value.

Do not confuse *venerable* with *veritable*: truly; very much so; genuine.

WANTON (WAHN tuhn) *adj.* without regard for what is morally right; reckless; unjustifiable

In criminal law, the prosecution must prove that a defendant accused of first-degree murder acted with *wanton* disregard for human life.

> 66 If you suppress the exorbitant love of pleasure and money, idle curiosity, iniquitous purpose, and *wanton* mirth, what a stillness there would be in the greatest cities." —Jean de La Bruyére

A closely related word is *want*: lack or scarcity. A wanton person possesses a want of scruples, probity, and moral rectitude.

Quiz Time (1.1–1.3)

Directions: Match each numbered word in the left column with its lettered definition in the right column. The answer key begins on page 89.

Quiz 1.1

1.	alacrity	a.	break or gap
2.	chagrin	b.	resentment
3.	curmudgeon	c.	cure-all
4.	demagogue	d.	cheerful willingness
5.	enigma	e.	miserly and rude person
6.	harbinger	f.	approval or permission
7.	hiatus	g.	mystery or puzzle
8.	panacea	h.	disappointment or humiliation
9.	sanction	i.	political agitator
10.	umbrage	j.	omen of future event

Quiz 1.2

1.	appease	a.	assent to passively
2.	acquiesce	b.	avoid
3.	countervail	c.	cater to the base desires
4.	deprecate	d.	confuse
5.	eschew	e.	convert
6.	obfuscate	f.	express disapproval of
7.	pander	g.	go back on a promise
8.	proselytize	h.	pacify
9.	renege	i.	respect and admire
10.	venerate	j.	use equal force against

Quiz 1.3

1.	choleric	a.	believing easily
2.	credulous	b.	impoverished
3.	ephemeral	c.	indifferent
4.	halcyon	d.	lasting only a short time
5.	indigent	e.	peaceful and serene
6.	laudable	f.	praiseworthy or commendable
7.	loquacious	g.	prominent or significant
8.	phlegmatic	h.	reckless and unjustifiable
9.	salient	i.	talkative
10.	wanton	j.	temperamental

99 Need-to-Know SAT Words

ABHOR (ub HOR) *v.* to hate intensely; despise; detest

> ✎ Although I am dispassionate about sports in general, I *abhor* the game of golf as a complete waste of time as well as prime real estate.

The sports "fan" in the sentence above finds golf to be *abhorrent*, although he is indifferent about sports in general.

A similar word is *loathe*.

Do not confuse *abhorrent* with *aberrant*: deviating or divergent (e.g., from the norm)

ABSTRUSE (ub STROOS) *adj.* difficult to comprehend or understand

Similar words include *esoteric* and *recondite*.

Do not confuse *abstruse* with *obtuse*: dull in perception or intellect. The distinction is illustrated in this sentence:

> ✎ The vacuous and *obtuse* young man barely made it through high school; academic subjects such as algebra and social studies were far too *abstruse* for him.

ACCOLADE (AK uh layd) *n.* an expression of approval or praise; laudatory notice or recognition, such as an award or prize

> ✎ Every aspiring stage actor dreams of receiving *accolades* from leading theater critics after a Broadway debut.

> ✎ The Olympic gold medalist was showered with *accolades* after her record-breaking performance; however, the laudatory efforts of the silver medalist, who also bettered the previous world record, went completely unnoticed.

An accolade is a means of paying *homage* or expressing one's *esteem* or *reverence*. A similar word is *obeisance*.

AMALGAMATION (uh mal guh MAY shun) *n.* the process or result of combining or mixing two or more things

> ✎ For dinner at the cafeteria, a dubious *amalgamation* of leftovers was given the euphemistic label "meat loaf."

The verb form is *amalgamate*.

A closely related word is *alloy*: a mixture of two metals for the purpose of increasing strength. Both words are used commonly in metallurgy to refer to the process or result of melting and combining metals.

Distinguish *amalgamation* from two similar but distinct words:

multifarious: diverse, having many elements or parts

mosaic: a matrix of various elements and parts, especially various colored tiles

AMELIORATE (uh MEEL yuh rayt) *v.* to make better or improve

The word is commonly confused with three related words: *mitigate*, *alleviate*, and *abate*, all of which refer to a lessening in harshness, severity, or amount (as opposed to making better or improving). This distinction is illustrated in the following trilogy of sentences:

✎ Beachfront parking is inadequate to accommodate the influx of weekend tourists; the city can *ameliorate* its tourist appeal by constructing a new parking lot.

✎ The city can *mitigate* (or *alleviate*) the beachfront parking problem by constructing a new parking lot.

✎ The parking problem will not *abate* until the influx of tourists becomes an efflux at the conclusion of the holiday weekend.

AMORPHOUS (uh MOR fus) *adj.* having no definite form or character; shapeless or characterless

✎ The baggy look favored by many young gang members gives them an *amorphous* appearance as well as allowing them to conceal weapons..

The word is derived from the Latin word *morph* (form).

Although the word is now used broadly (as in the sentence above), it was initially used in geology and chemistry, as defined here:

(geology) occurring in an unstratified and uncrystalline mass

(chemistry) not crystalline in structure

ANATHEMA (uh NATH eh muh) *n.* a person or thing condemned, accused, damned, cursed, or generally loathed.

✎ The adulteress Hester Prynne, the main character in *The Scarlet Letter*, is probably the best known example of an anathema (*adulteress* and *anathema* both begin with the letter "A").

A similar word is *pariah*: an outcast.

Do not confuse *anathema* with *anesthesia*: any drug that dulls the senses.

ANECDOTE (AN ek doht) *n.* a brief narrative of an amusing or interesting event

A personal anecdote relates an incident from the storyteller's personal experience. The adjective form is *anecdotal*.

> ❝ That when a man fell into his *anecdotage*, it was a sign for him to retire." —Benjamin Disraeli

The word bears no relation to *antidote*: a remedy or cure for a poison or other harmful substance.

A teller of anecdotes (storyteller) is referred to as a *raconteur*.

ASPERSION (uh SPER zhun) *n.* an insulting or derogatory remark; a slanderous, defamatory statement

The word is usually used in some form of the idiomatic expression "to cast aspersions."

The definition of the word is a bit at odds with the following variation of a familiar adage:

> ❝ Sticks and stones may break my bones, but a*spersions* will never hurt me."

A related word is *asperity*: roughness or sharpness of manner or tone.

ASSUAGE (uh SWAYJ) *v.* to pacify or soothe; to lessen another's fear, distress, or pain

> ✎ A skydiving instructor might attempt to *assuage* a student's fears by citing statistics showing that skydiving mishaps occur very rarely.

It is the fear or distress that is assuaged, not the person himself or herself.

Do not confuse *assuage* with *appease*. While both acts serve to calm or pacify, the former placates a demanding person, while the latter calms a fearful or distressed person.

ATTENUATE (uh TEN yoo ayt) *v.* to weaken or make thin

> ✎ The jeweler *attenuated* the raw gold into a long chain.

The adjective form is *tenuous*: thin, weak, insubstantial, unsupported. A good antonym of tenuous is *tenacious*: holding firm and fast, as with a strong grip (the noun form is tenacity).

Related words include: *tentative* (experimental, unsure); *tensile* (stretched or strained); as well as several anatomical "stretching" words—such as *tendon*, *tentacle*, and *tensor*.

AUSPICE (AW spis) *n.* a favorable sign or omen; (*auspices*) sponsorship or patronage; an emblem or symbol

> ✎ High scores on standardized tests might be an *auspice* of future academic success.

The adjective form is *auspicious*.

> ✎ Being accepted by the college of your choice is an *auspicious* occasion—one that portends a favorable or promising future.

As indicated above and illustrated in the following sentences, the word also has two other meanings:

> ✎ Under the *auspices* of the local art guild, the widely touted and celebrated sculptor created a masterpiece for the town square. The laudatory sculpture, patterned after the colorful state *auspice*, was met with accolades from all.

BEHOOVE (bih HOOV) *v.* to be incumbent upon, suited to, or proper for

This unusual but frequently used word comes to us form the Old English word *beholf* (to need).

> ✎ It *behooves* us to get out of the rain before our clothes become soaking wet.

> ❝ I believe it would *behoove* divorce-ridden America to learn of the devotion to family that exists amongst the primitive people." —Thomas A. Dooley, *The Edge of Tomorrow*

BELEAGUER (beh LEE ger) *v.* to surround; besiege

The word has a strong military connotation and is often used in the context of war or battle, either in the literal or figurative sense.

The word is commonly misused to refer to weariness or fatigue. The following sentence underscores the proper use of the word:

> ✎ *Beleaguered* by enemy troops, the weary soldiers finally admitted defeat and surrendered their garrison.

The adjective form is *belligerent*: hostile; warlike; aggressive.

BESMIRCH (bih SMERCH) *v.* to soil or tarnish, especially a person's honor or reputation; to defile

> ✎ One pejorative remark about the city councilman by the popular local newspaper columnist forever *besmirched* his reputation among the townspeople.

Similar words include *denigrate*, *deprecate*, and *calumniate*.

BILIOUS (BIL ee us) *adj.* irritable or irascible; unpleasant or distasteful

> The word was originally used in medicine to describe the indigestion caused by an excess secretion of bile by the liver.
>
> The word is now used figuratively as well. Did poet Ogden Nash use the word literally or figuratively in the following couplet?
>
> 66 A good deal of superciliousness Is based on *biliousness*." —Ogden Nash
>
> Similar words include *peevish* and *boorish*.

BRACKISH (BRAK ish) *adj.* having a somewhat salty taste, usually unpleasantly so

> Two related words are *saline* and *briny*. *Saline* is a neutral word which simply refers to salt.
>
> A synonym for brackish is *briny*, although *briny* is usually used to describe sea or ocean water.
>
> ✎ The Great Salt Lake in Utah is the world's most *briny* lake, and its water tastes even more *brackish* than my grandmother's vegetable soup.

BREVITY (BREH vih tee) *n.* briefness; conciseness

> According to the popular aphorism, "Brevity is a virtue." In Act 2 of Shakespeare's *Hamlet*, Polonius took this adage to heart:
>
> 66 Since *brevity* is the soul of wit, and tediousness the limbs and outward flourishes, I will be brief."
>
> A person known for brevity might be described as *pithy*, *sententious*, *terse*, *laconic*, or *succinct*.

CALLOW (KAL oh) *adj.* inexperienced; immature

> ✎ The *callow* teenager's voice trembled as he asked the girl he had a crush on to accompany him to the prom.
>
> Although the word suggests youth, an older person can also fittingly be described as callow:
>
> ✎ My parents are quite *callow* in the ways of the World Wide Web.
>
> Do not confuse *callow* with *fallow*: agricultural land left idle in order to restore productivity.
>
> A person who is callow in a particular endeavor might be referred to as a *neophyte* or *novice*.

CANVASS (KAN vus) *v.* to solicit votes, sales, opinions, etc.

> The word is usually used in reference to a geographical area, as in this sentence:

✎ Her summer job involved *canvassing* the residential neighborhoods to sell magazine subscriptions.

However, the word can be used in other contexts as well, as in this sentence:

❝ A *canvass* of opinion in Congress had convinced him [President Johnson] that the country was in no mood for progressive words on race." —Doris Kearns, *Lyndon Johnson and the American Dream*

The word is unrelated to *canvas*: a sturdy cloth used as a covering.

CELERITY (suh LAYR ih tee) n. quickness; swiftness

❝ Time, with all its *celerity*, moves slowly to him whose whole employment is to watch its flight." —Dr. Samuel Johnson

Two closely related but distinct words are:
dispatch: a quick or speedy sending off
alacrity: cheerful readiness or willingness; briskness
The word bears no relation to either *celebrity* or *celery*.

COZEN (KOH zun) v. to cheat; swindle; deceive; defraud

✎ Unsophisticated elderly people are particularly susceptible to the ruse of the *cozening* "financial advisor."

❝ Idiots may be *cozened* twice." —John Dryden

Similar words include *dupe* and *beguile*.
A person who engages in *cozenage* might be referred to as a *rogue*, *mountebank*, or *charlatan*.

CYNOSURE (SIH no zher) n. the center of attention or interest; a celebrity

✎ The English professor's current *cynosure* are the writers of the American Renaissance.

✎ From her first encounter with the Prince of Wales to her tragic death, Princess Diana was the *cynosure* of the paparazzi.

A similar word is *luminary*; a prominent person. *Luminary* is derived from the Latin word *lumin* (light). A *luminous* object catches a person's attention for its brightness.

DEARTH (DERTH) n. scarcity; lack; insufficiency

The word is used in referring to quantity (either amount or number), but not size.
The opposite of dearth is *plethora*.

✎ At the present time, a *plethora* of high-paying computer engineering jobs go unfilled, due to a *dearth* of qualified recent graduates.

Similar words include *paucity*, *poverty*, and *want*.

DECIMATE (DES uh mayt) *v.* to kill or destroy all or a large proportion of

✎ Untold animal and plant species have been *decimated* by clearcutting in the rainforests.

The word is derived from the Latin word *dec* (tenth). The word was original used to describe the selection and killing of every tenth person, as in war or in genocide.

DILATORY (DIL uh tor ee) *adj.* delaying or procrastinating; designed or intended to bring about delay

✎ I apologize for being *dilatory* in my duties, but I assure you that there are exigent circumstances to justify the delay.

The word is used commonly in law to refer to tactics and strategies used by lawyers to delay court proceedings, as in this sentence:

✎ To expedite the legal proceedings, the no-nonsense judge admonished the overzealous advocates to refrain from employing their arsenal of *dilatory* tactics.

DISPATCH (dis PACH) *v.* to send off, especially quickly

✎ The coach *dispatched* orders from the sidelines.

The word is also used as a noun, as in this sentence:

✎ A prolific artist produces works with great *dispatch* or *celerity*.

In the television series *Taxi*, Louie's job title with the taxicab company was "dispatcher"; he was in charge of sending taxis to pick up customers.

DURESS (dyoo RES) *n.* compulsion or procurement by threat, coercion, or restraint

Prisoners and hostages under *duress* can often be coerced to issue false confessions and other statements.

✎ Patricia Hearst was convicted of armed robbery and served time in prison despite her claim that she was a hostage of the Symbionese Liberation Army and acted under *duress*—the fear that they would kill her if she did not participate in the crime.

EFFACE (ih FAYS) *v.* to obliterate, wipe out, or rub out

Do not confuse effacing with marring or disfiguring. Effacing serves to remove the face of, while the other two acts damage or alter but do not remove.

✎ Years of use had *effaced* the design of the floor tiles.

A self-effacing person is overly modest in speaking of his or her own qualities and accomplishments.

"Face" words such as *efface* and *facade* are unrelated to "eff" words such as *efficacy* (capability)and *effect*.

EGREGIOUS (uh GREE jyus) *adj.* shocking, extraordinary, or outstanding in a bad way

✎ Introducing the venerable and eminent guest speaker by a derogatory epithet was an *egregious* error.

❝ There is no more *egregious* fallacy than the belief that order requires central direction." —Milton Friedman, *Newsweek*

Two similar word are *flagrant* and *glaring.*

EMINENT (EM uh nint) *adj.* distinguished; high in stature or rank; prominent

Accomplished and highly respected scholars, jurists, politicians, and diplomats are often described as *eminent.*

❝ Censure is the tax a man pays to the public for being *eminent.*" —Jonathan Swift

The noun form is *eminence.* Some monarchs prefer to be addressed as "Your Eminence."

Do not confuse *eminent* with these two words:

imminent: about to happen; impending; threatening

immanent: existing within the mind; inherent or indwelling

EPITHET (EP ih thet) *n.* a word or phrase describing a person used instead of or added to the person's name; an insulting or derogatory characterization

Here are a few well-known epithets: Alexander the Great, Tarzan the Ape Man, The King (Elvis Presley).

❝ I was on Grandpa's side, even if he was a failure. But I still wondered why he deserved that *epithet.*" —Walter Cronkite, *Reader's Digest*

Do not confuse *epithet* with these words:

epitaph: an inscription on a monument in memory of a deceased person

epigram: a clever, pithy saying; aphorism

ESPOUSE (eh SPOWZ) *v.* to advocate, support, promote, or argue for

❝ ...we must continue to perfect here at home the rights and the values which we *espouse* around the world. —Jimmy Carter

The word is related, albeit archaically, to *spouse* (marriage partner). A person who espouses is a defender, as a man might be viewed as a defender of his spouse (wife).

Similar verbs are *vindicate* and *champion*.

EVANESCENT (eh vuh NES unt) *adj.* fleeting; fading quickly; passing away; vanishing

✎ The *evanescent* bliss of a gluttonous cheesecake binge always gives way to a somewhat sick feeling.

The verb form is *evanesce*.

Similar words include *ephemeral*, *transient*, and *transitory*.

Do not confuse *evanescent* with *effervescent*: bubbling; lively.

EXACERBATE (eg ZAS er bayt) *v.* to increase in harshness or severity; aggrevate; worsen

✎ His high blood pressure, due mainly to obesity, was *exacerbated* by his stressful job.

The word also has another meaning: to irritate or embitter another's feelings.

✎ A caustic, derisive remark can *exacerbate* another person's feelings while also *exacerbating* any ill will between the two people.

A closely related word is *exasperate*: to annoy, irritate, or infuriate.

EXCULPATE (eks KUL payt) *v.* to free from blame; clear from a charge of fault or guilt; vindicate

✎ Not so much as a scintilla of evidence has been found which might *exculpate* the defendant from guilt.

An *exculpatory* clause in a contract releases one party from fault for specified events which may occur during performance of the contract.

A contrary word is *culpable*: at fault; blameworthy; responsible.

FOMENT (foh MENT) *v.* to instigate; stir up; incite; stimulate; arouse

Foment is a flexible word, useful in both a positive and a negative sense, as illustrated by these two sentences:

✎ The jealous ingenue did her best to *foment* a quarrel between her ex-boyfriend and the popular cheerleader.

✎ According to some botanists, indulging your houseplants with mellifluous music *foments* their growth and development.

Similar words include *impel*, *exhort*, *kindle*, *facilitate*, and *goad*.

FOPPISH (FAH pish) *adj.* excessively vain about one's dress, manner, or general appearance; overly refined

> A foppish person is a *fop.*
> *Foppery* are the clothes and demeanor of a foppish person.
>
> ✎ In Neil Simon's *The Odd Couple*, Felix is the fastidious and foppish roommate, and Oscar is the slovenly and slightly churlish one.
>
> A foppish person's manner of dress might be described as *dapper, spruce, chic, natty, rakish,* or *swank.*
> Two related words—*prudish* and *priggish*—refer to an excessive concern with manner and appearance as they relate to morality.
> Three other related words—*punctilious, meticulous,* and *fastidious*—refer more to a penchant for neatness and precision than to vanity.

FORENSIC (fuh REN sik) *adj.* pertaining to debate or rhetoric; suitable as evidence in a court of law

> The word has two related but distinct meanings, as suggested by the definition above.
> The academic art of debate and rhetoric is sometimes referred to as *forensics.*
> In criminology, the field of *forensics* involves the preservation of evidence to ensure its usefulness and integrity in court.
> The field of *forensic medicine* involves the application of medical knowledge to legal proceedings, especially the observation of a body's physical condition for evidentiary purposes and expert opinions.

GARRULOUS (GAYR yoo lus) *adj.* excessively talkative or wordy.

> ✎ My *garrulous* friend always runs up a large phone bill.
>
> Similar words include *loquacious, verbose,* and *voluble.*
> A related but distinct word is *glib*: fluent in speech or written expression but without care or thought.
> Do not confuse these "gabby" words with words such as *bombastic* and *grandiloquent* (see the next entry below).

GRANDILOQUENT (gran DIL uh kwent) *adj.* given to using pompous, high-sounding language

> A *grandiloquent* person may come across as *arrogant, haughty,* and *supercilious.*

❝ I am creating a certain image of man of my own choosing...This helps us in understanding...the content...of such rather *grandiloquent* words as anguish, forlorning, despair." —Jean-Paul Sartre

A similar word is *bombastic*.

ICONOCLAST (y KAHN oh klast) *n. one* who attacks cherished beliefs or traditions

The adjective form is *iconoclastic*.

✎ To his parents' chagrin, the *iconoclastic* young man rejected organized religion; not only was he vehemently reproached for his maverick ideas, he became an anathema among his churchgoing family members.

The word is derived from the Latin (and Greek) word *icon* (image); originally, an iconoclast was one who would demonstrate his rejection of conventional beliefs by destroying sculptures that served as religious icons.

IMPECUNIOUS (im peh KYOO nee us) *adj.* lacking money; penniless; indigent

✎ Without a sponsor, a spendthrift is likely to be perennially *impecunious*.

"Pecun" words, which relate to money, can be quite confusing, as suggested below.
The opposite of *impecunious* is not *pecunious* (*pecunious* is not a word).
Do not confuse *impecunious* with *pecuniary*: monetary or pertaining to money.
An *impecunious* person is said to be in a state of *penury*: poverty, destitution, or indigence.

IMPETUOUS (im PEH chyoo us) *adj.* impulsive; rash; spontaneous

An impetuous person would probably not be considered *timorous* (fearful) but might be considered *temerarious* (foolishly bold).

✎ *Impetuous* young lovers often behave in a *puerile* (childish and foolish) manner; they might be seen skipping in the rain without an umbrella or talking baby talk to each other.

An impulsive and foolhardy person is often described as "an impetuous fool."

IMPUDENT (IM pyoo dunt) *adj.* rude; brazen

❝ Folly will always find faith wherever impostors will find impudence." —Christian Nestell Bovee

Similar words include *insolent*, *audacious*, and *impertinent*.
The noun form is *impudence*.
Synonyms of *impudence* include *effrontery*, *audacity*, *insolence*, and *impertinence*.

Do not confuse *impudent* with *imprudent* (careless; reckless; indiscreet) or with *impotent* (not potent).

IMPUNITY (im PYOO nih tee) *n.* privilege; license; exemption

> 66 To praise princes for virtues they are lacking in is a way of insulting them with *impunity*." —La Rochefoucauld

Do not confuse *impunity* with *impugn*: to challenge; call into question; contradict
Similar words include *franchise* and *sanction*. All three words suggest officialism, authority, and formality.

INDOLENCE (IN doh luns) *n.* laziness; aversion to exertion; slothfulness; sluggishness

The adjective form is *indolent*.

> ✎ My next door neighbor is forty years old and still lives with his parents at their house; this is a sign of either terminal *indolence* or frugality gone amuck.

A similar word is *torpor* (*adj torpid*).

INTRANSIGENT (in TRAN si junt) *adj.* stubborn; unwilling to compromise; inflexible

> ✎ During the corporation's policy-making conference, the *intransigent* board member did not ingratiate himself among the other members of the board of directors.

The antonym *transigent* is not commonly used.
Similar words include *intractable*, *refractory*, and *contumacious*.
Related but distinct words are *importunate*, *pertinacious*, and *inexorable*, all of which involve unflagging (unwavering) persistence.

INTREPID (in TREP id) *adj.* fearless; courageous

> ✎ Most of the mountain climbers stayed behind, fearing an approaching storm; however, a few *intrepid* members of the expedition forged ahead to reconnoiter the next mountain face.

A related word is *trepidation*: fear
Do not confuse *intrepid* with *tepid*: luke warm; neither hot nor cold.

INUNDATE (IN un dayt) *v.* to flood or overflow; deluge; overwhelm

The word is similar in meaning to *beleaguer* and *besiege* but is distinct in its suggestion of a *flowing*.

✎ To foment controversy, the disgruntled employee posted on the company's intranet a haranguing commentary about being unfairly passed over for promotion; the surprising result was an *inundation* of support from coworkers and a formal apology from the company's CEO.

❝ What *inundation* of life and thought is discharged from one soul into another through [the eyes]." —Ralph Waldo Emerson

INVIDIOUS (in VID ee us) *adj.* likely to create ill will, animosity, or envy

✎ By his *invidious* remarks about who he thought were the best and worst athletes on the team, the impertinent outfielder threatened the collegial relationship among all the team members.

Do not confuse *invidious* with *insidious*: wily; crafty; sly; treacherous.

JOCULAR (JAHK yuh ler) *adj.* not serious; joking; facetious; jesting

✎ Many of the party guests left early, annoyed by the host's incessantly *jocular* and ribald banter that soon grew repugnant.

A closely related word is *jocose*: given to joking; playful; lighthearted.
Do not confuse *jocular* and *jocose* with *jocund*, which carries a somewhat different meaning: cheerful, merry.

❝ Night's candles are burnt out, and *jocund* day Stands tiptoe on the misty mountaintops." —Shakespeare

JUXTAPOSE (juk stuh POHZ) *v.* to put side by side, usually in order to compare or contrast

The noun form is *juxtaposition*.
Do not confuse the meaning of juxtaposition with that of *nexus*: a connection or linking.

❝ The human face is really like one of those Oriental gods: a whole group of faces *juxtaposed* on different planes; it is impossible to see them all simultaneously." — Eric Hoffer

LANGUISH (LANG gwish) *v.* to lose strength or vitality; weaken; become feeble, droop; fade

The noun form is *languor*, and the adjective form is *languid*.

✎ The Scandinavian tourists *languished* in the summer Mediterranean heat.

A person who is *languishing* has been *enervated* (deprived of strength and vitality).
Another word with a related but distinct meaning is *wizened*: shriveled or withered.

LURID (LOOR id) *adj.* sensational or shocking; shining with an unnatural glow; gruesome or revolting

> As suggested above, *lurid* is a flexible word with three related but distinct meanings. The first one is the most common and is illustrated by this sentence:
>
> ✎ Despite their lack of veracity and credibility, the *lurid* stories found in the tabloid magazines appeal to the prurient interests of even the most incredulous reader.
>
> Do not confuse *lurid* with *livid*: enraged; extremely angry.

MALADROIT (mal a DROYT) *adj.* bungling; awkward; clumsy

> A maladroit person would properly be described as a *lout, oaf,* or *boor* (or as *loutish, oafish,* or *boorish*).
> A person might be maladroit either in social or physical lack of grace. The waiter in the following sentence is twice maladroit:
>
> ✎ Our neophyte waiter spilled soup on us, then dismissed his clumsy act by thanking us for wearing cheap blouses.
>
> Two similar words are *gauche* and *ungainly*.
> The opposite of *maladroit* is *adroit*: graceful; skillful; tactful.

MARSHAL (MAR shul) *v.* to put in proper order; assemble; arrange clearly

> The word is usually used in military parlance; for example:
>
> ✎ A military commander *marshals* his troops for a final advance against the enemy.
>
> The word is also used as a noun: an officer charged with maintaining order.

MAUDLIN (MAWD lin) *adj.* overly sentimental; foolishly tearful

> ✎ The raconteur brought his lachrymose audience to tears with his *maudlin* story about the little boy who ran away from home with his dog.
>
> Maudlin people are sometimes labeled "romantic fools" or "hopelessly romantic."
> A similar words is *mawkish*.
> A related word is *lachrymose*: easily brought to tears (though not necessarily for sentimental reasons).

MELLIFLUOUS (meh LIF loo us) *adj.* sweet sounding; flowing smoothly

> The *mellifluous* tones of wind chimes were carried on the breeze.
>
> ❝ Much of what we hear strikes us as dissonance or as noise, and what falls within a certain range we find sweet, intellectually satisfying and *mellifluous*." —Diane Ackerman, *A Natural History of the Senses*

The word usually involves sound, but not always, as this sentence illustrates:

✎ The poet's thoughts flowed *mellifluously* onto the paper.

A similar word is *sonorous*: pleasing to the ear.

MIASMA (my AZ muh) *n.* noxious, dangerous, or unwholesome emissions, atmosphere, or influence

✎ By the end of a typical Saturday evening, the popular night club becomes a *miasma* of smoke, licentiousness and, most noxious of all, disco music.

The adjective form is *miasmic*.

✎ Environmentalists are fighting for the abatement the *miasmic* conditions created by the local pharmaceutical factory.

Because of its adverse effects on health, a miasma might be described as *deleterious*, *pestiferous*, or *virulent*.

An offensive smelling miasma or effluent might be described as *malodorous*, *noisome*, *rank*, or *mephitic*.

MULTIFARIOUS (mul tuh FAYR ee us) *adj.* greatly diversified; having various parts, elements, or forms

✎ My *multifarious* job is interesting and challenging, since I wear many hats and rarely perform the same task twice in a given day.

A related word is *multifaceted*: having many aspects or phases:

✎ I envy those *multifaceted* performers who can sing, play an instrument, dance, and act.

NEFARIOUS (neh FAYR ee us) *adj.* extremely wicked

This paraphrased line from a *Wizard of Oz* song has lost it's original alliterative quality:

❝ Ding, dong, the witch is dead. Which old witch? The *nefarious* witch!"

Similar words include *flagitious* and *depraved*.

NEPOTISM (NEP uh tiz um) *n.* favoritism bestowed upon family members or close friends, especially in business or poltics.

✎ The unspoken policy of *nepotism* in the company made advancement of non-relatives virtually impossible.

✎ Would it be considered *nepotism* for a president to appoint his own wife as the nation's health care czar, even if she isn't paid for her services?

Nepotism can also be characterized as *patronage*: financial support of others by a wealthy or powerful person. However, patronage does not require favoritism toward friends or relatives.

OBSTREPEROUS (ub STREP er us) *adj.* resisting control in an unruly, noisy, boisterous manner

Obstreperousness is characterized by both noise and lack of control.

✎ A crowd of people at a concert, sporting event, or demonstration can sometimes become *obstreperous* and, if growing violent, riotous.

✎ An individual person can also be *obstreperous*, as a drunken bar patron who is thrown out by a bouncer for behaving *obstreperously*.

A similar word is *recalcitrant*: unruly; resisting authority. However, a recalcitrant person is not necessarily noisy or clamorous.

OSTRACIZE (AHS truh syz) *v.* to banish, exile, or exlude by general consent

Ostracization usually results from an adverse judgment against a person and is a demonstration or means of *reproof*, *reproach*, *reprobation*, or *censure*.

✎ Widely *ostracized* for the deaths of his wife and her freind, O.J. Simpson became an expatriate of sorts, a "victim" of pandemic censure.

✎ For his aquiescence in Hitler's heinous crimes, the once venerable German dignitary was *ostracized* from his homeland for life.

PANDEMIC (pan DEM ik) *adj.* affecting a majority of a nation or the world

A related word is *epidemic*, meaning widespread (but not necessarily nationwide or globally). The distinction is illustrated in this sentence:

✎ Because the AIDS virus has already attained *epidemic* status, the federal government should increase funding for AIDS medical research before the virus reaches *pandemic* proportions.

Although the word is usually used in reference to a disease, it can be used figuratively as well, as in this sentence:

✎ Immediately after the Federal Reserve Board announced a significant hike in the key interest rate, a *pandemic* sense of doom was felt throughout the financial world.

PEREGRINATION (per uh gruh NAY shun) *n.* a journey or travel

> ✎ With his laptop computer, modem, and a little help from satellite communications technology, the senator can send and receive e-mail during his *peregrinations* and junkets.

The verb form of the word is *peregrinate*.
A related word is *peregrine*: foreign; alien; from another country.
Other related words include:
  migrate: to relocate
  emigrate: to move away to another place
  immigrate: to move to from another place
  pilgrimage: travel to a place of special significance

PLENARY (PLEE nuh ree) *adj.* absolute, complete, or full

A despot or dictator is said to have *plenary* political power over his domain.
An assistant store manager might be given *plenary* decision-making power while the manager is away.
The word also has a related but distinct meaning in business and politics: attended by all qualified members.

> ✎ The President's "State of the Union" address is one notable example of a *plenary* session of Congress—it is attended by all qualified members of Congress.

PORTEND (por TEND) *v.* to indicate in advance; foretell; predict

The adjective form is *portentous*, as illustrated in this sentence:

> ❝ I was thirty. Before me stretched the *portentous*, menacing road of a new future."
> —F. Scott Fitzgerald, *The Great Gatsby*

Similar words include *bode*, *forebode*, *presage*, *augur*, and *prophesy*. These words are not used the same in grammatical construction, however. For example:

> ✎ *Foreboding* storm clouds did not *bode* well for the camping trip; they *portend* an unpleasant weekend.

> ✎ The campers ignored a prior *presage*: the local meteorologist's prediction that a storm was impending.

The noun form is *portent*: an omen or prophetic sign, especially of something momentous or wonderful.

PRESAGE (PREH sij) *n.* anything that foreshadows future events; an omen or sign of what is to come

The word is derived from *sage*: a very wise or knowledgeable person.

✎ A middle-east oil embargo might be a *presage* or omen of rising prices at the gas pump. Only the members of the oil cartel can prophesy when such a *presage*— or its progeny—might occur.

❝ Books are...the symbol and *presage* of immortality." —Henry Ward Beecher

A similar word is *harbinger*.

Do not confuse *presage* with the related word *prescience*: firsthand foreknowledge of future events, as opposed to a mere prediction or prophecy(*adj prescient*).

PROFLIGATE (PRAHF luh git) *adj.* recklessly extravagant or wasteful; shamelessly immoral

✎ While Marie Antoinette wallowed in her ostentatious lifestyle, the destitute churls around her grew enraged by her *profligate* spending.

A profligate person such as Marie Antoinette could be referred to as a *wastrel*.

A related word is *spendthrift*: one who spends money extravagantly and wastefully.

Another related word is *prodigal*: wasteful in the use of money.

Profligate can also carry a related but broader meaning: shamelessly immoral or dissolute (indifferent to moral restraints).

PROPITIOUS (proh PISH us) *adj.* favorable to; advantageous

Conditions or circumstances are propitious if they tend to promote, facilitate, or work to one's advantage.

✎ A tailwind is *propitious* in an airplane's reaching its destination in as short a time as possible.

✎ A youthful electorate might be *propitious* for the liberal candidate in the upcoming election.

A similar word is *auspicious* (promoting success; favorable)

Do not confuse *propitious* with *propiteous*: pitiful.

PUNCTILIOUS (punk TIL ee us) *adj.* exacting in the observance of niceties and formalities of conduct

A punctilious person is likely to be a punctual person, always on time for his or her appointments and parleys.

A punctilious person is also likely to punctuate his or her sentences properly.

A similar word is *foppish*: excessively vain about one's dress, manner, or general appearance.

Other similar words include *fastidious* and *meticulous*.

QUANDARY (KWAHN duh ree) *n.* a perplexing or difficult situation; dilemma; predicament; "catch-22"

> ✎ The bride-to-be was in a *quandary* as to how to marshal her bridesmaids, family members, and future in-laws at the wedding so as to avoid indignation or ill will.

A similar word is *imbroglio*.
A word with a similar but distinct meaning is *conundrum*: a puzzle or mystery.

QUERULOUS (KWER uh lus) *adj.* full of complaints; whining

> ✎ The *querulous* vanpool member complained so incessantly about her job during the daily commute that eventually she was ostracized by the vanpool and had to drive her own car to work.

A similar word is *peevish*.
Do not confuse *querulous* with *query*: to inquire or question.

REPUDIATE (rih PYOO dee ayt) *v.* to reject, disown, or cast off as unbinding, non-authoritative, or without force

> A person can repudiate an accusation, a rule or order, or an idea or principle, as illustrated in the following sentences:

> ✎ The accused defendant categorically *repudiated* all indictments against him.

> ✎ The miasma exuding from the teenager's bedroom closet belied his *repudiation* of the house rule about laundering one's own dirty clothes on a weekly basis.

> ❝ Is man an ape or an angel? I am on the side of the angels. I *repudiate* with indignation and abhorrence these newfangled theories [referring to Darwin's Theory of Evolution]." —Benjamin Disraeli

RETICENT (RET ih sent) *adj.* reluctant to speak; reserved

> ✎ Intimidated by the ostensible grandeur of the law school classroom, the first-year student was *reticent* about participating in class discussions.

To interpret a popular adage: "The *reticent* wheel does not get the grease."
A similar word is *taciturn*.

RETINUE (RET ih noo) *n.* a group of attendants or servants

> The word refers to a group of assistants, not to an individual.

> ✎ Surrounding herself with a *retinue* gave the movie star a false sense of security; these acolytes were not her real friends but merely self-interested lackeys who enjoyed basking in her fame.

The word is derived from *retain* (to keep or possess).

A similar word is *entourage*.

Similar words which refer to an individual servile attendant include *acolyte*, *minion*, *lackey*, and *sycophant*.

RHAPSODIC (RAP soh dik) *adj.* exaggerated or exalted enthusiasm, especially as expressed in writing, speech, or music

✎ By *rhapsodizing* about the mundane chore of fence painting, Huck Finn convinced others to do the job for him.

✎ The Gershwin musical composition *Rhapsody in Blue* brilliantly juxtaposes a blues motif and a *rhapsodic* mood.

RUMINATE (ROO min ayt) *v.* to think over; ponder; mull over; "chew on"

The adjective form is *ruminant*.

The noun form is *rumination*, as illustrated in the following sentence:

✎ While the others at the table decided quickly on their choice of entree, Roberta announced her choice only after prolonged and pensive *rumination* and vacillation.

The word is derived from the zoological noun *ruminant*, a suborder of cud-chewing mammals which includes cattle and deer.

SALUBRIOUS (suh LOO bree us) *adj.* favorable to or promoting health; healthful

✎ We basked in the *salubrious* waters of the mineral pools.

The noun forms are *salubrity* and *salubriousness*.

A similar word is *salutary*.

Salubrious, *salutary*, and *healthful* do not mean "healthy"; for example:

✎ You might improve your health by taking *salubrious* (healthful) vitamin supplements.

Also, do not confuse *salutary* with *salutatory*, which pertains to saluting or obeisance (a show of respect or honor).

SANGUINE (SANG gwin) *adj.* hopeful; confident; optimistic; cheerful

❝ The *sanguine* hopes, which I had not shared, that Germany would collapse before the end of the year, failed." —Winston Churchill, *Triumph and Tragedy*

A similar but stronger word is *ardent*: eager, zealous, fervent.

The word also has another meaning: ruddy or reddish, as in skin complexion.

SCHISM (SIZ um) *n.* a split, division, or disunion

> The word is usually used in reference to politics, religion, or other ideological concerns.
>
> The secession of the Southern states from the Union preceding the Civil War was a *schism*.
>
> A word that is similar but distinct in meaning is *chasm*: a deep gap, split, or abyss. *Chasm* is used to describe a physical split, while *schism* is used to describe an abstract one.

SCINTILLA (sin TIL uh) *n.* a spark or trace; shred; small particle; tiny bit

> ✎ The investigator has not found a *scintilla* of evidence to implicate the accused as an accomplice in last week's chicanery.
>
> A related but distinct word is *scintillate*: to emit sparks; to flash, sparkle, or twinkle.
>
> ✎ Some people find a good book of fiction as *scintillating* as others find skydiving or racing down a ski slope.
>
> Similar words include *iota*, *mite*, and *whit*.

SURFEIT (SER fit) *n.* excess; overindulgence, especially in eating or drinking

> ❝ Sensual delights soon end in loathing, quickly bring a glutting *surfeit*, and degenerate into torments when they are continued and unintermitted." —John Howe
>
> ✎ After the *surfeit* of surfing music which inundated the air waves during the mid-1960s, the Beach Boys and their progeny were left behind in the musical "wake" of the Monterey Pop Music Festival.
>
> Similar words include *nimiety*, *glut*, and *plethora*.
>
> The word is also used as a verb: to satiate; indulge in to excess; fill completely; stuff; cloy.

TEMERITY (tuh MAYR ih tee) *n.* rash or foolhardy boldness; audacity; effrontery

> ✎ *Temerity* nearly cost the ardent but neophyte spelunker his life.
>
> The adjective form is *temerarious*, not to be confused with *timorous*: fearful.
>
> A temerarious person would also be considered *impetuous* (impulsive).

TEMPORAL (TEM puh rul) *adj.* pertaining to time, especially the present time; short-lived or transitory (as opposed to eternal); secular (worldly) as opposed to spiritual (not of the world)

> ✎ History informs us that peace among nations is *temporal*; it is humankind's nature to wage war against one another.

Two closely related words are:
ephemeral: fleeting; short-lived; temporary
evanescent: fleeting; fading quickly; passing away; vanishing

TORPOR (TOR per) *n.* a state of suspended activity powers; dormancy; sluggishness or lethargy

> *Torpor* can suggest either an absence or a slowness of activity.

> ✎ Prolific writers, musicians, and artists sometimes lapse into a period of *torpor*, allowing for a rejuvenation of creative powers and the germination and incubation of new ideas.

The adjective form is *torpid*.
A similar word is *indolence*.

TRIBULATION (trib yoo LAY shun) *n.* a great suffering, distress, or trouble

> *Tribulation* is a strong word, suggesting crushing and oppressive difficulties.

> ✎ The many trials and *tribulations* on the road to success test the mettle of a man or woman; what doesn't kill you makes you stronger.

A similar word is *throe* (usually *throes*), as illustrated in this sentence:

> ✎ Still in the *throes* of his daughter's untimely death, he found it impossible to function in his job.

TRUNCATE (TRUNG kayt) *v.* to shorten by cutting off a portion

> ✎ To meet the publishing deadline, the newspaper editor simply *truncated* the lengthy article rather than taking the time to abridge it.

> ✎ The Christmas tree was too tall for the room, so we *truncated* it by sawing off ten inches from the trunk.

Similar words are *lop* and *crop*.

TURGID (TER jid) *adj.* swollen; inflated; bombastic; pompous

> The word can be used literally or figuratively, to describe expression or attitude, as in this sentence:

     ❝ Spare me, I pray, your *turgid* rhetoric and bootlicking protestations." —S.J. Perelman, *The Road to Miltown*

UNCTUOUS (UNK choo us) *adj.* oily; fervently and overly pious or moralistic; having a suave, smooth, and insincere manner

The word is used in the tactile sense as well as to describe a person's disposition or behavior, as illustrated in the first sentence below:

✎ The *unctuousness* of the fitness guru's exhortations was exceeded only by his *unctuous*-appearing hairpiece.

❝ ... his voice had changed from rasping efficiency to an *unctuous* familiarity with sin and with the Almighty." — Sinclair Lewis, *Babbitt*

The word is derived from *unction*: the act of anointing with oil in religious ceremonies or primitive medical treatments.

USURP (yoo SERP) *v.* to take control or seize and hold by force or without right

The word is usually used in the context of government, politics, or the military.

✎ The incendiaries succeeded in *usurping* the office of prime minister, not through brute force but by sabotage and sedition.

VACUOUS (VAK yoo us) *adj.* expressionless; empty-headed or simpleminded

As the word suggests, a vacuous person is characterized by a vacuum between the ears.

✎ The hunky but *vacuous* "model-actor" never reached the final round of auditions for the role of lead actor, who the screenplay described as "a street-wise yet distinguished thirty-something male."

A similar word is *inane*, which is generally used to refer to a person's thought's or expressions rather than the person himself or herself.

VERITABLE (VAYR ih tuh bul) *adj.* truly; very much so; genuine

✎ The nonpartisan public interest organization grew so powerful that it became a *veritable* juggernaut of political clout.

Closely related words include:

    verity: the state or quality of being true

    verify: to prove the truth of; confirm

    verisimilitude: the appearance of truth

Do not confuse *veritable* with *venerable*: worthy of respect, praise, or honor.

VILIFY (VIL ih fy) *v.* to belittle or speak slightingly of in the extreme; slander; defame

> 66 Our ignorance of history makes us *vilify* our own age." —Gutave Flaubert

The noun form is *vilification*.
Similar words include *malign*, *disparage*, *chide*, *berate*, and *asperse*.

VIRULENT (VEER yoo lunt) adj. poisonous; extremely injurious; deadly

The word is derived from *virus*.

> The cornerstone and creed of the incumbent's campaign platform is to work toward eliminating all *virulent* effluents and toxins throughout the county.

A similar word is *deleterious*.
Do not confuse *virulent* with *virile*: masculine strength.

WANGLE (WANG gul) *v.* to obtain or accomplish something by trickery, scheming, or deception

> A *wangler* gets what he wants through *chicanery*, especially by "wagging" the tongue. In fact, *wangle* is derived from the word *wag*.

> The husband's *wangling* divorce lawyer left the former wife both indigent and indignant.

Similar words include *chicane*, *extort*, and *coerce*.

ZEALOUS (ZEL us) *adj.* overly enthusiastic or passionate, especially in devotion or activity

> The *overzealous* new employee appeared maladroit by attempting tasks in which he was inexperienced.

The word *zealot* is often used to refer to a religious fanatic.
Excessive *zealotry* can lead to idolatry.
The word is derived from *zeal*: zest, vim, vigor.
Similar words include *fervent* and *ardent*.

Quiz Time (1.4–1.7)

Directions: Match each numbered word in the left column with its lettered definition in the right column. The answer key begins on page 89.

Quiz 1.4

1.	abhor	a.	banish or exile
2.	ameliorate	b.	despise
3.	attenuate	c.	free from blame
4.	beleaguer	d.	improve
5.	decimate	e.	kill or destroy
6.	exculpate	f.	seize without right
7.	ruminate	g.	slander or defame
8.	usurp	h.	surround or besiege
9.	ostracize	i.	think over or ponder
10.	vilify	j.	weaken or make thin

Quiz 1.5

1.	amorphous	a.	advantageous
2.	bilious	b.	awkward or clumsy
3.	brackish	c.	boisterously unruly
4.	callow	d.	favorable to health
5.	egregious	e.	hopeful or confident
6.	intransigent	f.	irritable
7.	invidious	g.	likely to create ill will or envy
8.	maladroit	h.	shockingly or flagrantly bad
9.	obstreperous	i.	unwilling to compromise
10.	pandemic	j.	worldwide or universal
11.	plenary	k.	without definite form
12.	propitious	l.	salty
13.	salubrious	m.	inexperienced or immature
14.	sanguine	n.	insincere or overly smooth
15.	unctuous	o.	absolute or complete

Quiz 1.6

1.	abstruse	a.	complaining or whining
2.	dilatory	b.	delaying or procrastinating
3.	evanescent	c.	difficult to understand
4.	impetuous	d.	exacting in formalities
5.	impudent	e.	extremely injurious or deadly
6.	jocular	f.	fleeting or fading
7.	punctilious	g.	impulsive or spontaneous
8.	querulous	h.	not serious
9.	reticent	i.	reluctant to speak
10.	virulent	j.	rude or brazen

Quiz 1.7

1.	accolade	a.	dormancy or sluggishness
2.	anathema	b.	a dilemma or predicament
3.	celerity	c.	an unhealthful influence
4.	dearth	d.	attendants
5.	epithet	e.	excess or overindulgence
6.	impunity	f.	a journey or travel
7.	miasma	g.	foolhardy boldness
8.	peregrination	h.	an expression of approval
9.	quandary	i.	great suffering or distress
10.	retinue	j.	privilege or license
11.	scintilla	k.	a descriptive label
12.	surfeit	l.	a person or thing condemned
13.	temerity	m.	quickness
14.	torpor	n.	scarcity or insufficiency
15.	tribulation	o.	a small particle

99 Need-to-Know GRE Words

ACOLYTE (AK oh lyt) *n.* a servile attendant; assistant; helper

> 66 The faith of sophisticates goes to large electronic machines with computer printouts on cathode-ray tube terminals, attended by white-coated *acolytes*." —Adam Smith, *Esquire*

Similar words, which refer to servile followers, include *lackey*, *proselyte*, *minion*, *retinue*, and *entourage*.

ADAMANT (AD uh munt) *adj.* insistent; unwavering

> ✎ The little boy was *adamant* about getting an ice cream cone at the shopping center. His peevish whining and incessant foot-stomping indicated indubitably that he would not take "no" for an answer.

Many words are similar in meaning—for example: *resolute*; *tenacious*; *intent*; *intractable*; *contumacious*; *intransigent*; *importunate.*
Words that are contrary in meaning include: *irresolute*; *ambivalent*; *vacillating*.
The word *adamant* is unrelated to *Adam Ant*—either the 1960s cartoon super-hero insect or the English pop music star.

APPROBATION (ap ruh BAY shun) *n.* official approval; commendation

> 66 Conscience is...reason...accompanied [by] the sentiments of *approbation* and condemnation." —William Whewell

Two similar words are *sanction* and *imprimatur.*
The opposite of approbation is *reprobation* (or *disapprobation*).
The verb forms are *approbate* (approve) and *reprobate* (disapprove).
Approbate is not used as a noun. However, *reprobate* can be used as a noun to refer to an unprincipled or wicked person, as in this sentence:
A *reprobate* should be disapprobated, reprobated, or condemned, not approbated or commended.

ASCRIBE (uh SKRYB) *v.* to attribute to or refer to

> 66 Woe to him who has accustomed himself from his youth up to find something capricious in what is necessary and who would *ascribe* something like reason to Chance...." —Goethe

The word is derived from the Latin word *scrib* (write). A *scribe* is an official or professional copyist, recorder, notary, or scrivener, or other writer.

✎ I *ascribe* my intelligence to my parents, but I *ascribe* my knowledge of English vocabulary to Noah Webster and other such *scribes*.

Do not confuse *ascribe* with *describe*.

AUSTERE (aw STEER) *adj.* rigorous; difficult; severe; forbidding

The word is usually used to characterize abstract ideas, as in this sentence:

❝ Too *austere* a philosophy makes few wise men." —Seigneur de Saint-Evremend

Two similar words are *recondite* and *abstruse*. Do not confuse *abstruse* with *obtuse*: dull or slow-minded.

An *obtuse* person might have trouble grasping *austere* and *abstruse* ideas.

BASTION (BAS chyun) *n.* a fortress or stronghold

✎ In an increasingly chaotic world, the mortician found the morgue to be his last *bastion* of solitude.

A related word is *bastille*: a fortress or castle, often used as a prison.

In architecture, the word is used more precisely to refer to a projection from an outer wall of a fortification designed to defend the adjacent perimeter.

Other words that describe fortification or protection of a structure or area include:

berm: a mound of earth piled up against a wall or road

buttress: an extra thickness in a wall designed to add strength

bulwark: a strong defensive wall structure

rampart: a small mound of earth used defensively in battle

BOORISH (BOR ish) *adj.* ill-mannered; unrefined; rude

✎ In the movie *The Absent Minded Professor*, lounge singer Buddy Love's boorish demeanor contrasted sharply with the genteel disposition of his alter ego, the professor.

A boorish person might be referred to as a *churl* or *curmudgeon*.

Boorish can also mean clumsy or clownish.

Similar words are *churlish*, *impudent*, *insolent*, and *peevish*.

BUMPTIOUS (BUMP shus) *adj.* overly and offensively self-assertive

A *bumptious* patron at an amusement park might push and shove his way to the front of a line, "bumping" into people as he does so.

✎ The ambitious and *bumptious* news reporter may achieve his goals, but he will probably alienate friends and colleagues along the way.

Similar words include *bodacious*, *brazen*, *audacious*, and *overbearing*.

BURGEON (BER jun) *v.* to begin to grow or develop, especially suddenly; bloom; sprout; thrive

> The adjective form is *burgeoning*, as illustrated in this sentence:

> ✎ A relatively young but *burgeoning* high-tech company could pose a threat to its larger and more established rivals.

> The word is usually used with an *-ing*, either as a verb or an adjective (as in the sentence above). It can also be used as a noun to refer to a bud or sprout of a plant.

> Two similar words include:

> *effloresce*: to bloom or flower, or blossom

> *luxuriate*: to prosper, grow, or produce profusely

> Do not confuse *burgeon* with *bourgeois*: belonging to the social middle class.

CAJOLE (kuh JOHL) *adj.* to persuade by flattery or by promises; entice; taunt

> ✎ Car salesmen typically *cajole* customers into buying cars with hackneyed and insipid one-liners such as: "My boss is going to fire me for practically giving this car away to you, but I like you, so I'm going to do it anyway." The best place to watch people cajole one another, however, is at a singles bar.

> Similar words include *wheedle*, *coax*, *inveigle*, and *lure*.

> The word bear no relation to *Cajun*: a French dialect and subculture of Louisiana.

CANT (KANT) *n.* any special language used by a particular group, class, or profession; slang; jargon

> Consult a computer hackers' dictionary to explore the hacker's own distinct *cant*. Ebonics—the distinct African-American English form—is another form of *cant*.

> The word also refers to insincere, pious, or sanctimonious statements and platitudes, as in this sentence:

> ❝ Of all the *cants* in this *canting* world, though the *cant* of hypocrites may be the worst, the *cant* of criticism is the most tormenting." —Lawrence Stone

> Similar words include *lingo*, *vernacular*, and *argot*.

CHAUVINISM (SHOH vuh nih zum) *n.* unreasonable devotion to one's race, country, or sex

> ✎ During the 1960's, the term "male chauvinist pig" became the mantra for the burgeoning feminist movement.

> ❝ Patriotism has reappeared, along with its scruffy half brothers, xenophobia and *chauvinism*." —Lance Morrow, *Time*

> A related word is *jingoism*: excessive patriotism.

CHIMERICAL (kih MAYR ih kul) *adj.* imaginary; wildly fanciful; unreal; impossible

> ✎ Professional athletes past their prime sometimes attempt to realize their *chimerical* dream of once again being the best in the world at their sport. Olympic swimmer Mark Spitz and boxer Sugar Ray Leonard are two notable examples.

The related word *impracticable* refers not to something impossible or imaginary but rather to a goal or action that is unfeasible or unrealistic.

Similar words include *illusory* and *phantasmal*.

COQUETTISH (koh KET ish) *adj.* alluring; enticing; coy (feigned shyness)

> ✎ The young girl's *coquettish* ways lured many suitors and broke many hearts.

The word *coquette* is usually used in referring to an attractive young lady. A coquette need not cajole in order to get what she wants.

Other words used to refer to an attractive or alluring person or thing include *prepossessing*, *winsome*, *voluptuous*, *comely*, and *fetching*.

Another word which describes a *coy* person (one who pretends to be shy) is *demure*.

A genuinely shy person would also be described as *diffident*.

CORPULENCE (KOR pyoo luns) *n.* excessive fatness; obesity

A related word is *corpse*, which refers to a dead body. Hence, the following sentence:

> ✎ The solicitous wife warned her overweight husband: "You are going to be a *corpulent corpse* one day soon if you don't lose some weight."

DEIGN (DAYN) *v.* to condescend; to deem another worthy or fit in accordance with one's own sense of self-worth, stature, or dignity; to grant or allow

A person who deigns might be described as *supercilious*, *pretentious*, *haughty*, or *consequential*.

> ✎ The conceited, consequential executive *deigned* to dine with members of her staff on Secretary's Day.

DELETERIOUS (del eh TEER ee us) *adj.* harmful or injurious to physical or mental health

> ✎ The new factory may be salutary for the local economy, but the hazards from the factory's *deleterious* effluents outweigh its economic benefits.

Similar words include *noxious*, *pestiferous*, *virulent*, *pernicious*, *pestilential*, and *toxic*.

Do not confuse deleterious with these two words:
dilatory: intentionally causing a delay
diligent: hard-working or industrious

DESULTORY (DES uhl tor ee) *adj.* lacking order or consistency; rambling; disjointed; passing randomly from one thing to another

✎ Many ostensibly brilliant works of literature result not from inspired creativity but rather simply from a *desultory* frame of mind.

Similar words include *discursive*, *incoherent*, and *incongruous*.
Related words which suggest unpredictable or erratic behavior include *whimsical*, *capricious*, and *mercurial*.

DIFFIDENCE (DIF ih duns) *n.* lack of self confidence or faith in one's own ability; timidity or shyness

✎ Diffident people may go to great lengths to extricate themselves from public speaking obligations, which can be tumultuous ordeals for them.

❝ Now Giant Despair had a wife, and her name was Diffidence." —John Bunyan

The word is unrelated to *different* (not similar) and *indifferent* (unconcerned, disinterested).

DINT (DINT) n. force; power

❝ Now you weep; and, I perceive, you feel the *dint* of pity." —Shakespeare

Similar words include *puissance* (*adj puissant*) and *potency* (*adj potent*)
The word also has a more common meaning: dent, nick, or scratch. Both definitions are illustrated in this sentence:

✎ Although it felt as though the other car hit mine with the *dint* of a locomotive, my car suffered only a few *dints*.

DISCURSIVE (dis KER siv) *adj.* rambling from subject to subject; digressive

✎ The *discursive* vagrant ranted about anything and everything, but ranted nothing intelligible.

A similar word is *desultory*.
Another related word is *cursory*: performed quickly and superficially (as in a cursory reading of a magazine article)
A related word is *cursive*: flowing handwriting in which the letters of words are joined together.

In rhetoric and philosophy, the word has a more particular meaning: proceeding from reason rather than intuition. This definition is derived from the noun *discourse*: communication, discussion, or exchange of ideas, through conversation.

DUPE (DOOP) *n.* a person who is easily fooled

> 66 If [a man] pretends to be [your *dupe*], who is the biggest *dupe*—he or you?"
> —Jean de La Bruyére

A dupe may be described as *credulous* and *gullible* (overly trusting or believing).
A dupe might be duped by a *charlatan* or *mountebank* (a fraud).
A person who has been duped has been *beguiled* (defrauded or deceived).

EBULLIENT (eh BYOO lee int) *adj.* overflowing (bubbling over) with excitement, enthusiasm, or fervor

> ✎ Motivational "experts" and others who peddle panaceas and snake oils feed upon the pervasive *ebullience* among their would-be proselytes.

Similar words include *vivacious* and *effervescent*.
Related words which are a bit stronger (describing a passionate person) include *fervent*, *ardent*, *fervid*, *smitten*, and *zealous*.
A related word is *sanguine*: optimistic; hopeful; cheerful.

ELYSIAN (ih LIZH un) *adj.* blissful; heavenly; delightful

> 66 [T]his life of mortal breath is but a suburb of the life *elysian*, whose portal we call death." —Henry Wadsworth Longfellow

The word is derived from the mythological *Elysium* (or *Elysian Fields*), a place where the dead were said to abide in peace and bliss.
A similar word is *beatific*: blissful; bestowing or providing bliss or happiness.

EMENDATION (ee men DAY shun) *n.* improvement or correction of errors

> ✎ To be included in the next magazine issue, the callow intern's egregious article requires prompt *emendation*.

The verb form is *emend* or *emendate*.
A similar word is *ameliorate*.
Do not confuse *emend* with *amend* (to alter), which does not require improvement or correction.

ENGENDER (en JEN der) *v.* to bring about, cause, or produce

> ✎ An ebullient attitude at the workplace *engenders* the same among one's coworkers.

Here are two closely related words:
precipitate: to cause directly or immediately
facilitate: to help in bringing about; promote; assist
Other similar words include *incite*, *kindle*, and *spur*.
The word is unrelated to *gender* (sex, either male or female).

ENNUI (ahn WEE) *n.* a feeling of discontent or weariness; boredom

> ❝ Necessity is the constant scourge of the lower classes, *ennui* of the higher ones." —Arthur Schopenhauer

Similar words include *tedium* and *pall*.
To enliven and rejuvenate a person suffering from *ennui*, one might prescribe a dose of scintillation, titillation, or jubilation.

FASTIDIOUS (fas TID ee us) *adj.* difficult to please; finicky

> ❝ [T]he *fastidious* formal manner of the upper middle class is preferable to the slovenly easygoing behavior of the common middle class. In moments of crisis, the former know how to act, the latter become uncouth brutes." —Cesare Pavese

Similar words include *meticulous* and *punctilious*.
The word is closely related to *fast*: to abstain from eating. An overly fastidious person might resort to fasting rather than partaking of the fodder that is available.

FODDER (FAH der) *n.* course food, especially for livestock

The word is widely used figuratively to refer to any source of fuel for human thought or endeavor.

> ✎ The indiscretions of celebrities and other public figures are *fodder* for tabloid journalists.

> ❝ [Our country's military draft deferment tests] are reminiscent of Hitler's twin system of eugenics and education—weed out the intellectually deprived by conscripting them for cannon *fodder*." —Adam Clayton Powell

A similar word is *provender*.
Another related word is *pabulum*: any nourishment for animals or plants.

FULMINATE (FUL mih nayt) *v.* to explode or erupt violently or noisily; to denounce or condemn vehemently

> As suggested by the two definitions, the word may be used literally or figuratively.
> Active volcanoes fulminate, but so do peevish people and volatile situations (as in the following sentence):
>
> 66 What began in the morning as familiar Kissinger *fulminations* exploded by late day into a full-scale governmental crisis." —Charles Colson, *Born Again*
>
> A closely related word is *culminate*: to termination at the climax or highest point. Thus, a volcanic activity culminates in a fulmination.

GLIB (GLIB) *adj.* fluent in speech or writing, but without thought, restraint, or sincerity

> The word pertains to substance, not quantity; hence, a glib person is not necessarily loquacious or garrulous (talkative).
> Certain people, including salespeople and politicians, are notoriously glib.
>
> 66 The more gross the fraud, the more *glibly* will it go down and the more greedily will it be swallowed...." —Christian Nestell Bovee

IGNOMINIOUS (ig noh MIN ee uhs) *adj.* disgraceful; dishonorable; contemptuous

> This word originated from and means the opposite of the word *noble*. It has nothing to do with ignorance.
>
> ✏ The sort of *ignominious* knavery that permeates the legal profession in the United States today is actually sanctioned by our courts.
>
> Similar words include *ignoble* and *contemptible*.
> Do not confuse *ignominious* with *ignorant*: lacking knowledge.

INCORRIGIBLE (in KOR ih juh bul) *adj.* unmanageable; unruly; uncontrollable; incapable of being reformed

> The word is often used by people who wish to control the behavior of others.
>
> ✏ A frustrated young mother whose child refuses to behave might scold the child: "You're *incorrigible*! You take after your father, you know."
>
> 66 The idealist is *incorrigible*: if he is thrown out of his heaven he makes an ideal of his hell." —Nietzsche
>
> The antonym *corrigible* (easily reformed or corrected) is not as widely used.
> Similar words include *obdurate*, *contumacious*, and *refractory*.

INCUMBENT (in KUM bint) *adj.* pressed or emphatically urged; currently in office

> In the first definition above, the word is always used in the idiomatic expression "it is incumbent upon (on)....", as in this sentence:

> 66 Care of the poor is *incumbent* on society as a whole." —Baruch (Benedict) Spinoza

> *Incumbent* is also used to refer to a current holder of an office or position (usually political), especially in the context of a race for election against a challenger.

> ✎ The *incumbent* and popular senator will have no trouble defeating her little-known challenger in the next election.

INEFFABLE (in EF uh bul) *adj.* incapable of being expressed in words or spoken; inexpressible

> ✎ *Ineffable* joy overcame him at the sight of his dog which had been missing for several days.

> *Ineffable* and *unspeakable* are not synonymous. The latter is generally used to describe evil or immoral acts so offensive to one's sensibilities that they cannot be discussed.

> The antonym *effable* (expressible or utterable) is not as widely used.

> Do not confuse *effable* with *affable*: agreeable or friendly.

INGENUOUS (in JEN yoo us) *adj.* acting or speaking in a candid manner; innocent, naive, or unsophisticated

> ✎ Naive in the ways of office politics, the *ingenuous* young employee continually transmitted sensitive information, tacitly understood by others to be confidential, among various departments. The contagion was finally quelled when he quit his job to return to college.

> 66 The officers, however, were quite entranced with the *ingenuous* simplicity of the islanders, their piety...and their anxiety not to offend." —H.E. Traude, *History of Pitcairn Island*

> An ingenuous young girl is an *ingenue* (the word is not used to describe ingenuous males).

> The noun form is *ingenuousness* (not *ingenuity*).

> Do not confuse *ingenuous* with *ingenious*: inventive (*n* ingenuity).

INVECTIVE (in VEK tiv) *n.* vehement protest, attack, or abuse with words

> ✎ Overreacting to his colleague's remarks about the efficacy of Senator Burns' plan to balance the budget, Burns launched into an *invective* tantamount to character assassination.

The word can also be used as an adjective. It is no fun being at the receiving end of an *invective* harangue.

A related word, *vexation*, refers either to an irritation or annoyance or to the state of being irritated or annoyed.

ITINERANT (y TIN er unt) *adj.* traveling from place to place, especially for work.

✎ An *itinerant* construction worker moves from place to place depending on where work is available.

The word *itinerary* refers to a travel schedule or plans.

Itinerant can also be used as a noun.

The adjective *itinerate* can be used instead of *itinerant*.

Similar words include *nomadic* and *peripatetic*.

Another related word is *peregrinations*: journeys or travels.

KNAVERY (NAY ver ee) *adj.* trickery; deceit; crafty dealing; dishonesty

A *knavish* person is not someone who is simply given to telling lies, but rather one who relies on deceit in dealings with others. Knavery revealed is often met with reprobation.

Many politicians and lawyers are considered to be *knaves*.

Similar words include *chicanery*, *guile*, and *duplicity*.

LACHRYMOSE (LAK ruh mohs) *adj.* given to shedding tears (crying); tearful; mournful

A person who is easily moved to tears is lachrymose.

The word is also used figuratively to describe a person with a sad or mournful disposition.

A closely related word is *melancholy*: sadly sentimental.

Other words used to refer to a person who is sad or mournful include *lugubrious*, *woeful*, *plaintive*, *elegiac*, and *doleful*.

LACONIC (luh KAH nik) *adj.* brief and to the point; expressing much in few words; terse; concise

❝ 'If it ain't broke, don't fix it,' drawls Winegartner in the *laconic* accent of his native Springfield, Missouri." —Carol E. Curtis, *Forbes*

A similar word is *pithy* (given to expression in terse, clever sayings and aphorisms). Both words can refer to either a person or a statement, although they differ somewhat in meaning.

Another similar word is *sententious*.

Laconic is not synonymous with *taciturn* or *reticent*, both of which refer to a reluctance to speak rather than to the length and quality of the expression.

LIVID (LIV id) *adj.* enraged; extremely angry

✎ When accused falsely of embezzlement, the bookkeeper, who had always performed his duties with utmost probity, grew *livid* with anger and indignation.

The word is also used to refer to a pale, ashen, or bluish appearance.
A closely related word is *indignant*: angrily resentful.
Other similar words include *incensed* and *rabid*.

LUGUBRIOUS (luh GOO bree us) *adj.* dismal, depressing, or mournful (usually exaggeratedly so)

The word is usually used to describe a person's mood, but it can also be used to describe the mood created by a sound, as in the *lugubrious* tones of a particular instrument or the sound of a composition.

Similar words, which unlike *lugubrious* do not generally involve exaggeration, are *somber* and *melancholy*.

MAVERICK (MAV er ik) *n.* a person who takes an independent stance; a radical or non-conformist

The word was coined in the 19th century in reference to Charles Maverick, a Texas pioneer who refused to brand his cattle.
The word was popularized during the 1950s with the television show *Maverick*, a western about a non-conforming lawman.
A maverick might be described as *autonomous*: independent and self-governing.

MENDICANT (MEN duh kunt) *adj.* living by begging for money and food

The word is also used as a noun to refer to a beggar or one who lives off alms (donations) of others.
The act or practice of begging is referred to as either *mendicity* or *mendicancy*.
A mendicant might be but is not necessarily impoverished or indigent, as underscored by this sentence:

❝ Every genuinely benevolent person loathes almsgiving and *mendicity*."
—George Bernard Shaw

MERCURIAL (mer KYER ee ul) *adj.* volatile; given to changing moods suddenly

Mercury, the winged Greek god of commerce, possessed a number of characteristic traits; however, his volatile temper was the only trait that endured linguistically, as the definition above suggests.

✎ *Mercurial* young men with a low center of gravity are particularly suited for the sport of hockey, where assault with a deadly weapon is not only sanctioned but is part of the job description.

Similar words include *capricious*, *fickle*, and *whimsical*.

MORDANT (MOR dint) *adj.* biting or stinging (as in a remark or expression)

A mordant remark has a sharp, cutting effect on the listener and is often scornful and derisive.

Similar words include *caustic*, *trenchant*, *petulant*, and *acrimonious*.

A related word is *sarcastic*. A sarcastic remark is usually mordant in tone and effect but may carry some irony as well.

Another related word is *facetious*, which is often misused as a synonym for sarcastic. In fact, a facetious remark is one that is light-hearted or frivolous (although it may also be sarcastic as well).

Each of the following remarks might be interpreted as either mordant or facetious, depending on whether they were spoken in seriousness or in jest:

✎ "You look like hell today," Naomi remarked.
"You sure know how to hurt a guy," retorted Roger.

NUGATORY (NOO guh tor ee) *adj.* futile; worthless; of no real value

✎ Humankind's efforts to save itself from mass destruction at its own hands would be rendered *nugatory* by a collision with one fair-sized meteor.

A similar word is *vain*. The sentence above suggests that humankind's efforts to save itself might be in vain.

OBDURATE (AHB dyoo rit) *adj.* unyielding; stubborn; unmoved by persuasion, especially with respect to moral influence

✎ An *obdurate* bully may continue to pick fights with other boys despite repeated lectures by his school principal and by his parents.

Similar words include *incorrigible* and *refractory*.

A related word is *recidivistic*: returning to a life of crime—as in a recidivistic and obdurate drug dealer.

The word *obstinate* is similar but distinct in meaning. An obstinate person stubbornly adheres to a purpose or position, as illustrated in this sentence:

✎ Despite our pleading and our attempts to reason with him, the *obstinate* and suicidal "jumper" refused to come in from the edge of the building's roof.

ODIOUS (OH dee us) *adj.* deserving or causing hatred or scorn; detestable; despicable; offensive

> The noun form is *odium*: intense hatred or loathing; antipathy; obloquy
> Odium is directed at an *odious* object.
>
> > 66 Compromise is *odious* to passionate natures because it seems a surrender; and to intellectual natures because it seems a confusion." —George Santayana
>
> Both an anathema and a pariah would aptly be characterized as odious.
> Similar words include *abhorrent*, *repugnant*, and *loathsome*.
> Do not confuse *odious* with these unrelated words:
> > *odorous*: having a noticeable or strong smell (although an odorous object might have an odious odor)
> > *ode*: a lyric poem marked by exalted feeling
> > *odeum*: a hall or structure for theatrical or musical performances
> > *onerous*: burdensome; difficult

OSTENTATIOUS (aws ten TAY shus) *adj.* boastful; pretentious; showy

> People dress or act *ostentatiously* usually to impress others and to attract attention.
>
> > 66 The man who is *ostentatious* of his modesty is twin to the statue that wears a fig leaf." —Mark Twain
>
> Another word describing a boastful person is *vainglorious*: excessively proud of one's accomplishments
> The behavior of an ostentatious person can be referred to as *vaunting*.
> Another word describing a showy person is *flamboyant*.

PASTICHE (pas TEESH) *n.* an assortment or variety

> In music, art, and literature, the word is used to describe a work derived chiefly by combining techniques or ideas from other sources.
> The word is used more generally as well, as in this sentence:
>
> > 66 To many, Dutch society seemed a clumsy bourgeois *pastiche* of French culture." —Charles Wilson, *The Dutch Republic*
>
> Another word for pastiche is *paticcio*.
> Similar words include *potpourri*, *medley*, and *mosaic*.

PAUCITY (PAH sih tee) *n.* scarcity; insufficiency

> ✎ At the candy store one finds a myriad of confectionery delights but a *paucity* of salubrious foodstuffs.
>
> A related word is *pauper*: a penniless or indigent person.
> Two similar words are *poverty*, and *dearth*.

Two other related words are *impoverishment* and *indigence*. However, these words are used only to refer to financial poverty.

PEJORATIVE (puh JOR uh tiv) *adj.* negative in connotation; belittling

✎ The other students often refer *pejoratively* to the brightest student in the class by the epithet "teacher's pet."

A personal assistant whose job is to follow orders and blindly serve another person might be referred to in a pejorative manner as a "yes-man" or "bootlick."

Similar words include *deprecatory*, *derisive*, and *opprobrious*.

PENCHANT (PEN chunt) *n.* strong liking or taste for something; tendency or inclination to favor something

A fastidious person has a penchant for tidiness.

A prodigious person has a penchant for spending money.

A risible person has a penchant for laughter.

Similar words include *bent* and *propensity*.

PENITENT (PEN eh tunt) *adj.* regret for an offense, wrongful act, or sin committed

The opposite of penitent is *impenitent* (not regretful for wrongdoing)

Penitence is not necessarily accompanied by acts of *atonement* (making right), although it is usually accompanied by a sincere intent to atone.

❝ Penitence condemns to silence. What a man is ready to recall, he would be willing to repeat." —Francis Herbert Bradley

PENURIOUS (puh NYOO ree us) *adj.* extremely stingy; miserly

The noun form is *penuriousness*, not *penury*. *Penury* refers to a state of indigence or impoverishment. The distinction is underscored in this sentence:

✎ The *penurious* miser ignores the pleas of the mendicant who wallows in *penury*.

Similar words include *frugal*, *parsimonious*, and *niggardly*.

PERFIDY (PER fih dee) *n.* deliberate breech of trust or faith

Adulterous affairs are considered *perfidious* acts when engaged in surreptitiously.

❝ There is a confidence necessary to human intercourse, and without which men are often more injured by their own suspicions, than they could be by the *perfidy* of others." —Edmund Burke

The adjective form is *perfidious*.

The word is often used to describe seditious (undermining) acts against a government.

PERFUNCTORY (per FUNG ter ee) *adj.* performed without care, interest, or enthusiasm

> ✎ Unpleasant tasks which are part of a daily routine are typically discharged (performed) *perfunctorily.*

A perfunctory act is not necessarily performed quickly, although haste does suggest indifference or lack of care.

Other words suggesting carelessness include *remiss* and *negligent.*

A stronger word—*wanton*—suggests recklessness.

Other words suggesting lack of interest include *diffidence, apathy,* and *insouciance.*

PERNICIOUS (per NISH uhs) *adj.* injurious; ruinous; hurtful

A disease can be pernicious, but so can an insult or a lie.

As suggested in the sentence above, *pernicious* can describe a person's actions or statements; however, it is not used to describe the person himself or herself. Hence, it is improper to refer to a person as *pernicious.*

Similar words include *deleterious* and *baleful.*

PERSPICACIOUS (per spih KAY shus) *adj.* insightful; astute; discerning; keen in mental perception

A perspicacious person may recognize subtle distinctions, fine points, and deeper meanings.

> ❝ *Perspicuity* is the framework of profound thoughts." —Marquis de Vauvenargues

A closely related word is *percipient*: able to see or perceive things clearly or easily.

Do not confuse either *perspicacious* or *percipient* with *perspicuous*: clear in expression; lucid (*n perspicuousness*).

PETULANT (PEH chyoo lunt) *adj.* irritable; irascible; grumpy

A petulant person is easily moved to show irritation, even over minor annoyances; hence, a petulant person is generally impatient as well.

> ✎ With a *petulant* turn of her head, she dashed off angrily without waiting to hear my explanation for the brief delay.

Similar words include *mordant, acrimonious,* and *peevish.*

PRECOCIOUS (preh KOH shus) *adj.* showing maturity beyond one's age, especially in children

A child mature beyond his or her age typically will engage in mischief; accordingly, the word is usually used narrowly to describe a mischievous child.

The word is also commonly applied too broadly to describe mischievous behavior by any person. The word is used properly here:

> 66 For *precocity* some great price is always demanded sooner or later in life."
> —Margaret Fuller

PRISTINE (pris TEEN) *adj.* pertaining to the earliest times; pure or unspoiled

The two definitions above are closely related, since the "earliest times" were indeed "pure" and "unspoiled" compared to civilization today.

> ✎ We bathed in the *pristine* waters of the mountain springs, then toured the nearby *pristine* archeological ruins.

Other words also referring to earlier times include *archaic, antediluvian,* and *primeval.*

Other words that refer to something pure or unspoiled include *undefiled, unsullied, uncultivated, virginal,* and *chaste.*

PRODIGAL (PRAH duh gul) *adj.* extremely wasteful, especially with money

> ✎ A person who has struggled through financial difficulties and worked long and hard to build wealth is less prone to becoming *prodigal* than one who comes into a large sum of money suddenly and without sacrifice.

A similar word is *profligate.*

A prodigal person could be referred to as a *wastrel* or *spendthrift.*

A good antonym is *frugal.*

PROGENITOR (proh JEN ih ter) *n.* ancestor; forefather; ascendant; predecessor

Although the word is usually used to describe a biological relationship, it is also used in a more general sense as a synonym for *predecessor* or *precursor,* as in the following sentence:

> 66 Men resemble their contemporaries even more than their *progenitors.*" —Ralph Waldo Emerson

PUGNACIOUS (pug NAY shus) *adj.* inclined to fight; quarrelsome; contentious; argumentative

> 66 It is unfair to blame man too fiercely for being *pugnacious*; he learned the habit from Nature." —Christopher Morley, *Inward Ho!*

A similar word is *truculent.*

Other words that describe a person who seeks to create chaos or disorder include *mutinous, seditious,* and *perfidious.*

A related word is *pugilistic*: pertaining to hand-to-hand combat (*n pugilism*). The rigors of military boot camp include hand-to-hand combat with *pugil* sticks.

PUNGENT (PUN junt) *adj.* sharp in taste or smell; acidic

A pungent food or beverage sharply affects the senses of taste or smell, although not necessarily in a bad way.

The word is also used more generally to describe a sharp, biting, or caustic statement or general personality, as in this sentence:

❝ If you would be *pungent*, be brief; for it is with words as with sunbeams—the more they are condensed, the deeper they burn." —Robert Southey

Other words suggesting a sharp or biting personality or remark are *mordant, acrimonious, caustic,* and *petulant.*

PUSILLANIMOUS (pyoo sih LAN ih mus) *adj.* cowardly; faint-hearted; timid

✎ The cowardly lion in *The Wizard of Oz* was the embodiment of *pusillanimity.* However, his award for bravery, bestowed by the Wizard, lionized him, transforming him into an intrepid and stalwart "king of the jungle." The epithet befit the beast who saved Dorothy from the wicked witch.

Similar words are *craven* and *timorous.*

RANCOR (RANG ker) *n.* malice; hostility; spite; resentment; animosity

Rancorous actions can be motivated by vengeance or merely by unjustified and unreasoned ill will toward another.

❝ ...the truth can only be reached by the expression of our free opinions, without fear and without *rancor.*" —Wendell Wilkie

Do not confuse rancor with *rank*: foul-smelling; malodorous; noisome.

RECONDITE (REK un dyt) *adj.* difficult to understand; obscure

✎ After having difficulty understanding epistemology, teleology, and other philosophical subjects, the college freshman changed her major from philosophy to something far less *recondite*—home economics.

Similar words include *esoteric* and *abstruse.*

Do not confuse recondite with *reconnoiter*: to investigate unknown territory ahead.

REPOSE (reh POHZ) *n.* rest; inner peace; tranquillity; serenity

The word is used to describe both physical stillness or rest and internal calmness or stillness.

A related word is *repository*: a receptacle or other place for storing things (i.e., a place of rest for things).

> " We combat obstacles in order to get *repose* and, when got, the repose is insupportable." —Henry Adams

A state of repose can be described as *tranquil*, *placid*, or *halcyon*.

RESPITE (REH spit) *n.* a brief rest or cessation; pause

Coffee breaks provide a *respite* from the rigors of the workplace.

The word bears no relation in meaning to *spite*, which refers to a malicious attempt to harm or humiliate.

Two related words are *torpor* and *dormancy*, both of which refer to a suspension of (pause in) activity.

Do not confuse respite with *repose*, which refers to a state of rest or peace rather than a temporary pause or break.

RIFE (RYF) *adj.* abundant; prevalent; widespread; commonly occurring

Although the word can be used to describe a frequently occurring phenomenon (in terms of time), it is usually used to describe a widespread one (in terms of physical space).

An old wooden house might be *rife* with termites, or a watermelon might be *rife* with seeds.

> ✎ The stand-up comedian's act was *rife* with ribald (obscene) jokes which fell flat on the prudish audience.

Two related words are *pandemic* (universal or worldwide) and *epidemic* (widespread).

RISIBLE (RIH zuh bul) *adj.* laughable, comical, or ludicrous; given to or easily aroused to laughter

Risible is a flexible word, as suggested by the two different meanings above.

> ✎ Popular fashions among teenagers often appear *risible* to adults.

> ✎ After a few drinks, she becomes quite *risible*, giggling and laughing at anything anyone says.

Another word referring to something ludicrous is *farcical* (a *farce* is a literary form involving *risible* situations).

Other literary forms and approaches to a subject that could be described as risible include *parody*, *lampoon*, *satire*, and *travesty*.

SARDONIC (sar DAH nik) *adj.* disdainful; contemptuous; scornful

> 66 The mood was *sardonic*, fatalistic, and melancholy. I could hear it in our black jokes: "Hey, Bill, you're going on patrol today. If you get your legs blown off can I have your boots?" —Philip Caputo, *A Rumor of War*

The word is derived from and refers to the Sardinian plant, whose ingestion purportedly resulted in uncontrollable laughter ending in sure death.

A sardonic remark might also be sarcastic or cynical.

Similar words include *mordant* and *trenchant*.

Two words referring to biting or stinging statements are *caustic* and *acrimonious*.

SATURNINE (SAT er neen) *adj.* characterized by a gloomy, dark, or sluggish disposition

> *Saturnine* on schooldays, schoolchildren suddenly turn ebullient Saturday morning.
>
> The word refers to the planet Saturn; specifically, to the astrological belief that bodily temperaments correspond to the positions of the planets.
>
> Other words suggesting a gloomy disposition are *sullen*, *despondent*, *melancholy*, and *lugubrious*.
>
> Other words suggesting sluggishness are *lethargic*, *indolent*, and *torpid*.

SAVANT (suh VAHNT) *n.* a person who has had profound or extensive learning or understanding; scholar

> This word is also defined more broadly to include people of high intelligence. Hence, the psychiatric terms "autistic-savant" and "idiot-savant" do not refer to a scholar but rather to a person with high intelligence in only one narrow area.
>
> A related word is the noun *savvy*: understanding, intelligence, or sense.

SEDITION (sih DIH shun) *n.* any act designed to incite others against the government or to resist lawful authority; treason

> "Men that distrust their own subtlety are, in tumult and *sedition*, better disposed for victory than they that suppose themselves wise." —Thomas Hobbes

Similar words include *insurgence*, *recalcitrance*, and *contumacy*.

An act of sedition is performed by an *incendiary*: a person who incites others to quarrel or behave disruptively.

SEDULOUS (SEH jyoo lus) *adj.* diligent; persevering; untiring; indefatigable

> ✎ "*Sedulous* and steady wins the race," said the laconic tortoise-savant to the hasty hare.

Similar words include *unflagging*, *assiduous*, and *unremitting*.

SOLICITOUS (suh LIH sih tus) *adj.* worried; concerned; anxious; distraught (especially over the well-being or safety of others)

> An overprotective mother might be described as unduly *solicitous* regarding the safety of her child.
>
> 66 In mere *solicitude* man remains essentially with himself, even if he is moved with extreme pity." —Martin Buber
>
> The word bears no relation to *solicit*: to petition or make a formal request.

SPECIOUS (SPEE shus) *adj.* seemingly reasonable or genuine, yet without true merit

> Credulous people readily believe *specious* arguments.
>
> 66 His voice was still soft and filled with *specious* humility." —Margaret Mitchell, *Gone With the Wind*
>
> A related word is *dubious*: of doubtful quality or integrity.

STOLID (STAHL id) *adj.* unconcerned; indifferent; dispassionate; unemotional; stoic

> The usually *stolid* young man turned lachrymose during the movie *Bridges of Madison County*, a point in his favor in the eyes of his coquettish date.
>
> Similar words include *insouciant* and *unperturbed*.

STRIDENT (STRY dunt) *adj.* harsh-sounding; shrill; grating

> The word relates to the disagreeable quality of a sound, not to its amplitude (loudness). Nevertheless, a strident sound is probably a loud one as well.
>
> The *strident* cacophony of the high school marching band slowly abated as they strode off the football field after their half-time show.
>
> A related word is *stentorian*: booming, resonant, or thundering.

STULTIFY (STUL tih fy) *v.* to cause to appear foolish; to impair or to render ineffectual or futile

> *Stultified* victims of practical jokes often feel vindicated for their embarrassment by reciprocating against the perpetrator.
>
> Pouring sugar into a automobile gas tank can completely *stultify* the car's operational ability.
>
> Do not confuse stultify with *stupefy*: to stun or make numb; to astound or amaze.

SUBJUGATE (SUB juh gayt) *v.* to subdue or conquer; enslave

> The word is derived from *subject*, as suggested in these sentences:

✎ The invading army quickly *subjugated* the unarmed villagers, who then became the vanquishing king's reluctant *subjects*. Some villagers joined the army's forces under duress, while others were *subjected* to torture and other wanton acts.

Similar words include *vanquish*, *quell*, and *quash*.

TACITURN (TAS ih tern) *adj.* silent; reserved; uncommunicative

❝ One learns *taciturnity* best among people without it, and loquacity among the *taciturn*." —Jean Paul Richter

The word is derived form the Latin word *tacit*, meaning silent.

In music notation, *tacit* signifies that the musician is to remain silent for a specified number of measures.

A related but less forceful word is *reticent*: reluctant to speak; reserved.

TANTAMOUNT (TAN tuh mownt) *adj.* equivalent; equal to; amounting to

✎ For about five seconds, this roller coaster gives the rider a weightless feeling *tantamount* to that of being in outer space.

Similar words include *commensurate*, *akin*, *cognate*, and *parity*.

A closely related word is *paramount*: greater than; superior to; more important than.

TORTUOUS (TOR choo us) *adj.* twisting; curving; winding; not direct or straight

The word is used literally (as in a *tortuous* hiking trail) as well as figuratively (deceitfulness or trickery).

❝ The *tortuous* road which has led from Montgomery to Oslo is a road over which millions of Negroes are traveling to find a new sense of dignity." —Martin Luther King, Jr.

A related word is *tort*, a legal term denoting a non-criminal wrongful act; a tortuous act may give rise to a civil law suit in which the victim seeks compensation for damages resulting from the offense.

Similar words include *serpentine* and *sinuous*.

Do not confuse tortuous with the unrelated word *torturous* (excruciatingly painful).

TRAVESTY (TRAV es tee) *n.* a comical and ludicrous parody; portraying something as ridiculous; a debased imitation

The word is used in literature to describe a burlesque imitation of a serious literary work.

Outside of the literary world, *travesty* is heard most commonly in characterizing legal proceedings, as in this sentence:

✎ The defendant's acquittal was a *travesty* of justice, in view of the overwhelming evidence of his culpability.

TRENCHANT (TREN chunt) *adj.* incisive; keen; penetrating

The word is usually used to describe either a person or a person's language.

✎ While I found the liberal pundit's analysis of the President's press conference to be quite *trenchant*, the conservative analyst's comments were downright insipid, in my opinion.

A similar word is *incisive*.

A related word is *whet*: sharp (a *whetstone* is used to sharpen blades).

TRUCULENT (TRUK yoo lunt) *adj.* fierce; cruel; brutal; ferocious

✎ "It's a *truculent* jungle out there!" exhorted the laconic and savvy executive to his faithful acolyte.
"I'm no stranger to *truculence*," retorted the lackey. "I grew up with three older brothers."

The word can also mean defiant or belligerent.

Other adjectives suggesting cruel or abusive talk or behavior include *vitriolic*, *acrimonious*, and *mordant*.

TURBID (TER bid) *adj.* clouded; muddy

❝ Clear writers, like clear fountains, do not seem so deep as they are; the *turbid* seem the most profound." —Walter Savage Landor

Related words include:
turbulent: agitating, tumultuous, causing or showing disorder
turbine: a machine rotor with blades driven by pressure.
Hence, the following sentence:

✎ The ship's *turbines* left *turbulent* waters in their wake, resulting in a *turbid* sea.

A similar word is *bemired* (derived from *quagmire* or *mire*, a murky swamp or bog).

TURPITUDE (TER pih tood) *n.* depravity; wickedness

✎ While some would label the rancorous acts of violence by young gang members as incorrigible *turpitude*, the sociologist would see those acts as a manifestation of an inner-city social quagmire.

There is no adjective or verb form of the word.

A person exhibiting turpitude might be described as *dissolute*, *base*, *sordid*, *amoral*, or *vile*.

UBIQUITOUS (yoo BIH kwih tus) *adj.* being everywhere, especially at the same time

> ✎ The fulminating volcano known as Cyclops to the islanders created a *ubiquitous* cloud of black ash that resulted in what has become known as "the year without a summer."

> ❝ Today's software, he argues, is too complicated and loaded with gizmos no one ever uses.... 'PCs should be more like pencils,' by which he means cheap, user-friendly and, above all, *ubiquitous.*" —*Time*, quoting Larry Ellison, CEO of Oracle Corporation

Similar words include *omnipresent*, *pandemic*, and *pervasive*.
Two words that are contrary in meaning are *insular* and *parochial*, both of which mean narrow or limited in scope.

VENAL (VEE nul) *adj.* able to be bribed or bought; corruptible

> ✎ Large corporations keep our *venal* political office holders in their back pockets, expecting legislative perquisites in exchange for campaign pork.

A similar word is *mercenary*.

> ✎ *Venal* people need not be inveigled, wheedled, or cajoled by any more creative means than a simple bribe.

This word bears no relation to *veins* (blood vessels) or to *venison* (deer meat).

VICISSITUDE (vih SIS ih tood) *n.* change or variation in the course of something—especially of circumstance or fortune in life

> ❝ Happy is the man who can endure the highest and lowest fortune. He who has endured such *vicissitudes* with equanimity has deprived misfortune of its power." —Seneca

> ✎ Many a Hollywood movie, including *Trading Places* and *Reversal of Fortune*, has been predicated on the notion of *vicissitude*.

VITUPERATE (vy TOO per ayt) *v.* to scold harshly and abusively

> ✎ The teacher's *vituperation* both stultified and stupefied the sensitive youngster, who had never before been castigated in front of his schoolmates.

The adjective form is *vituperative*, and the noun form is *vituperation*.
Similar words include *reproach*, *reprove*, *castigate*, and *censure*.

WINNOW (WIH noh) *v.* to separate, scatter, or disperse; to separate or sift out, especially good from bad

As illustrated in the following sentences, *winnow* has two related but distinct meanings.

✎ *Winnowing* their way through hundreds of applications, the scholarship committee finally chose a recipient.

❝ I want to laugh the powers-that-be out of existence in a great *winnowing* gale of laughter." —Samuel Nathaniel Behrman

Other words that suggest sifting include *sieve* and *percolate*.

A related word is *vagility*: the innate ability to disperse.

Quiz Time (1.8–1.11)

Directions: Match each numbered word in the left column with its lettered definition in the right column. The answer key begins on page 89.

Quiz 1.8

1. ascribe
2. burgeon
3. cajole
4. deign
5. engender
6. fulminate
7. stultify
8. subjugate
9. vituperate
10. winnow

a. bring about or cause
b. separate or scatter
c. condescend to another
d. explode violently
e. attribute to or refer to
f. impair or to render futile
g. persuade by flattery
h. begin to grow or develop
i. scold
j. subdue or conquer

Quiz 1.9

1. adamant
2. desultory
3. ebullient
4. elysian
5. ignominious
6. itinerant
7. lugubrious
8. pejorative
9. penurious
10. pristine
11. pusillanimous
12. sardonic
13. specious
14. tortuous
15. ubiquitous

a. being everywhere
b. blissful
c. cowardly
d. disgraceful or dishonorable
e. exaggeratedly mournful
f. extremely stingy or frugal
g. insistent
h. lacking order or consistency
i. negative in connotation
j. overflowing with enthusiasm
k. pure or unspoiled
l. scornful or bitter
m. seemingly true or genuine but not
n. traveling from place to place
o. twisting or curving

Quiz 1.10

1.	acolyte	a.	deliberate breech of trust
2.	approbation	b.	discontent or boredom
3.	diffidence	c.	improvement
4.	emendation	d.	inciteful act
5.	ennui	e.	lack of self confidence
6.	invective	f.	ludicrous imitation
7.	penchant	g.	assistant or helper
8.	perfidy	h.	official approval
9.	sedition	i.	tendency to favor something
10.	travesty	j.	vehement protest

Quiz 1.11

1.	chimerical	a.	abundant or prevalent
2.	ingenuous	b.	boastful or showy
3.	laconic	c.	brief and to the point
4.	nugatory	d.	candid or naive
5.	ostentatious	e.	diligent and persevering
6.	perfunctory	f.	extremely wasteful
7.	perspicacious	g.	futile or worthless
8.	precocious	h.	harsh-sounding
9.	prodigal	i.	imaginary or impossible
10.	rife	j.	insightful or astute
11.	risible	k.	laughable or ludicrous
12.	sedulous	l.	mature beyond one's age
13.	solicitous	m.	performed without care
14.	stolid	n.	unconcerned or indifferent
15.	strident	o.	worried or anxious

Quiz Time—Answers (1.1–1.11)

Quiz 1.1

1. d
2. h
3. e
4. i
5. g
6. j
7. a
8. c
9. f
10. b

Quiz 1.2

1. h
2. a
3. j
4. f
5. b
6. d
7. c
8. e
9. g
10. i

Quiz 1.3

1. j
2. a
3. d
4. e
5. b
6. f
7. i
8. c
9. g
10. h

Quiz 1.4

1. b
2. d
3. j
4. h
5. e
6. c
7. i
8. f
9. a
10. g

Quiz 1.5

1. k
2. f
3. l
4. m
5. h
6. i
7. g
8. b
9. c
10. j
11. o
12. a
13. d
14. e
15. n

Quiz 1.6

1. c
2. b
3. f
4. g
5. j
6. h
7. d
8. a
9. i
10. e

Quiz 1.7

1. h
2. l
3. m
4. n

5. k
6. j
7. c
8. f

9. b
10. d
11. o
12. e

13. g
14. a
15. i

Quiz 1.8

1. e
2. h
3. g

4. c
5. a
6. d

7. f
8. j
9. i

10. b

Quiz 1.9

1. g
2. h
3. j
4. b

5. d
6. n
7. e
8. i

9. f
10. k
11. c
12. l

13. m
14. o
15. a

Quiz 1.10

1. g
2. h
3. e

4. c
5. b
6. j

7. i
8. a
9. d

10. f

Quiz 1.11

1. i
2. d
3. c
4. g

5. b
6. m
7. j
8. l

9. f
10. a
11. k
12. e

13. o
14. n
15. h

4

Confounding and Confusing **Words**

This chapter will help you master many of the most confounding and confusing words in the English language. It's no coincidence these words are some of the test-makers' favorites. The words are divided into five lists:

33 That Will Confound You

33 That Look Deceptively Familiar

33 That Will Fool You

33 That Might Fake You Out

Words Easily Confused with Others—the Big Bad List!

Each list (except the last one) is presented in a multiple-choice format to help you ferret out those words that require your attention. Don't forget to take the quizzes at the end of the chapter to review the new words you learned here. Finally, keep in mind that some of the words here also appeared in sample sentences in Chapter 3; so if you glossed over them in Chapter 3, now is your chance to fix them in your memory.

33 That Will Confound You

Some of these 33 words are foreign words that have been adopted by English speakers; others are just strange-looking words. In any case, trying to guess the meaning of these words would be futile (unless you are well familiar with other languages). **Directions:** For each word in bold letters, select the word among three choices—(a), (b) and (c)—that is nearest in meaning. Answers and definitions begin on page 93.

1. **bijou**
    (a) theater (b) ornament (c) riverbank

2. **calumny**
    (a) aroma (b) slander (c) donation

3. **charlatan**
    (a) child (b) celebrity (c) fraud

4. **concierge**
    (a) attendant (b) knave (c) meeting

5. **connoisseur**
    (a) flirt (b) leader (c) critic

6. **conundrum**
    (a) flask (b) shell (c) mystery

7. **debauch**
    (a) float (b) corrupt (c) simplify

8. **dilettante**
    (a) amateur (b) enigma (c) peace

9. **fiat**
    (a) passport (b) nest (c) command

10. **gauche**
    (a) awkward (b) soaked (c) similar

11. **gossamer**
    (a) adamant (b) lightweight (c) copious

12. **hubris**
    (a) anger (b) pride (c) soil

13. **imprimatur**
    (a) tardiness (b) poverty (c) approval

14. **insouciant**
    (a) hot (b) inexperienced (c) carefree

15. **juggernaut**
    (a) warrior (b) ideology (c) waiter

16. **ken**
    (a) knowledge (b) honesty (c) ethos

17. **kudos**
    (a) array (b) admiration (c) vibration

18. **macabre**
    (a) gruesome (b) enslaved (c) untidy

19. **milieu**
    (a) laziness (b) remnant (c) environment

20. **mountebank**
    (a) quack (b) plateau (c) wealth

21. **nepenthe**
    (a) medicine (b) turbulence (c) fortress

22. **opprobrium**
    (a) dishonor (b) clarity (c) disagreement

23. **paramour**
    (a) cleanser (b) lover (c) artist

24. **peccadillo**
    (a) coincidence (b) concert (c) crime

25. **phalanx**
    (a) tomb (b) imitation (c) union

26. **philatelist**
    (a) collector (b) pilot (c) treasurer

27. **queue**
    (a) attraction (b) sequence (c) prohibit

28. **quotidian**
    (a) inquisitive (b) trite (c) subordinate

29. **raconteur**
    (a) gambler (b) outcast (c) storyteller

30. **spelunk**
    (a) unwind (b) explore (c) surrender

31. **succedaneum**
    (a) blossom (b) replacement (c) victor

32. **yen**
    (a) repetition (b) sick (c) desire

33. **zeppelin**
    (a) blimp (b) roundabout (c) secret

Answers and Definitions

1. **BIJOU** (BEE zhoo) *n* jewelry; an ornament or decoration; bauble **(b)**

2. **CALUMNY** (KAL um nee) *n* a false and malicious statement designed to injure the reputation of someone or something **(b)**

3. **CHARLATAN** (SHAR luh tun) *n* a person who intentionally deceives; fraud; quack **(c)**

4. **CONCIERGE** (kahn see AYRZH) *n* a person who has charge of a building's entrance; doorkeeper; janitor **(a)**

5. **CONNOISSEUR** (kah nuh SOOR) *n* an expert in the arts, able to pass critical judgment **(c)**

6. **CONUNDRUM** (kuh NUN drum) *n* an enigma; puzzle; mystery; riddle **(c)**

7. **DEBAUCH** (dih BAWCH) *v* to corrupt by sensuality; deprave; pervert; inveigle; defile (*n* debauchee, debauchery) **(b)**

8. **DILETTANTE** (DIL uh tahnt) *n* a person who dabbles in the arts for amusement **(a)**

9. **FIAT** (FEE aht) *n* a command or order **(c)**

10. **GAUCHE** (GOHSH) *adj* lacking social graces; tactless **(a)**

11. **GOSSAMER** (GAHS uh mer) *adj* sheer and light, like cobwebs; translucent **(b)**

12. **HUBRIS** (HYOO bris) *n* excessive arrogance, pride, or self confidence; conceit **(b)**

13. **IMPRIMATUR** (im prih MAH ter) *n* an official license, approval, or sanction, especially to be published or printed **(c)**

14. **INSOUCIANT** (in SOO see int) *adj* unconcerned; without a care; carefree; jaunty **(c)**

15. **JUGGERNAUT** (JUG er nawt) *n* a powerful belief, ideology, or institution that draws blind devotion **(b)**

16. **KEN** (KEN) *n* scope of knowledge **(a)**

17. **KUDOS** (KOO dohz) *n* praise; honor; glory **(b)**

18. **MACABRE** (muh KAHB) *adj* gruesome; grisly; morbid; grim; gory **(a)**

19. **MILIEU** (mil YOO) *n* surroundings or environment; ambiance **(c)**

20. **MOUNTEBANK** (MOWN tuh bank) *n* a fraud; charlatan; quack **(a)**

21. **NEPENTHE** (nih PEN thee) *n* a drug or drink to alleviate one's sorrows or woe **(a)**

22. **OPPROBRIUM** (uh PROH bree um) *n* disgrace or dishonor incurred from shameful conduct; infamy; ignominy **(a)**

23. **PARAMOUR** (PAHR ih moor) *n* an illicit lover; courtesan; philanderer; debaucher **(b)**

24. **PECCADILLO** (pek uh DIL oh) *n* a slight offense; minor crime; misdemeanor **(c)**

25. **PHALANX** (FAY lanks) *n* any group of people grouped closely together for a specific purpose (especially a military one) **(c)**

26. **PHILATELIST** (fil AT uh list) *n* a stamp collector **(a)**

27. **QUEUE** (KYOO) *v* to form a line or sequence, as in a parade or caravan **(b)**

28. **QUOTIDIAN** (kwoh TID ee un) *adj* commonplace, everyday, or trivial; occurring or returning daily **(b)**

29. **RACONTEUR** (rak ahn TOOR) *n* a skillful teller of stories and anecdotes **(c)**

30. **SPELUNK** (speh LUNK) *v* to explore caves **(b)**

31. **SUCCEDANEUM** (suk suh DAY nee um) *n* a replacement or substitute **(b)**

32. **YEN** (YEN) *n* yearning; desire **(c)**

33. **ZEPPELIN** (ZEP lin) *n* a flying lighter-than-air craft; dirigible; blimp **(a)**

33 That Look Deceptively Familiar

Each word in this list looks a bit like a more common word with which you are probably familiar. However, the two words are unrelated in meaning. **Directions:** For each word in bold letters, select the word among three choices—(a), (b) and (c)—that is nearest in meaning. Answers and definitions begin on page 96.

1. **abject**
   (a) hopeless (b) argue (c) goal

2. **adventitious**
   (a) accidental (b) favorable (c) initial

3. **annular**
   (a) periodic (b) round (c) weary

4. **apposite**
   (a) low (b) encouraging (c) suitable

5. **beatific**
   (a) happy (b) attractive (c) bold

6. **concomitant**
   (a) accompanying (b) anxious (c) strong

7. **condign**
   (a) unfit (b) appropriate (c) abbreviated

8. **dissemble**
   (a) destroy (b) hide (c) compare

9. **enervate**
   (a) interfere (b) weaken (c) invigorate

10. **feint**
    (a) modesty (b) dizziness (c) sham

11. **fraught**
    (a) fearful (b) full (c) imagined

12. **friable**
    (a) sturdy (b) fragile (c) flexible

13. **gambol**
    (a) skip (b) criticize (c) lose

14. **importunate**
    (a) absent (b) demanding (c) trivial

15. **inane**
    (a) anxious (b) illogical (c) motionless

16. **ingratiate**
    (a) humiliate (b) persuade (c) annoy

17. **motif**
    (a) theme (b) intuition (c) cause

18. **obeisance**
    (a) passivity (b) satisfaction (c) homage

19. **obloquy**
    (a) condemnation (b) fashion (c) duty

20. **obviate**
    (a) avoid (b) obscure (c) connect

21. **ovoid**
    (a) canceled (b) oval (c) evasive

22. **preciocity**
    (a) refinement (b) mischief (c) rarity

23. **predilection**
    (a) preference (b) prophecy (c) bribery

24. **protean**
    (a) flexible (b) strong (c) important

25. querulous
(a) whining (b) meddling (c) eccentric

26. reproach
(a) retreat (b) scold (c) return

27. reprobate
(a) ashamed (b) unscrupulous (c) likely

28. succor
(a) dependence (b) agility (c) assistance

29. tenebrous
(a) uncertain (b) gloomy (c) convenient

30. traduce
(a) insult (b) initiate (c) divide

31. unrequited
(a) unreturned (b) surplus (c) adored

32. unwonted
(a) discarded (b) stubborn (c) unusual

33. whet
(a) entice (b) sharpen (c) soak

Answers and Definitions

1. **ABJECT** (AB jekt) *adj* utterly hopeless (as in abject poverty); utterly despicable or servile **(a)**

2. **ADVENTITIOUS** (ad ven TISH us) *adj* accidental; by chance; casual **(a)**

3. **ANNULAR** (AN yoo ler) *adj* ring-shaped **(b)**

4. **APPOSITE** (AP uh zit) *adj* appropriate; suitable; apt; fitting **(c)**

5. **BEATIFIC** (bee uh TIF ik) *adj* bestowing or providing bliss or happiness; blissful **(a)**

6. **CONCOMITANT** (kahn KAH mih tunt) *adj* associated with; accompanying; connected **(a)**

7. **CONDIGN** (kun DYN) *adj* well-deserved, fitting, or adequate (punishment) **(b)**

8. **DISSEMBLE** (dih SEM bul) *v* to hide, conceal, or disguise **(b)**

9. **ENERVATE** (EH ner vayt) *v* to deprive of vitality; debilitate **(b)**

10. **FEINT** (FAYNT) *n* a deceptive movement (*v* feign) **(c)**

11. **FRAUGHT** (FRAWT) *adj* filled; stored; laden **(b)**

12. **FRIABLE** (FRY uh bul) *adj* easily crumbled **(b)**

13. **GAMBOL** (GAM bul) *v* to skip or leap playfully **(a)**

14. **IMPORTUNATE** (im POR chuh nit) *adj* making persistent demands **(b)**

15. **INANE** (in AYN) *adj* silly or nonsensical; vacuous **(b)**

16. **INGRATIATE** (in GRAY shee ayt) *v* to gain favor with another; to become popular with **(b)**

17. **MOTIF** (moh TEEF) *n* a literary, artistic, or musical device that serves as the basis for suggestive expansion; the basic element repeated throughout the work **(a)**

18. **OBEISANCE** (oh BAY suns) *n* a physical demonstration of respect (e.g., bowing or saluting) **(c)**

19. **OBLOQUY** (AH bluh kwee) *n* condemnation or verbal abuse, or the disgrace resulting therefrom; vituperation **(a)**

20. **OBVIATE** (AHB vee ayt) *v* to avoid by preventive measures; make unnecessary **(a)**

21. **OVOID** (OH voyd) *adj* egg-shaped **(b)**

22. **PRECIOSITY** (preh see AH sih tee) *n* fastidiousness or overrefinement; foppishness **(a)**

23. **PREDILECTION** (preh duh LIK shun) *n* partiality; preference **(a)**

24. **PROTEAN** (PROH tee un) *adj* able to take many forms or perform many functions; versatile; variable; changeable; mutable **(a)**

25. **QUERULOUS** (KWAYR yoo lus) *adj* complaining; whining; peevish **(a)**

26. **REPROACH** (ree PROHCH) *v* to find fault with; blame; scold; censure; vituperate **(b)**

27. **REPROBATE** (REP ruh bayt) *n* a depraved, unprincipled, or wicked person; *adj* corrupt, depraved, or amoral; *v* to severely disapprove; censure **(b)**

28. **SUCCOR** (SUK er) *n* help; relief; aid; assistance **(c)**

29. **TENEBROUS** (TEN uh brus) *adj* gloomy; dark; morbid **(b)**

30. **TRADUCE** (truh DOOS) *v* to speak maliciously and falsely of; defame; slander; **(a)**

31. **UNREQUITED** (un ree KWY tid) *adj* not reciprocated; unilateral **(a)**

32. **UNWONTED** (un WOHN tid) *adj* not customary; not habitual; unusual or rare **(c)**

33. **WHET** (WET) *v* to sharpen; make keen; intensify **(a)**

33 That Will Fool You

Each word in this list incorporates a common, everyday word, as a component of the word. However, the two words bear no relation in meaning to each other. **Directions:** For each word in bold letters, select the word among three choices—(a), (b) and (c)—that is nearest in meaning. Answers and definitions begin on page 99.

1. **accost**
    (a) evaluate (b) accumulate (c) confront

2. **ape**
    (a) amass (b) mimic (c) escape

3. **asseverate**
    (a) fracture (b) declare (c) remove

4. **badinage**
    (a) joking (b) fighting (c) healing

5. **beholden**
    (a) obvious (b) obligated (c) astonished

6. **consequential**
    (a) arrogant (b) satisfying (c) shocking

7. **copious**
    (a) abundant (b) imitated (c) endured

8. **craven**
    (a) desirous (b) vengeful (c) cowardly

9. **decorous**
    (a) layered (b) polite (c) gaudy

10. **disabuse**
    (a) enchant (b) protect (c) correct

11. **disport**
    (a) arrive (b) amuse (c) enlarge

12. **factitious**
    (a) counterfeit (b) verifiable (c) detailed

13. **factotum**
    (a) veracity (b) handyman (c) directory

14. **fatuous**
    (a) obese (b) captivated (c) foolish

15. **impassive**
    (a) unemotional (b) hurried (c) weak

16. **leaven**
    (a) decorate (b) raise (c) crush

17. **noisome**
    (a) odorous (b) loud (c) friendly

18. **officious**
    (a) savage (b) pushy (c) authoritative

19. **potable**
    (a) drinkable (b) moveable (c) credible

20. **privation**
    (a) solitude (b) hardship (c) panic

21. **prosaic**
    (a) eloquent (b) humble (c) ordinary

22. **pullulate**
    (a) reproduce (b) tremble (c) lift

23. **rakish**
    (a) learned (b) arrogant (c) stylish

24. **redress**
    (a) fix (b) conceal (c) confront

25. refractory
(a) bent (b) unmanageable (c) flawed

26. restive
(a) tranquil (b) impatient (c) joyous

27. ribald
(a) obvious (b) obscene (c) courageous

28. salutary
(a) hungry (b) healthful (c) obedient

29. supplicate
(a) augment (b) plead (c) mold

30. touchstone
(a) burden (b) conduit (c) gauge

31. untoward
(a) improper (b) bashful (c) clever

32. winsome
(a) distorted (b) appealing (c) confident

33. wizened
(a) rejected (b) scholarly (c) shriveled

Answers and Definitions

1. **ACCOST** (uh KAWST) *v* to approach and confront boldly **(c)**

2. **APE** (AYP) *v* to imitate, mimic, or impersonate **(b)**

3. **ASSEVERATE** (uh SEV er ayt) *v* to declare earnestly; assert; aver **(b)**

4. **BADINAGE** (BAD uh nij) *n* teasing conversation; jesting; banter; persiflage **(a)**

5. **BEHOLDEN** (bih HOL din) *adj* obligated or indebted **(b)**

6. **CONSEQUENTIAL** (kahn sih KWEN chul) *adj* self-important; pompous; arrogant; following as a result **(a)**

7. **COPIOUS** (KOH pee us) *adj* abundant; plentiful; replete; teeming; fraught **(a)**

8. **CRAVEN** (KRAY vun) *adj* cowardly; pusillanimous; faint-hearted **(c)**

9. **DECOROUS** (DEK er us) *adj* showing good taste and propriety; polite **(b)**

10. **DISABUSE** (dis uh BYOOZ) *v* to correct a false impression **(c)**

11. **DISPORT** (dis PORT) *v* to amuse **(b)**

12. **FACTITIOUS** (fak TIH shus) *adj* contrived; not genuine; artificial; counterfeit; sham **(a)**

13. **FACTOTUM** (fak TOH tum) *n* a handyman; one who performs various jobs **(b)**

14. **FATUOUS** (FACH yoo us) *adj* foolish; inane **(c)**

15. **IMPASSIVE** (im PAS iv) *adj* composed; without emotion; reserved **(a)**

16. **LEAVEN** (LEH vun) *v* to cause to rise or to make lighter (especially, bread dough); pepsidate; ferment **(b)**

17. **NOISOME** (NOY sum) *adj* having a foul or offensive odor; fetid; unwholesome **(a)**

18. **OFFICIOUS** (uh FISH us) *adj* pushy; meddlesome; intrusive **(b)**

19. **POTABLE** (POH tuh bul) *adj* suitable for drinking; drinkable **(a)**

20. **PRIVATION** (prih VAY shun) *n* lacking life's usual comforts; hardship; destitution; deprivation; want; penury **(b)**

21. **PROSAIC** (proh ZAY ik) *adj* unimaginative; mundane; commonplace; banal; insipid **(c)**

22. **PULLULATE** (PUHL yoo layt) *v* to swarm or teem; to breed or produce rapidly **(a)**

23. **RAKISH** (RAY kish) *adj* stylish; chic; swank **(c)**

24. **REDRESS** (REE dres) *n* setting right that which is wrong; compensation or remedy for a wrong **(a)**

25. **REFRACTORY** (rih FRAK tuh ree) *adj* stubbornly disobedient; unmanageable; unruly **(b)**

26. **RESTIVE** (RES tiv) *adj* restless; impatient **(b)**

27. **RIBALD** (RY buld) *adj* pertaining to profane or irreverent language or speech; obscene; indecent; mocking **(b)**

28. **SALUTARY** (SAL yoo tayr ee) *adj* promoting a beneficial purpose; wholesome; healthful; salubrious **(b)**

29. **SUPPLICATE** (SUP lih kayt) *v* to petition humbly for a favor; entreat; beg; plead; beseech; adjure; conjure **(b)**

30. **TOUCHSTONE** (TUCH stohn) *n* a test for measuring the quality of a thing (especially, precious metals) **(c)**

31. **UNTOWARD** (un TORD) *adj* unfavorable or unfortunate; unpropitious; annoyingly improper; uncouth; gauche; unseemly; indecorous **(a)**

32. **WINSOME** (WIN sum) *adj* attractive; winning **(b)**

33. **WIZENED** (WEE zind) *adj* shriveled; withered **(c)**

33 That Might Fake You Out

Each word in this list looks a bit like a more common word with which you are probably already familiar. On your test, you might second-guess the test-maker by rejecting the more intuitive meaning; if so, you would be wrong! Avoid the fake-out, and memorize these words!
Directions: For each word in bold letters, select the word among three choices—(a), (b) and (c)—that is nearest in meaning. Answers and definitions begin on page 102.

1. **abstemious**
   (a) stubborn (b) moderate (c) secretive

2. **adduce**
   (a) prove (b) kidnap (c) separate

3. **aggrandize**
   (a) roughen (b) empower (c) repair

4. **amass**
   (a) entangle (b) collect (c) pray

5. **belated**
   (a) late (b) ignored (c) favored

6. **chastise**
   (a) hurry (b) forgive (c) restrain

7. **coalesce**
   (a) estimate (b) unite (c) pacify

8. **contagion**
   (a) restriction (b) transmission (c) tyrant

9. **efficacy**
   (a) capability (b) constancy (c) honesty

10. **evince**
    (a) persuade (b) chop (c) defeat

11. **exigency**
    (a) summit (b) urgency (c) escape

12. **extirpate**
    (a) remove (b) mix (c) flood

13. **forestall**
    (a) precede (b) predict (c) prevent

14. **frenetic**
    (a) agitated (b) pastoral (c) unfriendly

15. **funereal**
    (a) toxic (b) sorrowful (c) explosive

16. **guile**
    (a) chicanery (b) impurity (c) bitterness

17. **insular**
    (a) rude (b) troubling (c) isolated

18. **largess**
    (a) generosity (b) leverage (c) comfort

19. **maculated**
    (a) purified (b) stained (c) empowered

20. **militate**
    (a) supervise (b) advocate (c) diminish

21. **nexus**
    (a) connection (b) illusion (c) future

22. **polemic**
    (a) cripple (b) adherent (c) magnate

23. **politic**
    (a) clever (b) biased (c) wordy

24. **prepossessing**
    (a) enticing (b) methodical (c) happy

25. **quiescent**
    (a) squeamish (b) passive (c) serene

26. **rapacious**
    (a) unsteady (b) greedy (c) adoring

27. **remnant**
    (a) problem (b) surplus (c) symbol

28. **requisite**
    (a) necessary (b) careless (c) privileged

29. **stricture**
    (a) monument (b) constraint (c) vessel

30. **tendentious**
    (a) biased (b) grasping (c) loving

31. **timorous**
    (a) punctual (b) prepared (c) shy

32. **urbane**
    (a) refined (b) silly (c) upset

33. **voluble**
    (a) unstable (b) buoyant (c) talkative

Answers and Definitions

1. **ABSTEMIOUS** (ab STEE mee us) *adj* refraining from or moderation in an activity, especially partaking of food and strong drink; abstinent; abstentious; temperate **(b)**

2. **ADDUCE** (uh DOOS) *v* to offer as reason or proof **(a)**

3. **AGGRANDIZE** (uh GRAN dyz) *v* to make larger, more powerful or important, or wealthier **(b)**

4. **AMASS** (uh MAS) *v* to collect or accumulate **(b)**

5. **BELATED** (buh LAY tid) *adj* too late **(a)**

6. **CHASTISE** (CHAS tyz) *v* to discipline or restrain in order to correct or avoid unwanted (usually immoral) behavior **(c)**

7. **COALESCE** (koh uh LES) *v* to unite; come together to form a whole **(b)**

8. **CONTAGION** (kun TAY jun) *n* communicability (transmission) of a disease or idea **(b)**

9. **EFFICACY** (EF ih kih see) *adj* effectiveness; capability; efficiency **(a)**

10. **EVINCE** (ee VINS) *v* to show or demonstrate clearly or convincingly **(a)**

11. **EXIGENCY** (AYG zih jin see) *n* urgency; emergency; pressing need or state requiring immediate action **(b)**

12. **EXTIRPATE** (EK ster payt) *v* to exterminate; ferret out and destroy **(a)**

13. **FORESTALL** (for STAHL) *v* to prevent or hinder by action in advance **(c)**

14. **FRENETIC** (fruh NEH tik) *adj* frenzied; agitated; frantic **(a)**

15. **FUNEREAL** (fyoo NEER ee ul) *adj* sorrowful; solemn; sad **(b)**

16. **GUILE** (GYL) *n* devious cunning; deceit; fraud; duplicity; trickery; chicanery **(a)**

17. **INSULAR** (IN suh ler) *adj* narrow minded; parochial; isolated **(c)**

18. **LARGESS** (lahr JES) *n* a generous bestowal of gifts **(a)**

19. **MACULATED** (MAK yoo lay tid) *adj* spotted; stained **(b)**

20. **MILITATE** (MIL uh tayt) *v* to operate either for or against something **(b)**

21. **NEXUS** (NEK sus) *n* the connection of a group or series **(a)**

22. **POLEMIC** (puh LEM ik) *n* a person who argues for or advocates a particular position (*adj* polemical) **(b)**

23. **POLITIC** (PAHL uh tik) *adj* shrewd; artful; prudent; expedient; judicious **(a)**

24. **PREPOSSESSING** (pree poh ZES eeng) *adj* attractive; appealing; captivating **(a)**

25. **QUIESCENT** (kwee ES unt) *adj* quiet; inactive **(c)**

26. **RAPACIOUS** (ruh PAY shus) *adj* plundering; greedy and excessive grasping **(b)**

27. **REMNANT** (REM nunt) *n* that which remains or is left over; relic **(b)**

28. **REQUISITE** (REH kwih zit) *adj* inherently required or necessary

29. **STRICTURE** (STRIK cher) *n* adverse criticism; limit or restriction **(b)**

30. **TENDENTIOUS** (ten DEN shus) *adj* biased; advancing a point of view **(a)**

31. **TIMOROUS** (TIM er us) *adj* fearful; timid **(c)**

32. **URBANE** (er BAYN) *adj* refined; elegant; polished; suave **(a)**

33. **VOLUBLE** (VAHL yoo bul) *adj* wordy; loquacious; verbose; garrulous **(c)**

Words Easily Confused with Others—the Big Bad List!

The English language is laden with pairs (and larger groups) of words that are easily confused with each other because they look and/or sound similar. The most testworthy of these words are all right here in this list for your reference. Note that most of these words also appear elsewhere in this book; thus, this list might serve as a convenient means of review.

abatement *adj* alleviation; lessening; mitigation
abeyance *n* cessation; discontinuation

aberration *n* a deviation from what is normal, common, or morally right
abhorrence *n* detesting; despising; loathing
apparition *n* a ghost, phantom, or other such appearance

abet *v* to assist
abut *v* to border upon; adjoin

abdicate *v* to give up; relinquish
abnegate *v* to deny oneself (e.g., a pleasure or right); to relinquish or give up
abrogate *v* to repeal; abolish

abjection *n* utter hopelessness; despicableness (*adj* abject)
abjuration *n* renunciation; giving up (*v* abjure)
adjuration *n* an earnest appeal; solemn urging (*v* adjure)
adulation *n* flattery; admiration

abrade *v* to irritate; chafe
upbraid *v* to scold; reproach; censure; reprove; reprimand

absolve *v* to release from an obligation; to free from blame
resolve *n* determination made, especially to solve a problem; *v* to determine to do something by will

accede *v* to adhere to an agreement
cede *v* to relinquish or give up something— especially, territory
exceed *v* to surpass
secede *v* to withdraw and split off from a group

adapt *v* to adjust
adept *adj* proficient

affable *adj* agreeable; friendly
effable *adj* expressible; utterable

alleviate *v* to provide relief; lessen
ameliorate *v* to improve

allude *v* to refer to indirectly
elude *v* to avoid; escape detection

allusion *n* indirect reference
delusion *n* error in judgment
illusion *n* error in vision

amend *v* to alter; change
emend *v* to correct or improve

amerce *v* to punish by inflicting an arbitrary penalty
immerse *v* to plunge completely into a liquid; dunk

amity *n* friendship
amnesty *n* a general pardon by a government for past offenses

amorous *adj* moved by sexual or romantic love
amorphous *adj* vague; shapeless

amulet *n* a good-luck charm (a safeguard against misfortune)
annulet *n* a ring-shaped molding or ridge

anaphora *n* in speech, repeating the first words of sentences
anathema *n* a thing cursed or condemned

anecdote *n* narrative of a particular incident; brief personal story
antidote *n* remedy to counteract a harmful substance (poison)

annunciate *v* to proclaim or promulgate
enunciate *v* to pronounce clearly

averse *adj* disinclined; unwilling
adverse *adj* opposing

apiary *n* a place where bees are kept
aviary *n* an enclosure for birds

apostate *n* one who defects from or abandons one's faith, church or principles.
prostate *n* male glandular organ
prostrate *adj* lying down; prone

apocalyptic *adj* describing a cataclysmic and violent event in which forces of good destroy those of evil
apocryphal *adj* describing a literary work of unknown authorship or doubtful integrity

apothecary *n* druggist; pharmacist
apotheosis *n* elevation of a mortal to the rank of god; deification; glorification

appraise *v* to determine a monetary value
apprise *v* to inform; notify

archetype *n* anything that serves as a model for (example of) all other similar things
prototype *n* the first of a type

ardent *adj* eager, zealous, fervent
arduous *adj* requiring great exertion; laborious; difficult

arrant *adj* downright; complete or total; unmitigated
errant *adj* wandering; deviating from the regular course

articulate *adj* clear and precise in expression
reticulate *adj* having a veined, fibrous, or netlike quality

ascend *v* to rise or climb
assent *v* to agree to

asperse *v* to slander, defame, or insult
disperse *v* to separate or scatter

auger *n* a tool for boring holes in wood
augur *v* to predict, presage; forebode; portend (*n* a soothsayer or prophet)

autonomic *adj* referring to movements produced by some internal stimulus
autonomous *adj* independent from external constraints; self-governing

avocation *n* minor occupation
invocation *n* a call for assistance to a spiritual power

banal *adj* commonplace; trite; hackneyed; unoriginal
bane *n* any cause of ruin or destruction, lasting harm or injury, or woe

baneful *adj* destructive or poisonous
baleful *adj* evil or destructive; sorrowful

biannual *adj* twice a year; semiannual
biennial *adj* every two years

broach *v* to open up; to mention a subject; propose; introduce
brooch *n* a decorative pin (jewelry item)

canvas *n* strong cloth for making tents
canvass *v* to solicit for orders, votes

capacious *adj* spacious; roomy
capricious *adj* impulsive; arbitrary
captious *adj* fault-finding; carping

censor *v* to criticize, object to, and possibly delete (from a broadcast or publication), especially on moral grounds
censure *v* to severely criticize or find fault with; reproach; reprove; rebuke; reprimand; scold

cite *v* to quote or refer to as authority; also, to summons for a court appearance
site *n* a place; location

climactic *adj* relating to climax
climatic *adj* relating to climate

collegial *adj* easy to work with; amiable
collegiate *adj* pertaining to college

commensurate *adj* proportionate; equivalent
commiserate *v* to empathize; sympathy; share sorrow

complacent *adj* self-satisfied; smug; content
complaisant *adj* willing to please (comply with)

condole *v* to express sympathetic sorrow
condone *v* to approve tacitly; overlook; forgive

congeal *v* freeze; coagulate
congenial *adj* gracious; warm-hearted; friendly
congenital *adj* from or existing at birth; inborn; innate

council *n* an assemblage or group gathered to confer
counsel *v* to advise

credible *adj* worthy of acceptance; having integrity; believable
credulous *adj* believing easily; gullible

deceased *adj* dead
diseased *adj* characterized by illness

delegate *v* to appoint; authorize; deputize
relegate *v* to transfer or consign to an inferior position

demagogue *n* a false leader
pedagogue *n* a teacher

demur *v* to delay
demure *adj* serious; grave; coy (feigning
shyness)

denigrate *v* to smear or blacken, especially
the reputation of another
deprecate *v* to express strong disapproval
depredate *v* to plunder; to rampantly
destroy and vandalize

denounce *v* to accuse or inform against
renounce *v* to give up a right or opinion;
retract; abdicate; repudiate

desecrate *v* to violate the sanctity of
desiccate *v* to dry up

device *n* tool; implement
devise *v* to give (a gift) of property

discreet *adj* tactful; prudent
discrete *adj* distinct; distinguishable;
separate

disillusioned *adj* free from illusion;
disenchanted
dissolution *n* a dissolving or breaking up

disparage *v* to speak ill of; belittle
disparate *adj* scattered; unrelated

dissident *adj* rebellious; dissenting
dissonant *adj* unpleasant or disagreeable;
discordant; clashing (especially sound)

dissolute *adj* lewd; licentious; morally lax
resolute *adj* determined; full of resolve

distrait *adj* absent-minded
distraught *adj* worried; anxious; upset

effervescent *adj* bubbling
efflorescent *adj* busting into bloom;
blossoming
evanescent *adj* fleeting; fading quickly;
passing away; vanishing

eminent *adj* distinguished; lofty
immanent *adj* inherent; indwelling;
invading all creation
imminent *adj* impending; about to happen;
threatening

empirical *adj* based upon experience or
observation
imperial *adj* pertaining to a state's
sovereign rule over persons or other states
imperious *adj* dictatorial; domineering

epic *n* great in size or extent; a type of
poem about a heroic adventure
epoch *n* a specific time period marked by
distinctive events or features

epigram *n* a clever, pithy saying; aphorism
epitaph *n* an inscription on a monument in
memory of a deceased person
epithet *n* a word or phrase describing a
person used instead of or added to the
person's name

escheat *v* to transfer title by default to the
state (government)
eschew *v* to avoid

evoke *v* to call up past emotions
inveigh *v* to denounce; censure
invoke *v* to call up a spirit or emotion for
assistance or inspiration
revoke *v* to take back; rescind; cancel;
annul

exacerbate *v* to increase the harshness, severity; aggravate; worsen
exaggerate *v* distort by overstatement
exasperate *v* to annoy, irritate, or infuriate

exigent *adj* urgent
exiguous *adj* meager; trifling; scanty

expatiate *v* talk at length
expatriate *n* exile
expiate *v* make amends for an offense or sin

expedient *adj* suitable for a particular purpose; practicable; fitting for one's advantage or interest
expeditious *adj* speedy; quick

explicate *v* to explain, interpret, or clarify
expurgate *v* to clean; remove offensive parts (of a book)
extirpate *v* to root up
extricate *v* to free; disentangle

factious *adj* given to dissent; hostile; seditious; insurgent
factitious contrived; not genuine; artificial; counterfeit; sham
fractious *adj* unruly; given to breaking rules

feculent *adj* relating to feces (excrement)
fecund *adj* fertile; productive; fruitful

felicitous apt; suitable; appropriate
filaceous *adj* composed of threads
fallacious misleading; deceptive; logically unsound

fervent *adj* adamant; feverish; impassioned
furtive *adj* sneaky; surreptitious

germane *adj* pertinent; relevant
germinal *adj* creative; pertaining to a germ; seminal

glutinous *adj* gluey; sticky; adhesive
gluttonous *adj* ravenous; indulgent

hapless *adj* unlucky; unfortunate
helpless *adj* unable to help oneself

hoard *v* to stockpile, collect, or accumulate for future use
horde *n* a crowd

hypercritical *adj* overly critical
hypocritical *adj* insincere

igneous *adj* caused or created by volcanic eruption or by fire
ligneous *adj* like wood; having the quality of wood

imprudent *adj* careless; reckless; indiscreet
impudent *adj* rude; insolent; audacious; brazen; impertinent

impugn *v* to challenge; call into question; contradict
impunity *n* privilege; license; exemption

incipient *adj* coming into being; nascent; inchoate
insipid *adj* tasteless; uninteresting; banal

incubate *v* to hatch; scheme
incubus *n* burden; nightmare
inculcate *v* to teach; indoctrinate

indict *v* to charge with an offense
indite *v* to compose or express in words

indigenous *adj* native to or characterizing a particular region

indigent *adj* poor; destitute
indulgent *adj* permissive; tolerating

indurated *adj* hardened; unyielding; obstinate
inundated *adj* flooded; overflowed

inevitable *adj* unavoidable
inexorable *adj* relentless; unyielding; implacable

ingenious *adj* inventive; clever (*n* ingenuity)
ingenue *n* a naive and unsophisticated young woman
ingenuous *adj* naive; unsophisticated (*n* ingenuousness)

insidious *adj* wily; crafty; sly; treacherous
invidious *adj* likely to cause, ill will, resentment, discontent

insolent *adj* rude; insulting; brazen; audacious
insular *adj* isolated; narrowly exclusive

inveigh *v* to criticize vehemently with words
inveigle *v* to lure or entice by inducements

jocose *adj* playful; jesting; humorous
jocular *adj* joking; not serious; jesting; facetious
jocund *adj* cheerful; merry

labile *adj* unstable; likely to change
liable *adj* responsible for a debt; owing

lassitude *n* weariness; depression; languor
latitude *n* leeway; freedom from limitation
platitude *n* commonplace or trite expression

lathe *n* a rotating tool for rounding wood objects
lithe *adj* flexible; supple; labile
loath *adj* averse; reluctant
loathe *v* to detest; hate

literal *adj* word for word; express
literate *adj* able to read
littoral *adj* pertaining to a coastal region (shoreline)

livid *adj* enraged; extremely angry
lurid *adj* sensational or shocking; shining with an unnatural glow; gruesome or revolting

macerate *v* waste away or fall apart; to soften by soaking in liquid
maculated *adj* spotted or stained
masticate *v* chew

meddlesome *adj* interfering; intrusive
mettlesome *adj* courageous; ardent
nettlesome *adj* prickly or barbed; annoying or vexing

mendacity *n* deceit or fraud (*adj* mendacious)
mendicancy *n* the practice of begging or living off alms (charity) of others

meritorious *adj* worthy of merit; of value
meretricious *adj* gaudy; tawdry; flashy

miscreant *n* an evil person
recreant *n* one who yields in combat and begs for mercy

multifarious *adj* greatly diversified; of various kinds
multiparous *adj* producing more than one offspring at a birth

obfuscate *v* confuse; muddle
obdurate *adj* stubborn; persistent

obloquy *n* condemnation or verbal abuse, or the disgrace resulting therefrom
obsequious *adj* overly servile or obedient
obsequies *n* funeral rites or ceremonies

odious: *adj* deserving or causing hatred or scorn; detestable; despicable; offensive
odorous: having a distinct or strong smell

onerous *adj* burdensome; difficult
ominous *adj* looming; threatening; foreboding; impending

opalescent *adj* iridescent; shining
opulence *n* luxury; extreme wealth

oratorio *n* a large multisectional musical form which is really an unstaged sacred opera
oratory *n* discourse or speech

pablum *n* banal (trite or hackneyed) intellectual ideas or writings
pabulum *n* any nourishment for an animal (or plant)

palatable *adj* agreeable; tasty
palpable *adj* obvious; evident; unmistakable

palette *n* a board on which a painter mixes pigments
palliate *v* gloss; veil; varnish
pallet *n* cot (small bed)
pallid *adj* pale; wan

paradigm *n* a model, example, or pattern
paragon *n* a model of perfection; an ideal

paramount *adj* highest in rank or value

tantamount *adj* equivalent in meaning, value, or effect

parity *n* equivalence; resemblance
parody *n* humorous imitation

parley *n* a conference or discussion
parlance *n* a way or manner of speaking
parlay *v* to bet one's winnings on a subsequent bet

patriarch *n* father and ruler of a family or tribe
patrician *adj* aristocratic; having the elegance of nobility

pedagogy *n* the science of teaching methods
pedology *n* the study of children

peremptory *adj* final; with authority; absolutely
preemptive *adj* claimed or initiated before or in preference to others

perquisite *n* fringe benefit, privilege, or bonus
prerequisite *n* necessary beforehand

perspicacious *adj* insightful; penetrating; astute
perspicuous *adj* clearly or plainly expressed
pertinacious *adj* stubborn; persistent
pertinent *adj* appropriate; relevant

plaintiff *n* party initiating a law suit
plaintive *adj* mournful; baleful

practicable *adj* feasible; capable of being put into practice
practical *adj* useful; sensible

preciosity *n* fastidiousness or overrefinement

precociousness *n* maturity beyond one's years

prescience *n* foreknowledge (of future events)

prescribe *v* to set forth a rule, policy, or course of action

proscribe *v* to prohibit; forbid

principal *n* chief; primary

principle *n* fundamental truth, axiom, or presupposition

prodigal *adj* wasteful; reckless with money

prodigious *adj* immense; enormous; extraordinary; marvelous (*n* prodigy)

profligate *adj* degenerate; depraved; lascivious

proliferate *v* to multiply; spread; breed

promulgate *v* to make known by announcement; proclaim; disseminate

propagate *v* to breed; reproduce; generate

propitiate *v* to appease

propiteous *adj* pitiful

propitious *adj* favorable to; auspicious; advantageous

provenance *n* origin or source

providence *n* destiny; fate; divine guidance

provident *adj* prepared; ready; thoughtful

provisional *adj* temporary; interim; tentative

pugnacious *adj* defiant; rebellious; belligerent

pungent *adj* sharp or acidic in taste or smell

repugnant *adj* repulsive; offensive; revolting

querulous *adj* full of complaints; whining; peevish

query *v* to inquire or question

rake *n* a wasteful or morally lax person

rakish *adj* stylish; sportive

refectory *n* a large dining hall (at a church, college, etc.)

refractive *adj* changing direction obliquely (as light when moving from one medium to another)

refractory *adj* stubborn; unmanageable

regime *n* a system of government (especially, the administration of a specific leader)

regimen *n* a prescribed routine or habit

requisite *adj* necessary; required; mandatory; indispensable

requite *v* to repay; compensate; recompense; remunerate

respectful *adj* showing respect; courteous

respective *adj* in the order (sequence) given

salient *adj* prominent or conspicuous: notable, significant, or important

saline *adj* pertaining to salt

satire *n* a literary form employing irony, ridicule, and sarcasm

satyr *n* a mythological deity, appearing as half-man, half-goat, and known for its riotous and lascivious behavior

sedentary *adj* staying in one place; inactive

sedimentary *adj* describing accumulation of material deposited by water, wind, or glaciers

seditious *adj* resistant to authority; unruly; defiant; insubordinate; factious
sedulous *adj* diligent; persistent; assiduous; industrious

sinewy *adj* strong; sturdy; tough
sinuous *adj* winding; twisted; serpentine

specie *n* a coin or coined money
species *n* type; sort; variety; kind

succor *n* aid; relief; assistance
succumb *v* to yield; give in

superfluent *adj* frictionless; easily flowing
superfluous *adj* adding nothing necessary or important; excess; unnecessary; surplus

supine *adj* lying on one's back
supple *adj* soft; pliable

synergy *n* teamwork; cooperation
syzygy *n* alignment of three celestial bodies

temerarious *adj* foolhardy; rash; audacious (*n* temerity)
timorous *adj* fearful; timid

temporal *adj* pertaining to time
temporary *adj* lasting for a time only
temporize *v* to avoid committing oneself in order to delay or gain time

tenacious *adj* holding firm and fast, as with a strong grip (*n* tenacity)
tendentious *adj* tending to; having a propensity to; leaning toward a direction

tentative *adj* temporary; uncertain

torpid *adj* inactive; sluggish; lethargic; phlegmatic
turbid *adj* clouded; muddy
turgid *adj* swollen; inflated

tortuous *adj* twisting
torturous *adj* cruelly painful

ululate *v* to wail; howl; lament loudly
undulate *v* to move in a wavelike motion

vagary *n* an impulse; whim; caprice
vagrancy *n* the condition of having no home; vagabondage
vague *adj* imprecise; obscure; nebulous

venal *adj* corrupt; capable of being bribed; mercenary
venial *adj* excusable; forgivable; trivial
venerable *adj* worthy of respect, praise, or honor

veritable *adj* truly; very much so; genuine
veracious *adj* truthful; honest; credible
voracious *adj* ravenous; gluttonous; rapacious

virile *adj* possessing masculine strength
virulent *adj* poisonous; extremely injurious; deadly

visceral *adj* physiological; felt in one's inner organs
viscous *adj* sticky; gluey

waiver *n* giving up of a claim or right
waver *v* to hesitate

Quiz Time (2.1–2.7)

Directions: Match each numbered word in the left column with its lettered definition in the right column. The answer key begins on page 116.

Quiz 2.1 (15 That Will Confound You)

1.	calumny	a.	command or order
2.	conundrum	b.	dabbler in the arts
3.	debauch	c.	excessive pride
4.	dilettante	d.	group with a common purpose
5.	fiat	e.	commonplace or everyday
6.	gossamer	f.	line up sequentially
7.	queue	g.	puzzle or mystery
8.	hubris	h.	malicious statement
9.	insouciant	i.	corrupt by sensuality
10.	juggernaut	j.	replacement or substitute
11.	milieu	k.	sheer and light
12.	peccadillo	l.	slight offense
13.	phalanx	m.	compelling ideology
14.	quotidian	n.	surroundings or environment
15.	succedaneum	o.	unconcerned or carefree

Quiz 2.2 (15 That Look Deceptively Familiar)

1.	abject	a.	appropriate or suitable
2.	adventitious	b.	associated with
3.	apposite	c.	avoid by prevention
4.	concomitant	d.	fastidiousness
5.	enervate	e.	by chance
6.	obeisance	f.	complaining or whining
7.	obloquy	g.	relief or assistance
8.	obviate	h.	gloomy or morbid
9.	protean	i.	unusual or rare
10.	preciosity	j.	condemnation or verbal abuse
11.	predilection	k.	demonstration of respect
12.	querulous	l.	deprive of vitality
13.	succor	m.	preference
14.	tenebrous	n.	utterly hopeless
15.	unwonted	o.	versatile

Quiz 2.3 (15 That Will Fool You)

1.	asseverate	a.	annoyingly improper
2.	badinage	b.	beneficial or wholesome
3.	disabuse	c.	correct a false impression
4.	factitious	d.	declare earnestly
5.	fatuous	e.	hardship or destitution
6.	noisome	f.	having a foul odor
7.	officious	g.	not genuine
8.	privation	h.	petition humbly for a favor
9.	pullulate	i.	profane or irreverent
10.	refractory	j.	pushy or intrusive
11.	restive	k.	restless or impatient
12.	ribald	l.	inane
13.	salutary	m.	stubbornly disobedient
14.	supplicate	n.	swarm or produce rapidly
15.	untoward	o.	teasing conversation

Quiz 2.4 (15 That Might Fake You Out)

1.	abstemious	a.	capability or efficiency
2.	aggrandize	b.	pressing need for action
3.	amass	c.	discipline or restrain
4.	chastise	d.	unite
5.	coalesce	e.	ferret out and destroy
6.	efficacy	f.	wordy
7.	exigency	g.	devious cunning or trickery
8.	extirpate	h.	fearful
9.	frenetic	i.	shrewd or artful
10.	guile	j.	inherently necessary
11.	militate	k.	operate for or against
12.	politic	l.	agitated
13.	requisite	m.	moderate or abstinent
14.	timorous	n.	to make more important
15.	voluble	o.	accumulate

Quiz 2.5 (Noteworthy Nouns from the Big Bad List)

1.	aberration	a.	crowd
2.	allusion	b.	cooperation
3.	anecdote	c.	manner
4.	horde	d.	destiny
5.	impunity	e.	abnormality
6.	miscreant	f.	story
7.	parlance	g.	evil doer
8.	providence	h.	dining hall
9.	refectory	i.	reference
10.	synergy	j.	privilege

Quiz 2.6 (Various Verbs from the Big Bad List)

1.	abrogate	a.	scold
2.	asperse	b.	insult
3.	dessicate	c.	demote
4.	impugn	d.	teach
5.	inculcate	e.	proclaim
6.	macerate	f.	gamble
7.	parlay	g.	waste away
8.	promulgate	h.	contradict
9.	relegate	i.	dry
10.	upbraid	j.	repeal

Quiz 2.7 (A Fistful of Adjectives from the Big Bad List)

1.	commensurate	a.	veined
2.	discrete	b.	inherent
3.	felicitous	c.	appropriate
4.	immanent	d.	naive
5.	ingenuous	e.	extraordinary
6.	meretricious	f.	sticky
7.	onerous	g.	burdensome
8.	prodigious	h.	gaudy
9.	reticulate	i.	separate
10.	viscous	j.	equivalent

Quiz Time—Answers (2.1–2.7)

Quiz 2.1

1. h	6. k	11. n
2. g	7. f	12. l
3. i	8. c	13. d
4. b	9. o	14. e
5. a	10. m	15. j

Quiz 2.2

1. n	6. k	11. m
2. e	7. j	12. f
3. a	8. c	13. g
4. b	9. o	14. h
5. l	10. d	15. i

Quiz 2.3

1. d	6. f	11. k
2. o	7. j	12. i
3. c	8. e	13. b
4. g	9. n	14. h
5. l	10. m	15. j

Quiz 2.4

1. m	6. a	11. k
2. n	7. b	12. i
3. o	8. e	13. j
4. c	9. l	14. h
5. d	10. g	15. f

Quiz 2.5

1. e
2. i
3. f
4. a

5. j
6. g
7. c
8. d

9. h
10. b

Quiz 2.6

1. j
2. b
3. i
4. h

5. d
6. g
7. f
8. e

9. c
10. a

Quiz 2.7

1. j
2. i
3. c
4. b

5. d
6. h
7. g
8. e

9. a
10. f

Academic
Challenge
(33 Fields—from Anatomy to Zoology)

To gauge the breadth of your vocabulary, the test-makers will strive to include on your exam words from many different academic fields. After studying this chapter, you'll be ready for them! The most testworthy words from 33 subject areas—from Anatomy to Zoology—are right here. You'll also find a total of 12 **"Quiz Time" quizzes** interspersed throughout the chapter to help you review the words you just learned. (Or you can take each quiz *before* studying the lists that immediately precede it.)

Note: Many of the words in this chapter could appropriately be included on several different lists. (For example, the word *baroque* is used in art, literature, and music.) However, *most* such words are included on only one list, along with a brief reference to the other areas to which the word refers. Some of the words in this chapter also appear as main entries elsewhere in this book.

Anatomy (the Human Body)

ABLATION (uh BLAY shun) *n* destruction of part of the body (especially, part of the brain)

AMBULATORY (AM byoo luh tor ee) *adj* able to walk or move about

ASPIRE (uh SPYR) *v* to breathe

AURAL (AH rul) *adj* pertaining to the ear or to the sense of hearing

DEGLUTITION (dee gloo TIH shun) *n* the act or process of swallowing food

HYPERTROPHY (hy PER truh fee) *n* abnormally large growth of a bodily organ

INCONTINENCE (in KAHN tih nuns) *n* the inability to control one's bodily urges and functions

LACUNA (luh KYOO nuh) *n* a cavity, hole, or gap in a bone (or in a plant's cellular tissue or a rock)

MANDIBLE (MAN duh bul) *n* the principal bone of the lower jaw

MYOPIC (my AH pik) *adj* nearsighted; unable to see clearly in the distance

OLFACTORY (ahl FAK tuh ree) *adj* pertaining to the sense of smell

PALATE (PAL it) *n* the roof of the mouth

PERISTALSIS (payr ih STAWL sis) *n* involuntary contractions that move food through the digestive system

SENTIENT (SEN shunt) *adj* having the power of one's senses

SOMATIC (so MAT ik) *adj* pertaining to the body

SURDITY (SER dih tee) *n* deafness

TACTILE (TAK tul) *adj* pertaining to the sense of touch

VESICLE (VES uh kul) *n* any fluid-filled sac in the body

VISCERAL (VIS er ul) *adj* physiological

Anthropology

ABORIGINAL (ab uh RIJ uh nul) *adj* native to a region; indigenous

ANTEDILUVIAN (an tee dih LOO vee un) *adj* anything ancient, primitive, or outdated (literally, "before the flood")

BIBELOT (BIB loh) *n* a small item of rarity, beauty, or curiosity; relic; artifact

CONJUGAL (KAHN joo gul) *adj* referring to the relationship between two married persons

CONSANGUINITY (kahn sang GWIN ih tee) *n* relationship by blood

DOWRY (DOW ree) *n* money or property given by the bride's family to the bridegroom at marriage

ETHOS (EE thus) *n* the fundamental (underlying) character of a culture or spirit

HUSBANDRY (HUZ bin dree) *n* exploitation of domesticated animals for consumption, load carrying, etc.

MIDDEN (MID un) *n* a dunghill or refuse heap

NOMAD (NOH mad) *n* a person who moves about in a seasonal pattern, especially in search of work and usually without a fixed home

NUPTIAL (NUP shul) *adj* pertaining to a marriage ceremony or to a marriage

PETROGLYPH (PET roh glif) *n* a prehistoric carving or drawing on stone

PHILISTINE (FIL ih steen) *n* a person who is extremely indifferent to culture or aesthetic refinement

PHYLOGENIC (fy loh JEN ik) *adj* pertaining to a race (or species, in biology)

PRIMOGENITURE (pry moh JEN ih ter) *n* the condition or fact of being firstborn of the same parents; seniority by birth among children of the same parents

RITE (RYT) *n* a formal ceremonial act or procedure, often part of solemn religious occasions

RUNIC (ROO nik) *adj* pertaining to the characters of any ancient alphabet

SEPT (SEPT) *n* a division of a tribe or clan

SEPULCHER (SEP uhl ker) *n* a burial tomb or receptacle for sacred relics

TOTEM (TOH tum) *n* an object or animal with which a tribe, clan or group of people identify in its rituals

VENDETTA (ven DET uh) *n* a private feud in which kin are obliged to seek revenge for wrongs done to relatives

Architecture

ANNULET (AN yoo lut) *n* a ring-shaped molding or ridge

BASTILLE (bas TEEL) *n* a fortification or castle, typically used as a prison

BASTION (BAS chyun) *n* a projection from an outer wall of a fortification designed to defend the adjacent perimeter

BULWARK (BUL werk) *n* a strong defensive wall structure

BUTTRESS (BUT rus) *n* an extra thickness or projection in a wall designed to strengthen it.

CANTILEVER (KAN tuh lee ver) *n* a structure that projects out beyond its supporting wall

CONCOURSE (KAHN cors) *n* an open space where several paths meet

CUSP (KUSP) *n* the point where two curves meet (e.g., the apex of a vaulted arch)

EDIFICE (ED uh fis) *n* a monument

FACADE (fuh SAHD) *n* the exterior front or face of a building

FENESTRATION (fen uh STRAY shun) *n* the scheme or pattern of windows in the design of a building

HERMITAGE (HER mih tij) *n* a private or secluded retreat; a hideaway

HOVEL (HUH vul) *n* a shed or poorly constructed or ill-kept house

IMBRICATE (IM brih kit) *adj* overlapping in a regular, orderly pattern

KIOSK (KEE ahsk) *n* an open summer house or pavilion; a small structure, with one or more open sides, used to vend merchandise

MAUSOLEUM (mah zuh LEE um) *n* a monumental tomb (for a dead person)

MEZZANINE (MEZ uh neen) *n* a low balcony above the ground floor of a building

OBELISK (AH buh lisk) *n* a tapering (narrowing) column that forming pyramid at the top

OCULUS (AH kyoo lus) *n* a round window

PERISTYLE (PER ih styl) *n* a colonnade or row of piers surrounding a building or courtyard

PORTAL (POR tul) *n* an impressive or monumental entrance or gate

REFECTORY (ruh FEK ter ee) *n* a large dining hall at a church, college, or other institution

ROCOCO (ruh KOH koh) *adj* ornate; highly decorative

ROTUNDA (roh TUN druh) *n* a dome-covered circular hall or building

VESTIBULE (VES tih byool) *n* an inner or middle room in a building

VOUSSOIR (voo SWAH) *n* a wedge-shaped stone used in making an arch or vault

Quiz Time (3.1)

Directions: Match each numbered word in the left column with its lettered definition in the right column. The answer key begins on page 170.

1.	ablation	a.	a person indifferent to culture
2.	aboriginal	b.	burial tomb
3.	bastille	c.	cavity, hole, or gap
4.	cantilever	d.	deafness
5.	concourse	e.	destruction of part of the body
6.	consanguinity	f.	division of a tribe
7.	husbandry	g.	fortification or castle
8.	imbricate	h.	highly decorative
9.	lacuna	i.	native to a region
10.	obelisk	j.	overlapping in a pattern
11.	palate	k.	projecting out from a structure
12.	philistine	l.	relationship by blood
13.	rococo	m.	roof of the mouth
14.	sentient	n.	having the power of one's senses
15.	sept	o.	sense of touch
16.	sepulcher	p.	space where several paths meet
17.	surdity	q.	tapering column
18.	tactile	r.	use of domesticated animals

Astronomy

AURORA (uh ROR uh) *n* a display of changing colored light high in the atmosphere

AZIMUTH (AZ uh muth) *n* a measurement of direction, expressed as an angle and measured clockwise from a celestial reference point

CORONA (kuh ROH nuh) *n* the faint halo-like outer portion of the sun's atmosphere

COSMOGONY (kahz MAH jun ee) *n* the study of the ultimate origins of physical systems

FACULA (FAK yoo luh) *n* a small, bright spot on the sun's surface

NADIR (NAY der) *n* the point on the celestial sphere directly below the observer

NEBULA (NEH byoo luh) *n* an irregular, diffuse interstellar cloud

OCCULTATION (ah kuhl TAY shun) *n* passage of one celestial object in front of another

PENUMBRA (puh NUM bruh) *n* the region of semi-shadow in an eclipse; the less dark outer region of a sunspot

PERTURBATION (per ter BAY shun) *n* disturbance in regular motion (usually orbiting) of a celestial body

PULSAR (PUL sar) *n* a collapsed star of extremely high density

SIDEREAL (sy DEER ee ul) *adj* having to do with the stars

SYZYGY (SIH zih jee) *n* straight alignment of three celestial bodies

UMBRA (UM bruh) *n* the region of total shadow in an eclipse; the dark centrer of a sunspot

ZENITH (ZEE nith) *n* the point on the celestial sphere directly overhead

Biochemistry

ABIOSIS (ay bee OH sis) *n* absence of life

ANTIGEN (AN tih jin) *n* a foreign substance (such as a virus) that enters the body, thereby stimulating the production of an antibody

ATROPHY (AT ruh fee) *n* a wasting away; diminution in the size of a cell, tissue or part

CARCINOGEN (kar SIN oh jin) *n* any cancer-causing substance

CATALYST (KAT uh list) *n* any substance which creates or increases the rate of a (chemical) change without itself being affected

CLASTIC (KLAS tik) *adj* causing or undergoing division into parts

CYTOLOGY (sih TAHL uh jee) *n* the study of cells

DESICCANT (DES ih kint) *n* any drying agent

DETRITUS (dih TRY tus) *n* decaying organic matter lying just below the surface

ENZYME (EN zym) *n* a protein which acts as a biological catalyst

IMMISCIBLE (ih MIS ih bul) *adj* not capable of being mixed

IONIZATION (y un uh ZAY shun) *n* the process of charging an electrically neutral atomic configuration by heat, electrical discharge, radiation or chemical reaction

LIPID (LIP id) *n* a fatlike substance that cannot be dissolved in water

OSMOSIS (ahs MOH sis) *n* diffusion of a substance in a liquid solution across a membrane

SUBSTRATE (SUB strayt) *n* any substance which is acted on or altered by an enzyme

SYMBIOSIS (sim bee OH sis) *n* the living together of two dissimilar organisms in a mutually beneficial relationship

SYNAPSE (SIN aps) *n* the junction, usually a tiny gap, between two neurons or nerve cells

SYNERGY (SIN er jee) *n* coordination of different elements to achieve a common end

SYSTEMIC (sis TEM ik) *adj* referring to or distributed throughout an entire organism

ZYGOTE (ZY goht) *n* a fertilized egg

Botany

AMBIPAROUS (am BIH per us) *adj* having both leaves and flowers

APHYLLOUS (ay FIL us) *adj* without leaves

ARBOREAL (ar BOR ee ul) *adj* pertaining to trees

AUTONOMIC (aw toh NAH mik) *adj* referring to movements produced by some internal stimulus

BIENNIAL (by EN ee ul) *n* any plant that blossoms or sprouts every two years; *adj* occurring every two years

CONIFER (KAHN ih fer) *n* a cone-bearing tree

CUTICLE (KYOO tih kul) *n* the waxy outer layer of a plant (or animal)

DECIDUOUS (dih SIH jyoo us) *adj* shedding all leaves at a certain season of the year

EPIDERMIS (eh pih DER mis) *n* the outermost layer of a plant (or animal)

FLORA (FLOR uh) *n* the plant population of a given region or period

FOLIAGE (FOL yij) *n* leaves of a plant or tree

FROND (FRAHND) *n* the leaf of a fern, palm tree, or banana tree

FRUTICOSE (FROO tih kohs) *adj* shrublike

GUTTATION (guh TAY shun) *n* exudation (sweating) of water droplets from plants in a humid atmosphere

HERBARIUM (er BAYR ee um) *n* a collection of dried or preserved plants

HERMAPHRODITE (her MAF roh dyt) *n* having both male and female organs

HIRSUTE (HER soot) *adj* covered with very long, soft hairs

HYDROPHYTE (HY droh fyt) *n* a plant normally growing in water or damp places

LIGNEOUS (LIG nee uhs) *adj* like wood; having woodlike qualities

PERENNIAL (per EN ee ul) *adj* in Botany, a plant that lives for two or more years; generally, continuing through the year; continuing without cessation or intermission; perpetual

PUBESCENT (pyoo BES int) *adj* covered with a soft down; arriving at puberty

SCANDENT (SKAN dint) *adj* characterized by a climbing growth

SEDGE (SEJ) *n* grasslike herbaceous plant, growing in wet areas

SYLVAN (SIL vun) *adj* living in the forest or woods; sylvestrine

TENDRIL (TEN drul) *n* a thin, modified stem used for climbing by twining or adhesion

TERRARIUM (ter AYR ee um) *n* a small glass enclosure for plants

TROPISM (TROH pih zum) *n* involuntary response—e.g., a stem's bending movement—to some external stimulus (such as water, sun or gravity)

VENTRAL (VEN trul) *adj* pertaining to the lower or inner surface (of a leaf, petal, etc.)

VERDANT (VER dunt) *adj* lush in vegetation (literally, green)

VIABLE (VY uh bul) *adj* able to live, develop, or thrive

Quiz Time (3.2)

Directions: Match each numbered word in the left column with its lettered definition in the right column. The answer key begins on page 170.

1.	arboreal	a.	diffuse cloud
2.	atrophy	b.	diminution in the size
3.	azimuth	c.	drying agent
4.	catalyst	d.	faint halo
5.	corona	e.	fertilized egg
6.	deciduous	f.	like wood
7.	desiccant	g.	lush in vegetation
8.	flora	h.	measurement of direction
9.	guttation	i.	mutually beneficial relationship
10.	immiscible	j.	not capable of being mixed
11.	ligneous	k.	pertaining to the stars
12.	nebula	l.	pertaining to trees
13.	sidereal	m.	plant population of a region
14.	symbiosis	n.	point directly overhead
15.	umbra	o.	shadow of an eclipse
16.	verdant	p.	shedding all leaves during a season
17.	zenith	q.	stimulating change
18.	zygote	r.	sweating of plants

Business, Economics, and Finance

ACCRUE (uh KROO) *v* to accumulate over time (e.g., interest or money owing)

ACTUARY (AK choo ayr ee) *n* a specialist or expert on statistics, especially in the area of insurance

AMORTIZE (AM or tyz) *v* to account for the reduction in the value of an asset over the period of ownership of the asset

ANNUITY (uh NOO ih tee) *n* a contract to pay a sum of money yearly or at regular intervals

APPRAISE (uh PRAYZ) *v* to assess the market value of an asset

ARBITRAGE (AR bih trahzh) *v* to take advantage of differing prices for the same security or commodity

ARREARS (uh REERS) *n* a debt due but unpaid

CONTRABAND (KAHN truh band) *n* goods illegally transported across a border (e.g., to avoid payment of taxes)

DEBENTURE (duh BEN cher) *n* a note by a company promising to pay a debt, backed by the general credit of the company

EMBARGO (em BAR goh) *n* an official prohibition or restriction of foreign trade by one nation against another

ENTREPRENEUR (ahn truh pruh nyoor) *n* someone who takes a risk in a business venture, usually as the business owner

ESCROW (ES kroh) *n* a temporary account established to hold funds pending the completion of an investment or purchase transaction

EXCHEQUER (EKS chuh kur) *n* the treasury of a state or nation

FISCAL (FIS kul) *adj* pertaining to the finances of a government or business

HEDGE (HEJ) *v* to offset the risk of loss (e.g., from market price fluctuations)

INSOLVENT (in SAWL vunt) *adj* where one's financial liabilities exceed one's assets

NEGOTIABLE (nuh GOH shee uh bul) *adj* transferable (from one party to another)

PECUNIARY (puh KYOO nee ayr ee) *adj* financial; monetary

PEONAGE (PEE uh nij) *n* a system of forced labor based upon debts incurred by workers

PROCURE (pro KYOOR) *v* to obtain through purchase

PROSPECTUS (pro SPEK tus) *n* a descriptive circular used in soliciting orders (e.g., for the purchase of stock or other securities)

REPATRIATION (re pay tree AY shun) *n* return of financial assets deposited in a foreign bank to a home country

SCRIVENER (SKRIV ner) *n* a professional or public copyist, scribe, or notary

SPECIE (SPEE shee) *n* money in the form of coins

SPENDTHRIFT (SPEND thrift) *n* a person who is overly free or undisciplined in spending money

SUBSIDY (SUB sih dee) *n* financial grant or aid

SURETY (SHOOR tee) *n* one who guarantees the performance (e.g., payment) on behalf of another

SYNDICATE (SIN dih kit) *n* a group of persons or businesses joined together in a cooperative effort to reduce risk and increase efficiency

UNDERWRITE (UN der ryt) *v* to access, select and reject risks, usually for the purpose of determining insurability and insurance rates

USURIOUS (yoo ZHOOR ee us) *adj* referring to an extremely high or unlawful rate of interest

VOUCHER (VOWCH sayf) *n* legally acceptable evidence of debt repayment; written evidence of authorization to make a purchase

WARRANT (WOR int) *n* a certificate giving the holder the right to purchase securities at a specified price for a specified time period

YIELD (YEELD) *n* the return on an investment (e.g., dividends or interest)

Civil Law

AFFIDAVIT (af ih DAY vid) *n* written declaration of fact, made under oath (or affirmation) of the party making it

AGENCY (AY jun see) *n* a relationship in which one party is legally authorized to act on behalf of another

ANNUL (uh NUHL) *v* to make or declare invalid or void

ATTEST (uh TEST) *v* to state a fact in writing and swear to its truthfulness

BARRISTER (BAYR ih ster) *n* a counselor-at-law; attorney; lawyer

BEQUEATH (buh KWEETH) *v* to make a posthumous gift by one's will

BREACH (BREECH) *v* to break a contractual promise

CHATTEL (CHAT ul) *n* any movable property (not attached to land)

CODICIL (KAH dih sul) *n* a legal document which adds to or changes the provisions of a will

CONSERVATOR (kun SER veh tor) *n* one who is authorized to handle the property and/or personal affairs of another who is incapable of doing so for himself or herself

DECEDENT (dih SEE dunt) *n* a deceased person

DEMUR (duh MER) *v* to claim that even if another party's facts are true there is no legitimate claim or legal recourse

EASEMENT (EEZ munt) *n* an interest in land giving the holder the right of access to or a particular use of the land

FIDUCIARY (fuh DOO shee ayr ee) *n* one charged with the legal responsibility for administering and/or managing another's assets

FRANCHISE (FRAN chyz) *n* a right or privilege granted by authority (especially, suffrage—the right to vote)

IMPEACH (im PEECH) *v* to discredit; to detract from a person's credibility or believability

INDEMNIFY (in DEM nuh fy) *v* to restore a victim of a loss to the same position as before the loss occurred

JURISDICTION (joor is DIK shun) *n* the authority (usually of a court) to hear and decide legal disputes

LIEN (LEE un) *n* a formal claim against property that has been pledged or mortgaged to secure the performance of an obligation

MITIGATE (MIT uh gayt) *v* to minimize or lessen the severity of damage

NOTARY (NOH tuh ree) *n* a person who is officially authorized to authenticate legal documents (contracts, deeds, etc.)

NOVATION (no VAY shun) *n* substitution of a new contract or obligation for an existing one

PROXY (PRAHK see) *n* authority to act (e.g., to vote) for another

QUITCLAIM (KWIT klaym) *v* to transfer or relinquish title in property to another without any representation as to one's legal authority to do so

RESCIND (ree SIND) *v* to cancel, nullify, revoke; retract; annul; to invalidate by subsequent action

REVOCABLE (ruh VOH kuh bul) *adj* capable of being revoked, canceled, or rescind

STIPULATE (STIP yoo layt) *v* to specify, require, or set forth a particular fact as a condition of an agreement

SUBPOENA (suh PEE nuh) *n* a court order compelling a witness to provide information or to be present at a court hearing

SUBROGATE (SUB roh gayt) *v* to substitute one party (e.g., a creditor) for another

TORT (TORT) *n* a non-criminal and non-contractual wrongful act committed against another

VEST (VEST) *v* to attain a right or interest without possibility of losing it

WAIVE (WAYV) *v* to voluntarily give up or surrender a right or privilege

Quiz Time (3.3)

Directions: Match each numbered word in the left column with its lettered definition in the right column. The answer key begins on page 170.

1.	accrue	a.	addition to a will
2.	affidavit	b.	responsibility for another's assets
3.	appraise	c.	formal claim against property
4.	chattel	d.	assess the market value of
5.	codicil	e.	authority to act for another
6.	exchequer	f.	cancel or revoke
7.	fiduciary	g.	court order to provide information
8.	fiscal	h.	permanently attain a right
9.	insolvent	i.	situation where debts exceed assets
10.	lien	j.	accumulate over time
11.	pecuniary	k.	financial or monetary
12.	proxy	l.	copyist or notary
13.	rescind	m.	guarantor
14.	scrivener	n.	unlawful interest rate
15.	subpoena	o.	written declaration of fact
16.	surety	p.	government or business finances
17.	usurious	q.	movable property
18.	vest	r.	treasury

Engineering and Construction

AUGER (AW ger) *n* a tool for boring holes in wood

BANISTER (BAN ih ster) *n* a vertical member used to support a handrail

BARB (BARB) *n* sharp point on a tool projecting in the opposite direction from the main point(s)

BATTEN (BAT un) *v* to reinforce (a slatted wall or door) with a cross-member

BERM (BERM) *n* a bank of earth piled up alongside a road or wall

BEVEL (BEH vul) *n* a non-right angle which one surface makes against another surface

BUSHING (BUH sheeng) *n* a sleeve or fitting used to connect two pipes or cables

CALIPER (KAL uh per) *n* a two-pronged instrument used to measure diameter or thickness of an object

CONDUIT (KAHN doo it) *n* a tube, pipe or channel for conveying a flowing substance, usually water

CRAMPON (KRAM pahn) *n* a hooked device used to lift heavy weights

CRIMP (KRIMP) *v* to bend or warp on object (e.g., metal or wood)

DOWEL (DOW ul) *n* a round peg used to joint wooden parts together

FLANGE (FLANJ) *n* a projecting rim, edge, collar or ring on a pipe or shaft

GLAZIER (GLAY zher) *n* one who cuts and fits glass panes for windows

LAMINATE (LAM ih nayt) *v* to build up material in layers

LASH (LASH) *v* to bind or fasten with a rope or cord; to whip

LATHE (LAYTH) *n* a machine for shaping circular forms (especially, pieces of wood)

MASONRY (MAY sun ree) *n* stonework

NIB (NIB) *n* any projecting piece or part

PITCH (PICH) *n* a dark, sticky substance used for roofing and paving

PITON (PEE tahn) *n* spike hammered into rock fissures or ice to aid in climbing

RASP (RASP) *n* an abrading tool made of steel

ROUT (ROWT) *v* to groove or hollow out

SHEAR (SHEER) *v* to cut metal with blades

SIPHON (SY fun) *v* to withdraw liquid by suction

SLAG (SLAG) *n* the residue of a blast furnace, used for roofing surfaces

SOLDER (SAH der) *v* to join together or patch metal parts with a melted metal alloy

SPLAYED (SPLAYD) *adj* fanned apart

STRUT (STRUT) *n* a type of structural brace

WINCH (WINCH) *n* a machine used to pull up heavy weights

Criminology (Crimes and Criminal Procedure)

ABDUCT (ab DUKT) *v* to carry off a person by force

ABSCOND (ub SKAHND) *v* to flee from a geographic area or to conceal oneself without authorization, usually for the purpose of avoiding legal proceedings.

ACQUIT (uh KWIT) *v* to relieve an accused from criminal charges

ALIBI (AL uh by) *n* an excuse intended to avert blame

ARRAIGN (uh RAYN) *v* to bring before a court of law to hear and answer charges

COLLUSION (kuh LOO zhun) *n* an agreement between two or more parties to defraud another of their property or rights

COMPLICITY (kum PLIH sih tee) *n* association with or participation in a crime

DURESS (dyoo RES) *n* actual or threatened force, violence, or imprisonment, causing another to act contrary to his or her will

EXTORT (eks TORT) *v* to demand payment based on threats

EXTRADITE (EKS truh dyt) *v* to deliver (give up) a criminal from one state or nation to another

FLAGITIOUS (fluh GIH shus) *adj* scandalous, villainous

FORGE (FORJ) *v* to counterfeit; to shape molten metal

ILLICIT (ih LIH sit) *adj* illegal

IMMUREMENT (ih MYOOR mint) *n* confinement within walls

INCENDIARY (in SEN dee ayr ee) *n* an agitator, especially one who stirs up discontent by starting fires

INCOGNITO (in kahg NEE toh) *adj* living under an assumed name

INDICT (in DYT) *v* to charge with a crime or accuse of wrongdoing

KLEPTOMANIAC (klep toh MAY nee ak) *n* a person who has a compulsive desire to steal

LARCENY (LAR suh nee) *n* theft of personal property

PECCADILLO (peh kuh DIL oh) *n* a slight or minor offense; misdemeanor

PECULATION (pek yoo LAY shun) *n* stealing or misuse of public money entrusted to one's care; misappropriation; embezzlement

PERJURE (PER jer) *v* to lie under oath, especially to give false testimony in court

PILFER (PIL fer) *v* to steal repeatedly (especially, from one's workplace)

POACH (POHCH) *v* to take fish or game unlawfully from private or preotected property

RECIDIVISM (rih SIH dih vih zum) *n* habitual repetition of or return to criminal activity

REGICIDE (REJ uh syd) *n* murder of a monarch (king or queen)

VANDALIZE (VAN duh lyz) *v* to deface, damage, or destroy property

VIGILANTE (vih juh LAN tee) *n* one who takes justice into one's own hands

Ecology (Meteorology, Soil Science, and the Environment)

AGRARIAN (uh GRAYR ee un) *adj* pertaining to agricultural land and its cultivation

BIOME (BY ohm) *n* a discrete region characterized by the same life forms and conditions

CATACLYSM (KAT uh klih zum) *n* a violent or overwhelming subversion of ordinary phenomena of nature (e.g., a flood, earthquake, or volcanic eruption)

DEBACLE (deh BAH kul) *n* a violent rush or flood of debris-filled waters; an overwhelming defeat

DIURNAL (dy YER nul) *adj* referring to or occurring during the daylight hours

EBB (EB) *v* to recede or fall back (as the tide)

EFFLUENT (EF loo unt) *n* waste matter emitted by a sewage treatment or industrial plant

ENDEMIC (en DEM ik) *adj* restricted to a particular habitat or geographic range

EOLIAN (ee OH lee un) *adj* affected by wind

ESTIVAL (ES tuh vul) *adj* pertaining to summer

FALLOW (FAL oh) *adj* left idle (uncultivated) to restore productivity, usually referring to land used for agriculture

FUMEROLE (FYOO mer ohl) *n* a hole or vent (of a geyser, volcano, or spring) from which fumes or vapor rises

HIBERNAL (hy BER nul) *adj* relating to winter

HUMIC (HYOO mik) *adj* derived from the soil

HUMUS (HYOO mus) *n* decayed or decaying organic material in the surface layers of soil

INDIGENOUS (in DIJ uh nus) *adj* native to a given area

LEACH (LEECH) *v* to separate a liquid from a solid (usually waste) by flowing or percolating water into surrounding soil

LITTORAL (LIT er ul) *adj* pertaining to a shore (coastline), particularly the area of the shore between the high- and low tide marks

MAELSTROM (MAYL strum) *n* a whirlpool

MATUTINAL (muh TOO duh nul) *adj* pertaining to or functioning in the morning

PEDOLOGY (pih DAHL uh jee) *n* the study of soils

PLUVIAL (PLOO vee ul) *adj* relating to rain; drizzly

QUAGMIRE (KWAG myr) *n* soft ground where footing is insecure; swamp; bog

SIMOON (sih MOON) *n* desert wind or duststorm

SPATE (SPAYT) *n* a sudden flood

SQUALL (SKWAWL) *n* a strong, sudden wind

VERNAL (VER nul) *adj* relating to the spring

VIRAZON (VEER uh zahn) *n* a sea breeze

ZEPHYR (ZEF er) *n* a gentle breeze; a west wind

Quiz Time (3.4)

Directions: Match each numbered word in the left column with its lettered definition in the right column. Answer key begins on page 170.

1.	abscond	a.	abrading tool
2.	arraign	b.	charge with criminal offense
3.	batten	c.	deliver a criminal to another state
4.	caliper	d.	derived from the soil
5.	complicity	e.	flee or to conceal oneself unlawfully
6.	debacle	f.	glasscutter
7.	extradite	g.	habitual return to crime
8.	fallow	h.	instrument to measure thickness
9.	glazier	i.	left uncultivated
10.	humic	j.	living under an assumed name
11.	incognito	k.	machine for shaping circular forms
12.	lathe	l.	participation in a crime
13.	littoral	m.	pertaining to a coastline or shore
14.	maelstrom	n.	reinforce
15.	masonry	o.	stonework
16.	rasp	p.	strong wind
17.	recidivism	q.	violent and destructive flood
18.	squall	r.	whirlpool

Gastronomy (the Art and Science of Good Eating)

BASTE (BAYST) *v* to moisten meat in its own juices during cooking

BRAISE (BRAYZ) *v* to cook first by searing, then simmering in a small amount of liquid

BRAN (BRAN) *n* the coat of a grain seed, used for cereal

BRAZIER (BRAY zhyer) *n* a pan for holding burning coals, used for open-flame cooking

CALORIE (KAL er ee) *n* a unit of heat (not of nutrition)

COLANDER (KAHL in der) *n* a perforated basket used to strain water-filled foods

COMESTIBLE (kuh MES stuh bul) *adj* fit for eating; edible

CONFECTIONERY (kun FEK shun ayr ee) *n* any sweet food comprised primarily of sugar

CUISINE (kwih ZEEN) *n* particular style of prepared food

CULINARY (KUL uh nayr ee) *adj* pertaining to cooking

DECANTER (deh KAN ter) *n* a narrow-necked glass container used to hold and serve wine

DESICCATE (DEH sih kayt) *v* to dry or dehydrate

ELIXIR (eh LIK ser) *n* a liquid essence said to contain healthful properties

GASTRONOMY (gas TRAHN uh mee) *n* the science of preparing and serving food

LARDER (LAR der) *n* a pantry; place where food is kept

PASTEURIZE (PAS chyoor yz) *v* to sterilize by raising and lowering temperature to prevent fermentation and growth of bacteria

PERCOLATE (PER koh layt) *v* to filter liquid though a permeable substance in order to extract the substance's essence

SERRATED (ser AY tud) *adj* saw-toothed (especially, a knife)

SIEVE (SIV) *v* to strain

SPIT (SPIT) *n* a pointed skewer to hold meat over coals or fire

TRIPE (TRYP) *n* the stomach and intestinal lining of an animal

TRUSS (TRUS) *v* to secure (hold together) with skewers or twine before cooking

TUREEN (ter REEN) *n* a large, deep pot used to serve soup and sauces

VIAND (VY und) *n* a dish or article of food serve at a fine meal; course

VINTNER (VINT ner) *n* a dealer in or producer of wines

ZEST (ZEST) *n* the outside rind of any citrus fruit which contains the essential oils used for flavoring

Geography

ACCLIVITY (uh KLIV ih tee) *n* an ascending slope

ACCRETION (uh KREE shun) *n* gradual addition of new land to old by deposit of sediment carried by the water of a stream

AGGRADE (uh GRAYD) *v* to build up a grade or slope by the deposit of sediment

ALLUVIAL (uh LOO vee ul) *adj* pertaining to sediment deposited by flowing water, usually at the bottom of a body of water

ALPINE (AL pyn) *adj* pertaining to great mountain heights

APEX (AY peks) *n* tip, point, or angular summit (of a mountain)

ATOLL (AT ahl) *n* a coral island

AVULSION (uh VUL shun) *n* rapid erosion of a shoreline during a storm

BENTHAL (BEN thul) *adj* pertaining to the deepest zone or region of the ocean

BERM (BERM) *n* a narrow shelf or ridge

CALDERA (KAWL dayr uh) *n* a crater formed at the top of a volcanic mountain

CATARACT (CAT uh rakt) *n* a waterfall of great volume in which the vertical flow is concentrated in one sheer drop

CONFLUENCE (KAHN floo ins) *n* the point of convergence and uniting of two streams

CORDILLERA (kor dil YAHR uh) *n* a system of mountain ranges

DEBOUCHURE (dih BOO shyoor) *n* mouth of a river or point at which tributaries connect with larger passages

EDDY (EH dee) *n* circular movement of water produced by counter currents

ESTUARY (ES choo ayr ee) *n* river basin affected by ocean tides, having a mixture of fresh and salt water

FELL (FELL) *n* a bare, uncultivated rocky hill or mountain

KAME (KAYM) *n* a short, conical, steep hill

LOTIC (LOH tic) *adj* pertaining to a flowing stream, river, or spring

MERIDIAN (muh RIH dee un) *n* a line of longitude, passing over both north and south poles

PIEDMONT (PEED mahnt) *adj* lying or formed at the base of a mountain

RIPARIAN (ry PAYR ee un) *adj* pertaining to a riverbank

SCARP (SKARP) *n* a steep slope or inland cliff

SEDIMENTARY (seh dih MEN tuh ree) *adj* describing accumulation of material deposited by water, wind, or glaciers

SPIT (SPIT) *n* a narrow strip of alluvial deposit projecting into the sea

TUNDRA (TUN druh) *n* a vast, cold, treeless region

Geology (Rock Formations, Minerals, and Metals)

ANODIZE (AN oh dyz) *v* to treat a metal in an electrolytic process so that it forms a protective coating of oxide

AVEN (AY vin) *n* a vertical shaft leading upward from a cave passage

BENEFICIATE (ben uh FISH ee ayt) *v* to improve the grade of ore by milling, sintering, etc.

CHATOYANT (shuh TOY unt) *adj* having the luster or glow of certain gems, particularly cat's-eye

DENUDE (dih NOOD) *v* to wear away or remove overlying matter from underlying rocks, exposing them to view

FACET (FAS it) *n* the polished surface of a gemstone; a flat surface of a rock fragment

FAULT (FAWLT) *n* a fracture in the earth's crust

HYALINE (HY uh leen) *adj* glassy; crystalline; transparent

IGNEOUS (IG nee us) *adj* produced by volcanic eruption or fire

KARAT (KAYR ut) *n* a unit for measuring the fineness of gold

LODESTONE (LOHD stohn) *n* a natural mineral containing iron that acts as a magnet

NACREOUS (NAY kree us) *adj* pearly; having the luster of mother-of-pearl

OBSIDIAN (ub SID ee un) *n* black volcanic rock

QUARRY (KWOHR ee) *v* to extract stone from the surface

SECTILE (SEK til) *adj* capable of being cut with a knife without breaking off in pieces

SHARD (SHARD) *n* a spikelike fragment of glass

TUFA (TOO fuh) *n* a soft porous rock formed from lime deposits in springs

VENTIFACT (VEN truh fakt) *n* a stone that has been shaped to some extent by the abrasion of wind-driven sand

VITREOUS (VIT ree us) *adj* having the luster of broken glass

Quiz Time (3.5)

Directions: Match each numbered word in the left column with its lettered definition in the right column. The answer key begins on page 170.

1.	alloy	a.	base of a mountain
2.	alluvial	b.	cook first by searing, then simmering
3.	assay	c.	division of geologic time
4.	avulsion	d.	filter liquid though a membrane
5.	braise	e.	fit for eating
6.	caldera	f.	fusion of two or more metals
7.	comestible	g.	layers
8.	culinary	h.	netted or having veins
9.	epoch	i.	pertaining to cooking
10.	estuary	j.	rapid erosion of a shoreline
11.	grotto	k.	river basin affected by ocean tides
12.	piedmont	l.	pertaining to a riverbank
13.	reticulate	m.	saw-toothed
14.	riparian	n.	pertaining to sedimentary deposits
15.	rugose	o.	test or examine minerals
16.	serrated	p.	underground cave
17.	sieve	q.	volcanic crater
18.	strata	r.	wrinkled or ridged

Government

AMNESTY (AM nis tee) *n* a general pardon by a government for past offenses

APPARAT (uh PAYR it) *n* the existing power structure or political organization

DESPOT (DES puht) *n* a ruler having absolute ruler; tyrant; dictator

EDICT (EE dikt) *n* an official order or proclamation having the force of law

HEGEMONY (heh JEM uh nee) *n* domination by one state over others

INSURGENCY (in SER jin see) *n* a minor revolt against a local government; uprising

JUNTA (HOON tuh) *n* a small group, usually composed of military officers, ruling a country in the absence of a civilian government

MANDATE (MAN dayt) *n* authority conferred on an elected official by the electorate

MORATORIUM (mor uh TOR ee um) *n* an officially declared stoppage or delay

OMBUDSMAN (AHM boods mun) *n* an intermediary between a citizen and the government who investigates complaints by citizens about government agencies or officials

POLITY (PAHL ih tee) *n* a system or form of government

POTENTATE (POH tun tayt) *n* a monarch, dictator, or similar person possessing great political power

RATIFY (RAT ih fy) *v* to approve officially; sanction

REFERENDUM (ref uh REN dum) *n* popular vote on either proposed legislation or a popular initiative

REGALIA (rih GAYL yuh) *n* emblems and trappings of a political or military office

REGIME (reh ZHEEM) *n* the government of a specific leader; administration

SECEDE (suh SEED) *v* to separate from an organized body of government

SUBJUGATE (SUB joo gayt) *v* to conquer or dominate a people or territory

SUBVERT (sub VERT) *v* to overthrow, ruin, corrupt, or otherwise undermine the stability or order of a government

SUFFRAGE (SUF rij) *n* the right to vote

THRALLDOM (THRAWL dum) *n* slavery; serfdom

TITULAR (TICH uh ler) *adj* in title only (e.g., a monarch or president); nominal, and without actual power or authority

TYRANNY (TEER uh nee) *n* absolute authority, usually exercised oppressively

USURP (yoo SERP) *v* to assume political power or office by force or without right

Linguistics

ALLITERATION (uh lih ter AY shun) *n* repeting the same sound at the beginning of words

ANACHRONISM (uh NAK ruh nih zum) *n* a word or expression not corresponding to the language of a given period of history; anything seemingly from another time

ANAGRAM (AN uh gram) *n* a word (or group of words) made up of the same letters as those of another word or group of words

APHASIA (uh FAY zhyuh) *n* loss of the ability to speak

ASSONANCE (AS uh nuns) *n* repetition of sounds, especially vowel sounds, in a word or phrase

CADENCE (KAY dins) *n* the rise and fall in pitch, volume, or stress in speech

COLLOQUIAL (kuh LOH kwee ul) *adj* informal spoken or written expression

CONNOTE (kuh NOHT) *v* to suggest or convey feelings or ideas in addition to the express meaning (denotation) of a word

DIALECT (DY uh lekt) *n* a distinctive regional variety of a language

ELOCUTION (el uh KYOO shun) *n* the study and practice of speaking properly and effectively in public oratory and in professional acting

EUPHONIC (yoo FAHN ik) *adj* having an agreeable or pleasing sound

EVOCATIVE (ih VAHK uh tiv) *adj* causing an emotional reaction in the listener (or reader)

EXPLETIVE (EKS pluh tiv) *n* any word used as a filler

IDIOM (ID ee um) *n* a phrase which has a special meaning apart from the individual words used in the phrase

INTONATION (in toh NAY shun) *n* the melodic pattern produced by the variation in pitch of the voice during speech

LEXICON (LEK sih kahn) *n* collection of vocabulary; dictionary

LOCUTION (loh KYOO shun) *n* any utterance, expression, or phrase

MNEMONIC (nee MAH nik) *adj* symbolic substitution or abbreviation, used for memorization (and in computer programming)

PARLANCE (PAR luns) *n* any particular manner of expressing oneself, using vernacular and idioms

PEJORATIVE (puh JOR uh tiv) *adj* negative in connotation

PERORATION (per uh RAY shun) *n* the concluding part of a public address or speech (especially, summing up and recapitulating key points and/or exhorting and uplifting the audience)

PHONETIC (fuh NET ik) *adj* based on sounds (e.g., the phonetic spelling of a word)

PIDGIN (PIH jun) *n* a mixture of different languages

POLYGLOT (PAH lee glaht) *n* a person who speaks or writes in several languages

PROEM (PROH um) *n* an introduction, preface, or preamble (in speech or writing)

PROSODY (PRAH suh dee) *n* the distinctive rhythm, stress, and intonation in a language (or of poetic verse)

REBUS (REE bus) *n* the representation of a word by pictures or symbols

RHETORIC (RET uh rik) *n* persuasion through argument

ROSTRUM (RAHS trum) *n* a platform for public speaking; dais

SEMANTIC (suh MAN tik) *adj* involving signs (especially, words) and the things (ideas) they are intended to signify

SYNTAX (SIN taks) *n* construction of a sentence; arrangement of words in a sentence.

TRANSCRIBE (tran SCRYB) *v* to reduce speech to a written form

Literature

ALLEGORY (AL uh gor ee) *n* a collection of extended metaphors in narrative form used as a device for teaching a lesson

ALLUSION (uh LOO zhun) *n* a reference in a literary work to an identifiable person, event, place, or literary passage

ANALECT (AN uh lekt) *n* a literary fragment or passage

ANTHOLOGY (an THAH luh jee) *n* a collection of selections from the writings of one or more authors

APOCRYPHAL (uh PAHK rih ful) *adj* of unknown authorship or doubtful integrity

BALLAD (BAL id) *n* a narrative poem meant for recitation or singing

BARD (BARD) *n* a prominent poet or other writer (of the Renaissance period)

COLOPHON (KAH luh fahn) *n* a publisher's and/or printer's distinctive emblem, monogram, or cipher

DENOUEMENT (day noo MAHN) *n* the final unfolding of a plot; the final resolution or outcome following the climax

DOGGEREL (DAW guh rul) *n* poetic verse of generally poor quality; verse characterized by a crude, rough, irregular, or burlesque style

ELEGY (EL uh jee) *n* a poem (or song) of mourning; a lament

EPIC (EP ik) *n* a literary work recounting the travels and deeds of a legendary (heroic) figure

EPITAPH (EP ih taf) *n* an inscription on a monument in memory of a deceased person

EUPHEMISM (YOO fuh mih zum) *n* a pleasant or complimentary word or phrase used instead of one that is harsh or derogatory to prevent the conveyance of a bluntly honest opinion

FIGURATIVE (FIG yoor uh tiv) *adj* metaphoric; not to be interpreted literally

FUSTIAN (FUS chun) *n* describing pretentious, pompous, or bombastic writing

LAMPOON (lam POON) *n* harsh satire, usually directed against a particular person

LITOTES (LY toh teez) *n* an understatement made for rhetorical emphasis

MASTHEAD (MAST hed) *n* a statement of the name, ownership, etc. of a publication

MISSIVE (MIS iv) *n* a letter, usually formal or official

MOTIF (moh TEEF) *n* a literary, artistic, or musical device that serves as the basis for suggestive expansion; the basic element repeated throughout the work

ODE (OHD) *n* a lyric poem marked by exalted feeling

OPUS (OH pus) *n* a literary or musical work

PARODY (PAYR uh dee) *n* a distorted and usually humorous imitation of a particular style of writing

PASTICHE (pas TEESH) *n* a compostition made up of bits from various sources; an imitation of another writer's style or technique, usually done for satirical or humorous purposes

PATHOS (PAY thohs) *n* the quality of evoking a feeling of pity or compassion (in literature, art, or music)

PSEUDONYM (SOO duh nim) *n* a fictitious name used by an author

SATIRE (SAT yr) *n* a literary form employing irony, ridicule, and sarcasm

SCHOLIAST (SKOH lee ast) *n* an ancient commentator or annotator of classic texts

TOME (TOHM) *n* a very large or scholarly work

TREATISE (TREE tis) *n* a comprehensive and systematic literary examination of a particular subject

VIGNETTE (vin YET) *n* a short, sketchy story

VITA (VEE tuh) *n* a brief, autobiographical sketch.

Quiz Time (3.6)

Directions: Match each numbered word in the left column with its lettered definition in the right column. The answer key begins on page 170.

1.	amnesty	a.	ancient commentator of classic texts
2.	anachronism	b.	conclusion of a speech
3.	analect	c.	dictionary
4.	apocryphal	d.	effective public speaking
5.	colloquial	e.	emblems of office
6.	colophon	f.	general pardon for past offenses
7.	despot	g.	informal expression
8.	elegy	h.	literary fragment or passage
9.	elocution	i.	of unknown authorship
10.	junta	j.	official or formal letter
11.	lexicon	k.	persuasion through argument
12.	missive	l.	poem or song of mourning
13.	peroration	m.	publisher's emblem
14.	regalia	n.	seemingly from another time
15.	rhetoric	o.	slavery
16.	scholiast	p.	small military group ruling a country
17.	secede	q.	to separate from a governmental body
18.	thralldom	r.	tyrant or dictator

Maritime Matters (Boating)

ATHWART (uh THWORT) *adv* transversely; from side to side

BALLAST (BAL ust) *n* any heavy material placed low in a ship (or other structure) to increase stability

BUOYANT (BOY ent) *adj* able to float

DREDGE (DREJ) *v* to deepen a channel by scraping or suction

FLOTSAM (FLAHT sum) *n* the part of a ship's wreckage found floating in the water

FURL (FERL) *v* to secure sails, awnings, or flags

HULL (HUL) *n* the outer body or shell of a ship

JETSAM (JET sum) *n* debris from a ship that has washed ashore; cargo thrown overboard to lighten a ship

LIST (LIST) *v* to tilt from side to side

MOOR (MOOR) *v* to fasten, tie down, or anchor a ship in its dock

PURSER (PER ser) *n* a clerk on a passenger ship in charge of safekeeping money and possessions of crew and passengers.

REGATTA (rih GAH tuh) *n* a boat race or series of boat races

SEXTANT (SEKS tunt) *n* a type of navigational instrument used on ships

SINUATE (SIN yoo ayt) *v* to maneuver in a series of curves around a set course, usually for evasive purposes

STAUNCH (STAWNCH) *adj* sturdy; watertight

TACK (TAK) *n* the direction a vessel takes in relation to the wind

ULLAGE (UL ij) *n* the empty space in a tank for holding liquid (e.g., fuel or water)

Mathematics

CONFLATE (kun FLAYT) *v* to integrate two separate sets to produce a single set

CONGRUENT (kahn GROO unt) *adj* equivalent; having exactly the same size and shape

CONJUGATE (KAHN joo git) *adj* having the same or similar properties

COROLLARY (KOR uh layr ee) *n* a theorem proved by a previously proved theorem

INNUMERATE (ih NOO mer it) *adj* mathematically illiterate

INTERPOLATE (in TER pul ayt) *v* to estimate a value of a function between two known values (by a method other than that defined by the equation or law that represents the function)

INVOLUTION (in vuh LOO shun) *n* the process of multiplying a quantity by itself a given number of times (i.e., taking a number to a "power")

ITERATION (ih ter AY shun) *n* one step in a sequence of repeated steps in the solution of a problem (iterative: *adj* repeating)

MATRIX (MAY triks) *n* a array of terms (numbers) arranged in columns and rows

ORDINAL (OR duh nul) *adj* indicating the order, position, or rank of an item among others in a group or set

PERMUTATION (per myoo TAY shun) *n* an operation on a set of elements (numbers) in which each element is replaced by itself or by some other element of the set

RATIOCINATION (ray shee oh NAY shun) *n* the act of drawing conclusions from premises; reasoning

SCALAR (SKAY ler) *n* an element of a set or field (e.g., of numbers)

STOCHASTIC (stuh KAS tik) *adj* referring to a sequence of uncertain outcomes over time (usually used in statistics and linear programming)

TERTIARY (TER shee ayr ee) *adj* third

Medicine and the Health Professions

ASTRINGENT (uh STRIN junt) *n* a substance that causes binding by contraction; a harsh, biting substance

BENIGN (bih NYN) *adj* harmless; gentle (as in a benign tumor)

CHRONIC (KRAH nik) *adj* continuous; constant; prolonged; recurring periodically

CONGENITAL (kun JEN ih tul) *adj* existing or dating from birth; inbred; inborn; innate

EMETIC (uh MEH tik) *n* any substance used to induce vomiting

FEBRILE (FEE bryl) *adj* feverish

GERIATRIC (jayr ee AT rik) *adj* relating to medical care and treatment of the elderly

HOSPICE (HAH spis) *n* a shelter for the sick, dying, or underprivileged (or for travelers)

MORBIDITY (mor BID ih tee) *n* the incidence or prevalence of disease (or death)

NATAL (NAY tul) *adj* pertaining to birth

PATHOLOGY (path AHL uh jee) *n* the study of the processes and causes of disease

PROGNOSIS (prahg NOH sis) *n* a medical prediction or forecast of the course of an illness and chances of recovery

PROSTHESIS (prah STHEE sis) *n* an addition to the end of (esp., an artificial limb)

QUARANTINE (KWOR un teen) *n* sequestration (isolation) of a person to prevent spread of disease (also used as a verb)

REMISSION (ree MIH shun) *n* abatement or lessening (of the symptoms of a disease)

SENESCENT (suh NES unt) *adj* growing old; aging

SYNCOPE (SING kuh pee) *n* a brief loss of consciousness; fainting or swooning

SYNDROME (SIN drohm) *n* a cluster of symptoms, all thought to be caused by the same disease or illness

VELLICATE (VEL uh kayt) *v* to cause convulsive twitching

VERTIGO (VER tih goh) *n* dizziness and the sensation of head-spinning

Quiz Time (3.7)

Directions: Match each numbered word in the left column with its lettered definition in the right column. The answer key begins on page 170.

1. astringent
2. ballast
3. conflate
4. congenital
5. conjugate
6. flotsam
7. furl
8. iteration
9. moor
10. morbidity
11. ordinal
12. prosthesis
13. senescent
14. sextant
15. stochastic
16. syncope
17. ullage
18. vellicate

a. artificial limb
b. binding by contraction
c. empty space in a tank
d. existing or dating from birth
e. to cause convulsive twitching
f. fainting or swooning
g. fasten or tie down a ship
h. growing old
i. having similar properties
j. stabilizing material placed low
k. incidence of disease or death
l. to integrate two separate sets
m. navigational instrument for ships
n. step in a sequence of repeated steps
o. order or rank
p. sequence of uncertain outcomes
q. to secure sails
r. wreckage found floating in water

Metaphysics and the Afterlife

ANAGOGIC (an uh GAHG ik) *adj* relating to spiritual or lofty ideals

ANIMISM (AN ih mih zum) *n* the belief that natural objects and phenomena possess souls or spirits

APOCALYPSE (uh PAH kuh lips) *n* a cataclysmic, violent event in which forces of good destroy those of evil

APOSTATE (uh PAH stayt) *n* one who defects from or abandons one's faith, church, or principles

APOTHEOSIS (uh pah thee OH sis) *n* the elevation of a mortal to the rank of deity (god); deification; glorification

ATONE (uh TOHN) *v* to reconcile wrongful acts (sins) through forgiveness

AUSPICE (AW spis) *n* a prophetic sign; omen

DEITY (DEE uh tee) *n* a divine or supreme being

ETHEREAL (ee THEER ee ul) *adj* nonmaterial; heavenly.

EXPIATE (EKS pee ayt) *v* to atone for one's wrongful acts (sins)

HALLOW (HAL oh) *v* to make holy; consecrate

HEATHEN (HEE thin) *n* a nonbeliever; pagan; infidel; kafir

HERESY (HAYR uh see) *n* a dissenting or unorthodox religious belief; sacrilege

KISMET (KIZ mut) *n* fate; destiny; fortune

MAMMONISM (MAM un ih zum) *n* the personification of material wealth as evil

MANITOU (MAN ih too) *n* a supernatural being that controls nature

ORACULAR (or AK yoo ler) *adj* prophetic; foretelling; portentous (oracle: *n* a divinely inspired utterance)

PERDITION (per DIH shun) *n* a place of damnation; hell

PIOUS (PY us) *adj* acting dutifully in reverence (whether or not genuine) to God

PRESCIENCE (PREH shuns) *n* direct acquaintance with the future, as opposed to fore-knowledge based on inference

RECREANT (REK ree unt) *adj* failing to maintain faith

SACRILEGE (SAK rih lij) *n* a statement or act that degrades that which is sacred; heresy

SACROSANCT (SAK roh sankt) *adj* sacred; holy inviolable; hallowed

SECULAR (SEK yoo ler) *adj* rejecting religion as necessary in understanding or interpreting the world

SERENDIPITY (sayr uhn DIP ih tee) *adj* unsought good fortune

VENERATION (ven er AY shun) *n* reverence; devotion

Military Science

ARMISTICE (AR muh stis) *n* a general truce; cessation of war

BELAY (buh LAY) *v* to cancel a command (also, to make secure or fast)

BIVOUAC (BIV wak) *n* a temporary encampment, usually with little or no shelter

BRASSARD (BRAS erd) *n* a distinctive insignia worn on the shoulder of a uniform to indicate task or rank

BREACH (BREECH) *n* an expedient passage through an obstacle

BRIGADE (brih GAYD) *n* a type of military unit; subunit of a battalion.

CAPITULATE (kuh PICH yoo layt) *v* to surrender

CITADEL (SIT uh dul) *n* a fortress or stronghold, especially for defending a city

CLANDESTINE (KLAN DES tin) *adj* secret; concealed

COUP (KOO) *n* a highly successful maneuver; a surprise attack

COVERT (KOH vert) *adj* secret; hidden

DEBARK (dee BARK) *v* to unload or leave a ship or aircraft

DECRYPT (de KRIPT) *v* to convert encrypted (coded) text to plain text through the use of a decoding system

DEFECT (duh FEKT) *v* to repudiate one's native country in favor of an opposing nation

DEPLOY (dih PLOY) *v* to send troops or equipment to a foreign area for duty

ESPIONAGE (ES pee uh nahzh) *n* spying to obtain information about a government's plans or activities

FORAY (FOR ay) *n* an incursion or raid

GARRISON (GAYR uh sun) *n* a fortified, secured area or building for stationing troops

INTERDICTION (in ter DIK shun) *n* disruptive action designed to prevent an enemy from gaining access to routes, areas, or supplies

MERCENARY (MER suh nayr ee) *adj* for hire; not motivated by political loyalty or allegiance

PERFIDY (PER fuh dee) *n* deceptive tactics that tend to destroy the basis for restoring peace

PREEMPTIVE (pree EM tiv) *adj* launched or initiated because of evidence that the enemy is about to move or attack

RECONNAISSANCE (rih KAH nuh suns) *n* observation of an area of military significance

SABOTAGE (SAB uh tahzh) *n* intentional destruction or obstruction aimed at disrupting military or government activities

SENTRY (SEN tree) *n* a soldier whose job is to maintain a watch against threats from the enemy

SHRAPNEL (SHRAP nul) *n* destructive fragments resulting from the explosion of a bomb or projectile

SORTIE (SOR tee) *n* an air mission

TRIAGE (TREE ahzh) *n* a method of ranking sick or injured people according to severity of sickness or injury for the purpose of determining priority of treatment

VANGUARD (VAN gard) *n* troops (forces) sent in advance; the forefront of an army

WAYLAY (WAY lay) *v* to lie in wait for the purpose of ambushing or intercepting

Music and Musicology

ANTHEM (AN thum) *n* a short choral song of a serious (e.g., religious or patriotic) nature

ARIA (AHR ee uh) *n* part of an opera, oratorio, etc., where the action is stopped and characters sing their reaction to the dramatic situation

BALLAD (BAL ud) *n* a (vocal) song whose words tell a story

BALLADE (buh LAHD) *n* an instrumental piece, usually long, that is lyrical and romantic in style

BAROQUE (buh ROHK) *adj* attempting to achieve artistic effect (in music, literature, or art) by startling and irregular movement in style and form

CADENCE (KAY duns) *n* a point of rest or conclusion; modulation in tone; measured movement

CADENZA (kuh DEN zuh) *n* an extended cadence just before a point of rest, allowing for a soloist to improvise or play a composed passage to display his or her technical ability

CANON (KAN un) *n* a musical form in which the voices enter successively with the same material; a round

CHORALE (koh RAL) *n* a hymn or psalm sung to a melody

CLARION (KLAYR ee un) *n* a shrill-toned trumpet

CODA (KOH duh) *n* passage added to the final section of a musical piece

CONCERTO (kun CHAYR toh) *n* a composition for a solo instrument (or group of instruments) and orchestra

CONSERVATORY (kun SER vuh tor ee) *n* a special school which offers instruction in all aspects of music

FORTE (FOR tay) *adj* strong; loud

FUGUE (FYOOG) *n* a musical form consisting of a number of imitative explorations of a theme

GLISSANDO (glih SAHN doh) *n* a series of ascending or descending notes played quickly so as to give the impression of sliding from the first to the last note

LIBRETTO (lih BREH toh) *n* the words or text for an opera, oratorio, etc.

MADRIGAL (MAD ruh gul) *n* a Renaissance form of unaccompanied choral music based on a nonsacred text

MELISMA (muh LIZ muh) *n* a florid melody with a free rhythm structure

NOCTURNE (NAHK tern) *n* a slow, quiet, lyrical piece

ORATORIO (or uh TOR ee oh) *n* a large multisectional musical form which is really an unstaged sacred opera

OSTINATO (ah stih NAH toh) *n* a repeated melodic pattern whose insistence becomes a characteristic of the piece

OVERTURE (OH ver cher) *n* an instrumental introduction to a musical play or opera

POLYPHONY (puh LIF uh nee) *n* the simultaneous combination of two or more melodies

PROSODY (PROH zuh dee) *n* the art of setting text to music

REPRISE (rih PRYZ) *n* repetition of a musical phrase

REQUIEM (REK wee um) *n* a composition written for a funeral Mass

SONATA (suh NAH tuh) *n* a musical piece composed for solo instrument, sometimes with piano accompaniment

SYNCOPATION (sing koh PAY shun) *n* a shifting of the normal accent (stress) in music, so that "offbeats" are stressed

TIMBRE (TIM ber) *n* the unique quality of a sound produced by a particular instrument or voice

TROUBADOUR (TROO buh dor) *n* a poet-musician of the Medieval period

Quiz Time (3.8)

Directions: Match each numbered word in the left column with its lettered definition in the right column. The answer key begins on page 170.

1.	apocalypse	a.	predictive of the future
2.	apostate	b.	added to the end of a musical piece
3.	armistice	c.	cataclysm in which good destroy evil
4.	baroque	d.	introduction
5.	cadenza	e.	cessation of war
6.	capitulate	f.	defector from one's faith
7.	clandestine	g.	disruptive military action
8.	coda	h.	dissenting religious belief
9.	ethereal	i.	extended musical pause for a solo
10.	heresy	j.	fate or destiny
11.	interdiction	k.	irregular movement in artistic style
12.	kismet	l.	lie in wait to ambush
13.	libretto	m.	lyrics for an opera
14.	oracular	n.	music for a funeral
15.	overture	o.	nonmaterial or heavenly
16.	requiem	p.	quality of a sound
17.	timbre	q.	secret or concealed
18.	waylay	r.	to surrender

Philosophy and Logic

AUTONOMY (aw TAH nuh mee) *n* independence from external constraints; self-determination

CANON (CAN un) *n* a rule, norm, tenet, or principle that is logically consistent

CORPOREAL (kor POR ee ul) *adj* relating to the body or to physical matter

DIALECTIC (dy uh LEK tik) *n* a question-and-answer method of investigation

DISCURSIVE (dis KER siv) *adj* characterized by analysis

EMPIRICAL (em PEER ih kul) *n* based on direct or practical observation and experience

EPICUREAN (ep ih KYOOR ee un) *adj* pertaining to the pursuit of pleasure

FALLACIOUS (fuh LAY shus) *adj* logically unsound; misleading or deceptive

HEURISTIC (hyoo RIS tik) *adj* serving to persuade through discovery and revelation rather than through logic or rhetoric

IMMANENT (IM uh nunt) *adj* existing within the mind; indwelling or inherent

IRREFRAGABLE (ih reh FRUG uh bul) *adj* irrefutable; undeniable

METAPHYSICS (met uh FIZ iks) *n* the philosophy of being; the study of being in its universal aspects

NIHILISM (NY uh liz um) *n* the belief that that there is no purpose to existence; rejection of established laws and institutions

NONSEQUITUR (nahn SEK wih ter) *n* that which does not follow logically

ONTOLOGY (ahn TAHL uh jee) *n* the branch of metaphysics dealing with the nature of existence (being)

PARADOX (PAYR uh dahks) *n* a seemingly contradictory assertion that may nevertheless be true or valid

POSTULATE (POS choo lut) *n* a hypothesis that cannot be demonstrated

PROLEPSIS (pro LEP sis) *n* a preconception or necessary assumption or principle; anticipation of possible objections in order to answer them; an error in chronology in which an event is dated before the actual time of occurrence

Physics

AMPLITUDE (AM plih tood) *n* height or depth (range) of the crest (or trough) of a wave

ATTENUATE (uh TEN yoo ayt) *v* to reduce in size or amount

BUFFER (BUF er) *n* a temporary storage area for data or signals as they pass from one system to another

CENTRIFUGAL (sen TRIF uh gul) *adj* conveyance outward by force from a rotating center

CRYOGENICS (kry oh JEN iks) *n* production and effects of extremely low temperatures

DAMP (DAMP) *v* to lessen a vibration

DECIBEL (DES uh bul) *n* a unit of measurement of the intensity (loudness) of sound

ENTROPY (EN truh pee) *n* the degree of disorder or tendency toward the breakdown of a system

FISSION (FIH zhun) *n* the process of splitting apart or disjoining

FULCRUM (FUL krum) *n* the point of pivot of a lever

GALVANIZE (GAL vuh nyz) *v* to excite (stimulate) by electrical current; to coat iron with zinc in order to prevent rust

INCANDESCENT (in kun DES unt) *adj* emitting light due to production of heat

JOULE (JOOL) *n* a unit of energy or work used in scientific measurement

KINETIC (kih NEH tik) *adj* produced, creating, or characterized by motion

LUMINOUS (LOO min us) *adj* giving off light

MODULATE (MAHJ yoo layt) *v* to vary

OPAQUE (oh PAYK) *adj* describing a material that is unable to transmit light

PARALLAX (PAYR uh laks) *n* a shift in the relative position of objects due to a change in perspective

PHOTIC (FOH tik) *adj* pertaining to light

QUANTUM (KWAWN tum) *n* a discrete and indivisible unit of energy

REFRACTION (ree FRAK shun) *n* the bending of a wave as it passes obliquely from one medium to another

RESONATE (REH zuh nayt) *v* to vibrate greatly as a response to an external stimulus

SONIC (SAH nik) *adj* pertaining to sound waves

SPECTRUM (SPEK trum) *n* the entire range of wavelengths produced when a beam of electromagnetic radiation is broken up into its array of entities

THERMAL (THER mul) *adj* pertaining to heat

TORQUE (TORK) *n* a force that produces a twisting or rotating motion

VISCOSITY (vis KAHS ih tee) *n* internal friction of a fluid; resistance to flow

Political Science

CABAL (kuh BAL) *n* a secret group of political conspirators

CADRE (KAH dray) *n* close-knit group of leaders who advocate particular views

CAUCUS (KAW kus) *n* a closed meeting, usually by a political party to plan a strategy

CLOUT (KLOWT) *n* political power or influence

COALITION (koh uh LIH shun) *n* an alliance of political parties or states based on a common purpose

GERRYMANDER (JAYR ee man der) *v* to alter voting district lines so as to further one's own interests in obtaining votes

GRAFT (GRAFT) *n* money or property gained through political corruption

INCUMBENT (in KUM bunt) *adj* currently in office; running against a challenger

JINGOISM (JING goh ih zum) *n* belligerent or excessive patriotism

JUNKET (JUNG kit) *n* a personal trip of a public official financed by public funds

NEPOTISM (NEP uh tih zum) *n* political favoritism toward friends and relatives, especially in granting favors

PARTISAN (PAR tih zun) *adj* advocating or favoring the views of one party

PLOY (PLOY) *n* a clever and deceptive maneuver designed to achieve an objective without revealing one's intent or goal

QUISLING (KWIZ leeng) *n* a traitor who collaborates with an enemy occupying his country

QUORUM (KWOR um) *n* the minimum number of members required to conduct business

STALWART (STAWL wert) *n* an unwavering, staunch supporter

Quiz Time (3.9)

Directions: Match each numbered word in the left column with its lettered definition in the right column. The answer key begins on page 170.

1.	caucus	a.	based on direct observation
2.	centrifugal	b.	question-and-answer investigation
3.	cryogenics	c.	closed meeting
4.	damp	d.	movement away from a rotating axis
5.	dialectic	e.	degree of disorder
6.	empirical	f.	existing within the mind
7.	entropy	g.	extremely low temperatures
8.	immanent	h.	giving off light
9.	joule	i.	internal friction of a fluid
10.	irrefragable	j.	minimum number required to vote
11.	junket	k.	necessary assumption or principle
12.	luminous	l.	subsidized trip of a public official
13.	nepotism	m.	political favoritism toward relatives
14.	prolepsis	n.	characterized by analysis
15.	quisling	o.	to lessen a vibration
16.	discursive	p.	traitor
17.	quorum	q.	undeniable
18.	viscosity	r.	unit of energy or work

Psychology

ANACLITIC (an uh KLIH tic) *adj* dependent on another person

ANGST (ANGST) *n* anxiety

CATAPLEXY (KAT uh plek see) *n* a sudden paralysis of all voluntary movement, resulting in a collapse of the entire body

CATHARSIS (kuh THAR sis) *n* a discharge of strong emotions

CATHEXIS (kuh THEK sis) *n* placing special emotional significance on an object or idea

DEREISTIC (der ee IS tik) *adj* not in accord with reality, experience, and logic

EMPATHY (EM puh thee) *n* the ability to participate in another person's feelings and experiences and to understand them

EUPHORIA (yoo FOR ee uh) *n* a feeling of well-being or happiness

GESTALT (guh SHTAWLT) *n* a unified whole, especially the human psyche, having properties distinct from the sum of its parts

IDIOTROPIC (id ee oh TROH pik) *adj* introspective

LIBIDO (lih BEE doh) *n* sexual or psychic energy

LUDIC (LOO dik) *adj* pertaining to play and playful curiosity

MISOGYNIST (mih SAH juh nist) *n* a person who hates women

NARCISSISM (NAR sih sih zum) *n* excessive love of oneself

NEUROSIS (nyer OH sis) *n* any mild emotional disorder

PLACEBO (pluh SEE boh) *n* a treatment that has no effect except in the patient's own mind

SUBLIMATE (SUB luh mayt) *v* to express repressed desires or wishes in acceptable forms

SUBLIMINAL (suh BLIM uh nul) *adj* beneath the threshold of consciousness

SURGENT (SER junt) *adj* extroverted

SURROGATE (SER uh gut) *n* a substitute

VICARIOUS (vy KAYR ee us) *adj* experienced indirectly through observation

Religion (Institutions and Customs)

ADVENT (AD vent) *n* signifying arrival

APOSTLE (uh PAH sul) *n* an agent or deliverer through which the will of the sender of a message is expressed

BENEDICTION (ben uh DIK shun) *n* a recitation of praise (to God)

CANON (KAN un) *n* a religious doctrine, code, or law, usually written

CHERUB (CHAYR ub) *n* a type of angel, represented as a child

CLERIC (KLAYR ik) *n* a member of the clergy; an ordained priest, minister or rabbi

CREED (KREED) *n* a system or formal statement of religious beliefs

DOXOLOGY (dahk SAH luh jee) *n* a hymn of praise (to God)

ECCLESIASTICAL (eh klee zee AS tih kul) *adj* pertaining to the church as an institution

ECUMENICAL (ek yoo MEN ih kul) *adj* universal; worldwide; pertaining to a unified whole

EXEGESIS (ek sih JEE sis) *n* analysis, interpretation, and criticism of a literary work (usually a sacred text), especially its metaphoric and symbolic patterns

IMPETRATION (im puh TRAY shun) *n* a petition; request; prayer

LAITY (LAY uh tee) *n* any persons other than clergy; laypersons

LITURGY (LIH ter jee) *n* the rites, practices, and ceremonies of religious worship

MARTYR (MAR ter) *n* a person who is persecuted—usually put to death—for defending his or her religious principles

ORTHODOX (OR thuh dahks) *adj* conventional; traditional

PENANCE (PEN uns) *n* a specific act of repentance for wrongful acts (sins)

PREDICANT (PRED uh kunt) *n* a preacher (curate, vicar, parson, minister, etc.)

SCHISM (SKIH zum) *n* a separation or division into groups or sects due to differing beliefs

SECT (SEKT) *n* a religious group deviating from orthodox faith

Sociology

ABLEISM (AY bul ih zum) *n* discrimination against mentally or physically disabled people

ACCULTURATE (uh KUL cher ayt) *v* to adopt the cultural traits and patterns of another group through continual firsthand exposure

ANOMIE (AN uh mee) *n* a societal condition in which the social norms have weakened or disappeared

ATOMISM (AT uh mih zum) *n* a society composed of clearly distinct elements and factions

CASTE (KAST) *n* a hierarchical social system, characterized by minimal social mobility

COHORT (KOH hort) *n* a group of individuals of the same age

DERACINATION (dih ras ih NAY shun) *n* uprooting from one's cultural or social environment

ENCULTERATION (en kuhl cher AY shun) *n* the process of learning the culture of one's own group or society by observation, experience, and instruction.

ETHNOCENTRIC (eth noh SEN trik) *adj* evaluating the behavior and values of others only according to the criteria of one's one ethnic group

GUILD (GILD) *n* an association for the promotion of common goals

LABEFACTION (LAB uh fak shun) *n* a decline in or weakening of public morality and social order

MORE (MOR ay) *n* a custom or folkway considered essential to the welfare of a society

SOLECISM (SAH lih sih zum) *n* a violation of accepted conventions or customs (especially in language or etiquette)

STIGMA (STIG muh) *n* an act or trait that is perceived as highly negative, setting the stigmatized person apart from others

TABOO (tab OO) *adj* prohibited behavior, where the prohibition is established through social custom

TELESIS (TEL uh sis) *n* planned progress through the use of both social and natural forces

YEOMAN (YOH man) *n* the owner of a small estate; a middle-class farmer

Quiz Time (3.10)

Directions: Match each numbered word in the left column with its lettered definition in the right column. The answer key begins on page 170.

1.	cataplexy	a.	involving the church as an institution
2.	caste	b.	group of individuals of the same age
3.	cohort	c.	association promoting a goal
4.	cherub	d.	analysis of a literary work
5.	creed	e.	ceremonies of religious worship
6.	dereistic	f.	decline in public morality
7.	ecclesiastical	g.	excessive love of oneself
8.	ecumenical	h.	extroverted
9.	exegesis	i.	formal statement of religious beliefs
10.	guild	j.	hierarchical social system
11.	idiotropic	k.	introspective
12.	labefaction	l.	not in accord with reality
13.	liturgy	m.	playful curiosity
14.	ludic	n.	substitute
15.	narcissism	o.	angel
16.	stigma	p.	sudden paralysis
17.	surgent	q.	trait perceived as highly negative
18.	surrogate	r.	universal or worldwide

Theater Arts and Public Speaking

DEBUT (day BYOO) *n* an actor's first performance

HAMARTIA (hah mar TEE uh) *n* a flaw in a tragic character

HARLEQUIN (HAR lih kwin) *n* masked, comic character

HISTRIONICS (his tree AH niks) *n* acting in highly theatrical or overly dramatic, exaggerated style

IMPRESARIO (im preh SAHR ee oh) *n* a manager, promoter, or sponsor for performing artists

LIBRETTIST (lih BRET ist) *n* writer of song lyrics for a musical

LOGE (LOHZH) *n* balcony seating area of a theater

MARQUEE (mar KEE) *n* sign on the front of a theater advertising a play

MINSTREL (MIN strul) *n* traveling entertainer of the medieval period

ODEUM (OH dee um) *n* a small theater or concert hall

PANTOMIME (PAN tuh mym) *n* acting without dialogue

PERIPETEIA (per uh pih TY uh) *n* a striking reversal in the action of a play

PROSCENIUM (pro SEE nee um) *n* the front part of a stage, marked off at top by an arch

REPERTORY (REH per tor ee) *n* a theatrical company

SCRIM (SKRIM) *n* a curtain that may be transparent or opaque, depending on how it is lit

SOUBRETTE (soo BRET) *n* a frivolous girl character, often a lady's maid

TABLEAU (tab LOH) *n* a stage picture created by actors posing motionless

Visual Arts—General/Sculpture

ARMATURE (AR muh cher) *n* a skeleton construction upon which a sculptor builds up a sculpture

BURNISH (BER nish) *v* to rub or polish to a high gloss

COLLAGE (kuh LAHZH) *n* artwork resulting from the piecing together of different, often unrelated, pieces of material

CONTRAPPOSTO (kahn truh PAH stoh) *n* a pose in which the parts of the body are twisted or distorted into opposite directions

CROP (KRAHP) *v* to trim off

CURATOR (KYER ay ter) *n* person in charge of the artwork in a museum

DOCENT (DOH sint) *n* a tour guide at a museum

ECTYPE (EK typ) *n* a replica of an original artwork

EMBOSS (em BAWS) *v* to create raised figures or designs on a surface

ETCH (ECH) *v* to partially eat away a glass or metal surface by using a chemical in order to create a design

FESTOON (fes TOON) *n* a decorative design of looped, curved lines

GILDED (GIL did) *adj* covered with a gold finish

GISANT (gee ZAHNT) *n* the sculptured representation of a deceased person, usually part of a monumental tomb

MEDIUM (MEE dee um) *n* the particular material used to create a picture or sculpture

MONTAGE (mahn TAHZH) *n* a combination of several pictures or parts of pictures blended into a single unit

MOSAIC (moh ZAY ik) *n* an illustration formed by a matrix of tiles or stones set in cement

PATINA (puh TEE nuh) *n* green film on the surface of bronze, resulting from exposure to atmosphere or chemicals

RELIEF (rih LEEF) *n* raised; projecting from a background surface

SLIP (SLIP) *n* a fluid mixture of clay and water used for pottery

TESSELLATED (TES uh lay tid) *adj* inlaid; mosaic

Visual Arts—Painting

ABOZZO (uh BOHT soh) *n* a sketch; in painting, the first outline or drawing on a canvas

CALLIGRAPHIC (kal uh GRAF ik) *adj* the free and rhythmic use of pen markings to approximate handwriting

CARICATURE (KAYR ih kuh choor) *n* a pictorial ridicule or satire in which the subject's physical characteristics are distorted

CARTOON (kar TOON) *n* a preliminary drawing or sketch

CHIAROSCURO (kee ahr uh SKYOOR oh) *n* the use of light and shade to give forms a three-dimensional appearance

CHROMA (KROH muh) *n* the distinctive quality, excluding color, that identifies a particular color

CURSIVE (KUR siv) *adj* freeflowing, in the manner of running handwriting

FICTILE (FIK tul) *adj* molded or capable of being molded into form by sculpture

FRESCO (FRES koh) *n* a mural painting on freshly laid plaster

IMPASTO (im PAHS toh) *n* heavy layers or strokes of paint, creating a rough surface with deep brushmarks

PALETTE (PAL ut) *n* the range of colors or pigments available to an artist; a wooden board used by a painter to hold paint while painting

SICCATIVE (SIK uh tiv) *n* a substance added to oil paint to make it dry more quickly

TEMPERA (TEM per uh) *n* pigment mixed with water and egg yolk or similar material

TONDO (TAHN doh) *n* a picture in the round

VARNISH (VAR nish) *n* a solution used as a protective coating over paint

VIGNETTE (vin YET) *n* an illustration that fades into the space around it without a definite border; also, a small illustration at the beginning or end of a chapter or book to fill up space

Quiz Time (3.11)

Directions: Match each numbered word in the left column with its lettered definition in the right column. The answer key begins on page 170.

1.	abozzo	a.	decorative design of looped lines
2.	burnish	b.	first outline or sketch
3.	chiaroscuro	c.	frivolous girl character
4.	ectype	d.	green film on the surface of bronze
5.	festoon	e.	heavy, rough strokes of paint
6.	gisant	f.	inlaid or mosaic
7.	hamartia	g.	masked, comic character
8.	harlequin	h.	overly dramatic acting style
9.	histrionics	i.	picture in the round
10.	impasto	j.	replica of an original artwork
11.	odeum	k.	rub or polish to a high gloss
12.	patina	l.	sculptured likeness of a dead person
13.	peripeteia	m.	small theater or concert hall
14.	repertory	n.	striking reversal in a play's action
15.	siccative	o.	substance to dry oil paint quickly
16.	soubrette	p.	theatrical company
17.	tessellated	q.	tragic character's flaw
18.	tondo	r.	use of shading to achieve depth

Zoology

AGONISTIC (ag uh NIS tik) *adj* displaying fighting behavior

ALIPED (AL uh ped) *n* an animal whose toes are connected by a membrane, serving as a wing (e.g., a bat)

APIARY (AY pee ayr ee) *n* a place where bees are kept

AVIARY (AY vee ayr ee) *n* an enclosure for birds

CARAPACE (KAHR uh pays) *n* a shell or protective covering over all or part of the back of certain animals (e.g., turtles and crabs)

DIURNAL (dy YER nul) *adj* referring to or occurring during the daylight hours

EQUINE (EK wyn) *adj* pertaining to horses; horselike

EWE (YOO) *n* a female sheep

FAUNA (FAW nuh) *n* the animal species of a given region or period

FORAGE (FOR ij) *v* to wander or rove in search of food; to collect food; *n* food of any kind for animals, especially for horses and cattle

HERPETOLOGIST (her pih TAHL uh jist) *n* a person who studies reptiles

ICHTHYOLOGY (ik thee AHL uh jee) *n* the study of fish

LEONINE (LEE uh nyn) *adj* pertaining to lions; suggestive of a lion

MATUTINAL (muh TOO duh nul) *adj* pertaining to or functioning in the morning

NIDUS (NY dus) *n* a nest in which insects deposit eggs

NOCTURNAL (nahk TER nul) *adj* pertaining to the darkness or to organisms active or functional at night

OMNIVOROUS (ahm NIV er us) *adj* eating both plants and animals

ORNITHOLOGY (or nih THAHL uh jee) *n* the study of birds

PABULUM (PAB yuh luhm) *n* any nourishment for an animal (or plant)

PREHENSILE (pre HEN sul) *adj* capable of grasping and holding

ROOKERY (RUH ker ee) *n* a breeding or resting place, especially for birds

SEDENTARY (SED in tayr ee) *adj* living in one place; not migratory

TAXIDERMY (TAK sih der mee) *n* preparing, stuffing, and displaying animal skins

TAXONOMY (tak SAH nuh mee) *n* the science or technique of classification (of animals, plants, etc.)

URSINE (ER syn) *adj* pertaining to bears; bearlike

VAGILITY (vuh JIL ih tee) *n* the innate ability to disperse

VESPIARY (VES pee ayr ee) *n* a nest of wasps

VESTIGIAL (veh STIJ yul) *adj* describing a body part that no longer functions usefully (*n* vestige)

VULPINE (VUHL pyn) *adj* pertaining to foxes; like a fox

Quiz Time (3.12)

Directions: Match each numbered word in the left column with its lettered definition in the right column. The answer key begins on page 170.

1.	agonistic	a.	a nest for insect eggs
2.	apiary	b.	animal species of a region
3.	carapace	c.	breeding place for birds
4.	equine	d.	capable of grasping and holding
5.	fauna	e.	classification of animals
6.	omnivorous	f.	displaying fighting behavior
7.	ornithology	g.	eating both plants and animals
8.	nidus	h.	innate ability to disperse
9.	pabulum	i.	non-functioning body part
10.	prehensile	j.	nourishment for an animal
11.	rookery	k.	pertaining to horses
12.	taxidermy	l.	place where bees are kept
13.	taxonomy	m.	preparing animal skins
14.	vagility	n.	shell of an animal
15.	vestigial	o.	study of birds

Quiz Time—Answers (3.1–3.12)

Quiz 3.1

1. e	7. r	13. h
2. i	8. j	14. n
3. g	9. c	15. f
4. k	10. q	16. b
5. p	11. m	17. d
6. l	12. a	18. o

Quiz 3.2

1. l	7. c	13. k
2. b	8. m	14. i
3. h	9. r	15. o
4. q	10. j	16. q
5. d	11. f	17. n
6. p	12. a	18. e

Quiz 3.3

1. j	7. b	13. f
2. o	8. p	14. l
3. d	9. i	15. g
4. q	10. c	16. m
5. a	11. k	17. n
6. r	12. e	18. h

Quiz 3.4

1. e	7. c	13. m
2. b	8. i	14. r
3. n	9. f	15. o
4. h	10. d	16. a
5. l	11. j	17. g
6. q	12. k	18. p

Quiz 3.5

1.	f	7.	e	13.	h
2.	n	8.	i	14.	l
3.	o	9.	c	15.	r
4.	j	10.	k	16.	m
5.	b	11.	p	17.	d
6.	q	12.	a	18.	g

Quiz 3.6

1.	f	7.	r	13.	b
2.	n	8.	l	14.	e
3.	h	9.	d	15.	k
4.	i	10.	p	16.	a
5.	g	11.	c	17.	q
6.	m	12.	j	18.	o

Quiz 3.7

1.	b	7.	q	13.	h
2.	j	8.	n	14.	m
3.	l	9.	g	15.	p
4.	d	10.	k	16.	f
5.	i	11.	o	17.	c
6.	r	12.	a	18.	e

Quiz 3.8

1.	c	7.	q	13.	m
2.	f	8.	b	14.	a
3.	e	9.	o	15.	d
4.	k	10.	h	16.	n
5.	i	11.	g	17.	p
6.	r	12.	j	18.	l

Quiz 3.9

1. c
2. d
3. g
4. o
5. b
6. a

7. e
8. f
9. r
10. q
11. l
12. h

13. m
14. k
15. p
16. n
17. j
18. i

Quiz 3.10

1. p
2. j
3. b
4. o
5. i
6. l

7. a
8. r
9. d
10. c
11. k
12. f

13. e
14. m
15. g
16. q
17. h
18. n

Quiz 3.11

1. b
2. k
3. r
4. j
5. a
6. l

7. q
8. g
9. h
10. e
11. m
12. d

13. n
14. p
15. o
16. c
17. f
18. i

Quiz 3.12

1. f
2. l
3. n
4. k
5. b

6. g
7. o
8. a
9. j
10. d

11. c
12. m
13. e
14. h
15. i

6

Flexibility Training
(Prefixes and Roots)

Memorizing words is one way to build your vocabulary. Another, and more flexible, way is to become familiar with the Latin, Greek, and Anglo-Saxon prefixes and roots from which most English words are derived. By learning prefixes and roots, you can take **educated guesses** at the meaning of new words and increase your odds of responding correctly to exam questions.

This chapter provides a handy list of the more commonly used prefixes and roots (in bold uppercase letters). For each one, the English meaning (in italics) and some illustrative testworthy words (and brief definitions) are provided. Many of these illustrative words appear elsewhere in the book.

Note: You'll discover that some of the illustrative words convey the meaning of the prefix or root quite clearly, while for others the connection is a bit strained, due to evolving meaning and use of words, roots, and prefixes over the centuries.

Prefixes to Pump Up Your Vocabulary

AB
from, away

abdicate *v* to give up; relinquish

abduct *v* to lead away by force; kidnap

abhor *v* to turn away from; loathe

abject *adj* utterly hopeless (all hope gone away)

abjure *v* to reject, disavow, or renounce under oath

ablution *n* washing away; cleansing

abnegate *v* to deny oneself (e.g., a pleasure or right); to relinquish or give up

abrogate *v* to repeal; do away with

abscond *v* to steal away and hide

abstergent *n* a cleanser

AD, AC, AF, AG, AL, AN, AP, AR, AS, AT
to, toward

accord *n* an agreement

adit *n* an entrance

adjunct *n* something joined to another thing

admonish *v* to strongly urge or caution

affiance *n* a promise to marry

affiant *n* a person who makes an affidavit (pledge)

aggrandize to make larger, more powerful or important, or wealthier

appease *v* to pacify; bring toward peace

arraign *v* to bring to justice; indict

arrogate *v* to claim or seize

assiduous *adj* diligent; industrious

attest *v* to offer testimony; testify

AMB, AMBI
around, about, both

ambidextrous *adj* able to use both hands with skill

ambient *adj* surrounding all sides

ambiparous *adj* having both leaves and flowers

ambivalent *adj* having conflicting emotions

ambulatory *adj* able to walk

AMPHI
two, both, on both sides

amphibious *adj* capable of living both on land and in water

amphibolic *adj* uncertain

amphibolous *adj* capable of having two meanings

amphorous *adj* having a hollow sound

ANA
through, up

anabasis *n* a journey upward; a military advance

anacephalize *v* to review; recapitulate

anachronism *n* a thing out of place in time

anagram *n* a word (or phrase) formed from the scrambled letters of another word (or phrase)

ANTE
before

antedate *v* to precede in time
antenuptial *adj* before marriage
antetype *n* an earlier type of something

ANTI
opposed, against

antidote *n* a remedy against a poison
antimony *n* opposition between two laws
antipathy *n* a strong feeling of dislike; hostility; aversion
antithesis *n* a contrast of ideas

APO
away from

apocrypha *n* writings of doubtful authority
apoplexy *n* a sudden loss of consciousness
apostasy *n* abandonment of or turning away from one's faith
apostle *n* a person sent away to deliver a message

BE
intensive, thoroughly, top, make or render

bedaub *v* to smear over
bedeck *v* to dress or cover up
befuddle *v* to confuse thoroughly
beguile *v* to deceive; trick
beleaguer *v* to surround, besiege, or blockade
berate *v* to scold harshly
bereave *v* to deprive or rob cruelly
besmirch *v* to soil; make filthy

BENE, BON
well, good

benediction *n* a blessing
benefaction *n* a gift; donation
benevolent *adj* good-hearted
bonify *v* to convert into good

BI
two, twice

bicameral *adj* composed of two parts or sides
biennial *adj* every two years
bipartisan *adj* cooperative (as between both political parties)
biped *n* any two-legged animal

CATA
down

cataclysm *n* a disaster—e.g., a flood (downward sweep of water)
catalyst *n* a substance or event that starts a reaction
cataract *n* a waterfall
catastrophe *n* a disaster

CIRC, CIRCUM
around

circuitous *adj* in a roundabout way
circumfluous *adj* flowing around
circumlocution *n* talk that is not to the point
circumscribe *v* to draw a line around
circumspect *adj* cautious; wary; watchful (looking around)
circumvent *v* to prevent; foil (encircle)

DE
down, away, from

debase *v* to lower in value
declinate *adj* having a downward slope; declining
denude *v* to strip bare
depose *v* to remove from a position

DIA
through

dialectic *n* argument through critical discussion
diatribe *n* a long, usually abusive, argument or lecture

E, EF, EX
out of

eczema *n* a breaking out of the skin
effervescent *adj* bubbling; lively
efflux *n* a flowing out
effusive *adj* pouring forth freely; gushing
emanate *v* to flow out
exacerbate *v* to make worse
expunge *v* to rub out; obliterate

EN, EM
in, into, on

embalm *v* to inject a preservative into a corpse's blood vessels
embark *v* to board a ship or train for a trip
embellish *v* to decorate or make beautiful
envelop *v* to assimilate (bring in as part of)
envenom *v* to poison
environ *v* to encircle

EP, EPI
upon, beside, among

epidemic *n* a spreading among a populace
epigram *n* a clever, pithy saying; aphorism

epistle *n* a letter (writing)
epitaph *n* an inscription on a gravestone
epithet *n* a word or phrase describing a person; a derogatory word or phrase used to show contempt
epitome *n* a person or thing that is typical of or characterizes a whole class; a summary of a topic or work

EU
good, well

eulogy *n* words of praise, especially for a deceased person
euphemism *n* a pleasant or complimentary word or phrase instead of one that is harsh or derogatory
euphony *n* a pleasing sound
euphoria *n* a feeling of well-being
euthanasia *n* mercy killing

EXTRA
beyond

extradite *v* to deliver (give up) a criminal from one state or nation to another
extraneous *adj* beyond that which is necessary; surplus
extrapolate *v* to deduce or infer an unknown (e.g., a quantity) from something that is known
extrovert *n* a person who is outgoing and concerned primarily with **external** things

HYPER
excessive, over, above

hyperbole *n* an exaggeration used to make a point
hypertrophy *n* abnormally large growth of a bodily organ
hyperventilate *v* to breathe excessively fast

HYPO
under, beneath, lower

hypocrite *n* a person who pretends to have certain different attitudes than those beneath the surface
hypodermic *adj* beneath the skin
hypoglycemia *n* low blood sugar
hypothesis *n* something assumed for the sake of argument

IL, IN, IM, IR
not

illiberal *adj* closed-minded (not liberal)
illicit *adj* not allowed; illegal (not legal)
impeccable *adj* flawless; perfect
implacable *adj* incapable of forgiveness or of being appeased or pleased (not placable)
inclement *adj* not mild, especially in reference to the weather
innocuous *adj* not harmful or injurious
insatiable *adj* incapable of being satisfied
irresolute *adj* unable to decide or make up one's mind (not resolute)

MAG, MAGNA, MAGNI
large, great

magnanimous *adj* noble or elevated in mind; generous
magnate *n* an important or influential person, especially in business
magnify *n* to cause to appear larger in size
magniloquent *adj* bombastic, pompous, or grandiose (as in talk or speech)
magnitude *n* greatness; extent

MIS, MISO
wrong, bad, hate

misanthrope *n* a hater of mankind
miscreant *n* an evil-doer
misnomer *n* a wrong name or designation
misogynist *n* a hater of women

NEO
new

neologism *n* a newly coined word
neonate *adj* newborn
neophyte *n* a novice; beginner

OB, OP, OC, OF
against, facing

disoblige *v* to offend, affront, or insult; to refuse or to act contrary to
obdurate *adj* stubborn; persistent
oblate *adj* flattened at a sphere's poles
objurgate *v* to denounce harshly
obloquy *n* condemnation or verbal abuse, or the disgrace resulting therefrom
occlude *v* to close out or block out
officious *adj* pushy; meddlesome; intrusive

PARA
beside, like, position

parable *n* a story with a lesson or moral
paradigm *n* a model or example
paradox *n* a seeming contradiction that may be true or valid
paragon *n* a model of perfection; an ideal
parallax *n* a shift in the relative position of objects due to a change in perspective
paramount *adj* above all others in position; supreme; most important
paraphrase *v* to reword
parody *n* a mocking imitation

PER
through, completely

percolate *v* to filter (liquid) through a membrane

perdition *n* entire loss; utter destruction; ruin

peremptory *adj* final; with authority; absolutely

perennial *adj* occurring every year or throughout the year; continuous

peregrinate *v* to walk through or travel, especially on foot

permeable *adj* allowing passage through

perspicacious *adj* insightful; penetrating; astute

pervade *v* to spread throughout

PERI
around

peripatetic *adj* walking around; itinerant

periphery *n* edge; boundary; outer region

peristalsis *n* involuntary contractions that move food through the digestive system

peristyle *n* a colonnade or row of piers surrounding a building or courtyard

POLY
many

polychromatic *adj* multicolored

polydemic *adj* native to many geographic areas

polygamous *n* having several spouses

polyglot *n* a speaker of several languages

polyhedron *n* a solid figure having many plane surfaces

polyphony *n* the simultaneous combination of two or more melodies

POST
after, behind, following

posterity *n* those who come after

postern *adj* situated at the rear

posthumous *adj* after death

PRE
before

preamble *n* an introductory statement

precedent *n* something similar occurring before

precocious *adj* having matured very early

preeminent *adj* above all others; supreme

premonition *n* a forewarning

prerequisite *adj* necessary beforehand

presage *n* a foreboding event or omen

preside *v* to occupy the leading position

PRO
forward, forth

procure *v* to get or gain

profess *v* to openly admit

prolific *adj* bringing forth fruit; highly productive

prolix *adj* needlessly prolonged or drawn out

proscribe *v* to prohibit or forbid (from the present time forward)

provisional *adj* temporary; interim; tentative

RE
back, again

recapitulate *v* to summarize

recompense *v* to pay back or compensate (for services, time, etc.)

reimburse *v* to repay (pay back)

reiterate *v* to repeat

requite *v* to repay; compensate; recompense; remunerate

SE
aside

secede *v* to withdraw

secern *v* to discriminate or set apart

secrete *v* to hide away or store away; to discharge or exude

sequester *v* to separate (from society); to retire from public life

SUB, SUC, SUP, SUS
under, beneath

subjugate *v* to bring under control

subpoena *n* a court order to appear at a proceeding

subsidize *v* to aid financially

subterfuge *n* an artifice used to deceive, especially to escape blame

subvert *v* to undermine (e.g., the government)

succumb *v* to yield (cease to resist) or submit

SUPER, SUPR
over, above, beyond

superable *adj* able to be overcome; conquerable

supercilious *adj* overbearing; haughty

superfluent *adj* flowing freely

superfluous *adj* unnecessary; surplus

supernal *adj* in a higher place; pertaining to things above; celestial; heavenly

SUR
upon, more

surfeit *v* to sicken from overindulgence

surrogate *n* a substitute

surtax *n* an additional tax

SYM, SYN, SYL, SYS
with, together

syllogism *n* an explanation as to how different elements (ideas) relate to one another

symbiotic *adj* mutually beneficial

syndactyl *adj* having webbed feet

syndicate *n* an association of persons for business purposes

syndrome *n* signs and symptoms occurring at the same time

synergistic *adj* cooperative (teamwork)

synopsis *n* a summary

TRANS
across, over

intransigent *adj* stubbornly unwilling to compromise

transcend *v* to cross over to a high level

transient not lasting or permanent; staying only a short time

transfuse *v* to pass from one to another

transgress *v* to go beyond a limit; to offend or sin

transhumance *n* seasonal migration

transit *n* the path (way) from one place to another (*adj* transitory)

traverse *v* to cross over—e.g., a bridge or stream

Branch Out with Word Roots

ACER, ACID, ACRI
bitter, sour, sharp

lacerated *adj* jagged; torn
acerbic *adj* bitter; irritating
acidify or acidulate *v* to make bitter, sour, or
  acidic
acrid *adj* stingingly bitter
acrimonious *adj* nagging; bitterly
  quarrelsome; caustic

AG, AGI, AGO
drive, do, go, move

agile *adj* quick; active
agog *adj* eager
cogent *adj* convincing; compelling
cogitate *v* to think or meditate
demagogue *n* a charismatic leader
  (especially a politician) who stirs up
  emotions in others
exigent *adj* urgent
pedagogy *n* the study of teaching methods
  and materials
prodigal *adj* extremely wasteful;
  extravagant

ALI, ALLO, ALTER
other

alias *n* an assumed name
alibi *n* proof of being elsewhere at the time
  a crime was committed
alienable *adj* transferable (to another)
allogrtaph *n* a signature or other writing
  inscribed by one person for another
altercation *n* a dispute, argument, or fight
altruistic *adj* unselfish

AM, AMA
love, friend

amatory *adj* expressing love
amiable *adj* friendly
amicable *adj* friendly; amiable
amity *n* friendship
enamor *v* to inspire to ardent love

ANIM
soul, mind

animadvert *v* to criticize
animosity *n* active hostility
equanimous *adj* even-tempered
magnanimous *adj* noble or elevated in
  spirit or mind; generous
pusillanimous *adj* cowardly; faint-hearted

ANTHROP
man (human beings)

anthropic *adj* pertaining to humankind
misanthrope *n* hater of humankind
philanthropy *n* charity; love of humankind

AUD, AUS
hear, listen

audible *adj* able to be heard
audient *adj* listening; paying attention
ausculate *v* to listen to sounds within a
  body cavity

AUTO
self

autocrat *n* an absolute monarch; despot
autonomous *adj* self-governing;
  independent in action

BELLI
war

antebellum *adj* existing before the war
bellicose or **belligerent** *adj* inclined to argue or fight; hostile

CAD, CAS, CID
fall

cadaver *n* corpse (dead body)
cadence *n* rhythmic movement in speech or music
cascade *v* to fall as a waterfall, especially a series of falls
decadence *n* deterioration, esp. in morality
recidivism *n* habitual return to criminal activity

CALOR
heat

caloric or **calorific** *adj* giving off heat
caudle *n* a warm, beneficial drink for an ill person
cauldron *n* a large kettle for heating
nonchalant *adj* indifferent; unconcerned

CANT
sing

cant *n* jargon used by a particular group or profession, especially politicians
cantata *n* a type of musical composition
canto *n* a division of a long poem; in music, the highest part
recant *v* to formally renounce one's previous beliefs

CAP, CEP, CEPT, CIP
take, seize

captation *n* an effort to gain something through flattery

captious *adj* calculated to entrap
captious *adj* finding fault; hypercritical
incipient *n* just beginning
precept *n* a maxim or principle

CAPIT, CAPT
head, cap

capitate *adj* forming a head; enlarged
capitation *v* a tax imposed by counting individuals (heads)
capitular *adj* relating to a heading, chapter, or section (of a book)
capitulate *v* to surrender or give up
recapitulate *v* to summarize

CARN
flesh

carnage *n* massacre or slaughter, as from a war or battle
carnal *adj* pertaining to bodily appetites or desires
carnivorous *adj* flesh eating
incarnate *n* the embodiment of a quality

CED, CES
yield, surrender, go

abscess *n* any inflamed, pus-filled part of the body
accede *v* to go along with; agree to
accession *n* going to (especially, to a position of authority, such as that of a monarch)
cede *v* to yield; admit
concede *v* to yield to; agree to
decedent *n* in law, a deceased person
incessant *adj* continual; unrelenting
intercede *v* to go between; mediate
recede *v* to go back; retreat
secede *v* to withdraw from a group

CENTR
middle, center

centrifugal *adj* tending to move away from the center

centripetal *adj* tending to move toward the center

concentric *adj* having a common center

eccentric *adj* off-centered or out of the ordinary, especially in manner of behavior

CERN, CRET, CREM
sift

discern *v* to distinguish one thing from others; discriminate

discrete *adj* careful about one's actions or words

excrement *n* matter expelled or ejected; waste

recrement *n* superfluous or useless matter

secrete *v* to hide away or store away; to discharge or exude

CIT
call, rouse

cite *v* to quote a passage; give legal notice to

incite *v* to stir up or start up; move to action

recite *v* to recall or repeat aloud

resuscitate *v* to bring back to life

suscitate *v* to arouse or excite

CLAM
shout, call out

acclaim *v* to shout approval

clamorous *adj* loud; noisy

declamation *n* speech

exclaim *v* to cry out abruptly

proclaim *v* to announce to the public

CLIN, CLIV
bend, slope

acclivity *n* an upward slope

declination *n* refusal; a downward slope

declivity *n* a downward slope

proclivity *n* a natural tendency

CLU, CLO
close, shut

cloistered *adj* living a sheltered life

occlude *v* to shut out; bar a passage; blockade

preclude *v* to prevent by prior action

recluse *n* a person who lives a solitary life; hermit

seclude *v* to hide, confine, or shut away

COGN
know

agnostic *adj* lacking knowledge

cognizant *adj* aware

connoisseur *n* an expert in the arts

incognito *adj* under an assumed name

prognostic *adj* knowing beforehand

reconnoiter *v* to survey an area for information (about an enemy's position)

CORD, COUR
heart

accord *n* a heart-felt agreement in mind or spirit

concord *n* an agreement

cordial *adj* warm-hearted; hospitable; friendly

CORP
body

corporeal *adj* pertaining to the body
corps *n* a group of people organized for a particular purpose
corpse *n* a dead body
corpulent *adj* excessively fat; obese

CRE
grow

accretion *n* growth in size
accrue *v* to gain or accumulate by natural tendency or advantage
excrescence *n* normal outgrowth (e.g., hair)
increment *n* increase or gain

CRED
trust, believe

accredit *v* to recognize as acceptable; approve and bring into trust or favor
credence *n* belief in the statements of others
credible *adj* believable
credulous *adj* believing easily; gullible
creed or **credo** *n* a formal statement of beliefs or principles
incredulous *adj* skeptical
miscreant *n* an evil person
recreant *n* one who yields in combat and begs for mercy

CUB, CUMB
lean back, lie down

encumber *v* to burden or hamper
incubus *n* a nightmare; something that burdens or oppresses one like a nightmare
incumbent *n* pressed or emphatically urged; current office holder

recumbent *adj* leaning back or lying down
succumb *v* to sink (cave in) under pressure; yield

CUL, CUR
care, care for

curator *n* a person who takes care of a museum or library
procure *v* to obtain
sinecure *n* a paid position without responsibility

CUR, COUR
run

cursory *adj* brief
courier *n* a messenger
discursive *adj* skimming over many unrelated topics
incursion *n* an unfriendly entry or raid
precursor *n* something that comes before; a forerunner

DAMN, DEMN
harm

endamage *v* to prejudice or bring loss
indemnify *v* to protect against loss or damage

DAT, DIT
give

antedate *n* a prior date
extradite *v* to deliver (give up) a criminal from one state or nation to another
mandate *n* an authoritative order; authority of an elected official conferred by the electorate
perdition *n* entire loss; utter destruction; ruin

DEC
comely (attractive)

decor *n* the decorative scheme of a room
decorous *adj* showing good taste and propriety
decorum *n* behavior and appearance

DEM
people

demagogue *n* a charismatic leader (especially a politician) who stirs up emotions in others
demigod *n* a person who has been elevated to the status of deity (god)
endemic *adj* indigenous; found only in a particular area
epidemic *adj* affecting many people
pandemic *adj* universal; worldwide

DENT
tooth

denticate *v* bite; chew; masticate
denticle *n* a small tooth or toothlike projection
dentigerous *adj* having teeth
indentured *adj* bound (by contract) to serve another
trident *n* a three-pronged spear

DIC, DICT
claim, say

abdicate *v* to formally relinquish or renounce an office or right
interdict *v* to prohibit with authority
maledictory *adj* speaking evil of someone
predicate *n* a statement contingent on something else
valediction *n* a farewell speech or utterance

vindicate *v* to clear from acccusation, blame, or suspicion

DIGN
worthy

dignify *v* to make worthy
disdain *n* rejection due to unworthiness
indignation *n* resentment and anger for not being treated as having worth

DOC
teach

docile *adj* easily instructed; obedient; tractable
doctrinaire *n* a visionary theorist; dogmatist
indoctrinate *v* to instruct in theories or beliefs

DOG, DOX
belief

dogmatic *adj* asserted without proof, usually arrogantly
doxology *n* a hymn of praise (to God)
orthodox *adj* conforming to conventional beliefs
paradox *n* a seeming contradiction that may be true or valid

DUC, DUCE, DUCT
lead

abduct *v* to kidnap (lead away)
adduce *v* to offer as reason or proof
aqueduct *n* a channel for transporting water
conducive *adj* tending to promote or lead to
educe *v* to draw out; infer
inductile *adj* not easily led or molded; inflexible

traduce *v* to disgrace unjustly; slander; vilify

viaduct *n* an arched roadway

DUR
hard, lasting

duress *n* coercion; restraint of will

indurate *v* to make hard or callous

obdurate *adj* stubborn; not easily persuaded

perdurable *adj* permanent; everlasting

EMPT
buy, take

coempt *v* to gain control by taking the whole quantity

peremptory *adj* authoritative and final (court order or command)

redeem *v* rescue; repurchase

ERR
wander

aberration or **aberrance** *n* deviation; departure from what is right

errant *adj* wandering; deviating from the regular course

errata *n* mistakes in writing or printing

EXTR
outward

extraneous *adj* foreign; not essential

extricate *v* to free; disentangle

extrinsic *adj* not essential

FAC, FEC, FIC
make, do, easy, face

efface *v* to make disappear

efficacious *adj* producing the result desired; effectual

facetious *adj* lightly joking; sarcastic

facient *n* a doer; agent

facile *adj* easily achieved

factious *adj* tending to produce dissension

factive *adj* making; causing

FAL
deceive

fallacious *adj* misleading; deceptive; logically unsound

fallible *adj* likely to be inaccurate or be deceived

FAT, FAB
speak

confabulate *v* to talk together; prattle

ineffable *adj* inexpressible; overwhelming

FER
bring, bear, carry

deference *n* courtesy; respect; yielding to

pestiferous *adj* carrying disease

proffer *v* to offer for acceptance

vociferous *adj* shouting noisily

FERV
boil

effervescent *adj* bubbling; vivacious

ferment *v* to excite

fervent *adj* showing great warmth of feeling

fervid *adj* burning; impassioned

fervor *n* intense heat or feeling

FID, FEAL, FEDER
trust, faith

affiance *n* a pledge to marry

affidavit *n* a written statement made under oath or by pledge

confide *v* to trust someone
diffident *adj* lacking self-confidence (faith
   in oneself)
fidelity *n* faithfulness; loyalty
fiduciary *n* one who holds something in
   trust for another
infidel *n* one who lacks faith; nonbeliever
perfidy *n* disloyalty; deceit

FIG
shape

effigy *n* an image, likeness, or
   representation of a person
feign *v* to pretend, invent, or fabricate
figment *n* an invention; something
   imagined

FILA, FILI
thread

filaceous *adj* composed of threads
filigree *n* fine ornamental design in gold or
   silver
filate *adj* threadlike; slender
filiferous *adj* bearing threads

FLAM, FLAG
fire

conflagrate *v* to burn up
flagrant *adj* outrageous; flaming into notice
flambeau *n* a flaming torch
flamboyant *adj* flowery; bombastic

FLOR
flower

effloresce *v* to blossom out
florid *adj* flowery; colorful; showy or gaudy
flourish *v* to grow luxuriantly

FLU
flow

affluent *adj* wealthy; prosperous; flowing
   freely
effluent *adj* flowing out
fluctuant *adj* unstable; fluctuating; moving
   like a wave
superfluous *adj* overflowing

FORT
strong, luck, chance

forte *adj* in music, strong
fortify *v* to strengthen physically
fortitude *n* patient endurance
fortuitous *adj* occurring by chance or
   accident; lucky

FRACT, FRANG
break

fractious *adj* unruly; tending to break rules
frangible *adj* easily broken
refract *v* to bend (break), as a ray as it
   passes from one medium to another

FRONT
front

affront *v* to insult openly
effrontery *n* shameless boldness; audacity;
   insolence

FUG
flee

fugacious *adj* fleeting; transitory
fugitive *n* one who flees (from justice)
refugee *n* one who flees to a safe place
subterfuge *n* an artifice (clever trick) used
   to deceive, especially to escape blame

FULG
flash

fulgent *adj* dazzlingly bright
fulgid *adj* glittery
fulminate *v* to explode violently

FUNCT
perform

defunct *adj* no longer functioning (or existing)
dysfunction *n* abnormal or impaired functioning
perfunctory *adj* performed without care

FUS
pour

diffuse *adj* widespread
effuse *adj* gushing; pouring out
infuse *v* to pour into
profuse *adj* pouring forth

GEN
beget, race

benign *adj* harmless; favorable; gentle
disingenuous *adj* insincere
engender *v* to bring about; to cause to exist
generic *adj* belonging to a type or kind
genial *adj* having a kind disposition; favorable to growth
genre *n* kind, type, or species
malign *v* to treat harshly or badly
progenitor *n* ancestor; forefather; ascendant
progeny *n* offspring; descendants

GEN
kind

benign *adj* harmless; favorable; gentle
disingenuous *adj* insincere

genial *adj* having a kind disposition; favorable to growth
malign *v* to treat harshly or badly

GERM
vital part

germane *adj* akin; closely related; pertinent
germinate *n* to begin to grow or develop from a seed of a living substance

GEST
carry, bear

gestate *v* to carry during pregnancy
gesticulate *v* to indicate by gestures while speaking
ingest *v* to put (food) into one's stomach

GNOS
know

gnome *n* a wise, pithy saying; a diminutive (small) person
gnosis *n* superior wisdom, especially acquired mystically
prognosis *n* a prediction of the course of a disease and chances of recovery

GRAD, GRESS
walk, step, degree

aggrade *v* to build up a slope by depositing sediment, as in a river
degression *n* degree or rank
digress *v* to step (move) away from temporarily, as from the subject; ramble
egress *v* to leave or exit
gradient *adj* moving by steps
gressorial *adj* adapted for walking
ingress *v* to step into or enter
retrograde *v* to move backwards; deteriorate; worsen; regress

transgress *v* to move over or beyond; to break some prescribed rule; to offend

GRAPH, GRAM
write

allograph *n* a forgery
calligraphy *n* the free and rhythmic use of pen markings to approximate handwriting
epigram *n* a witty, pithy, pointed statement
epigraph *n* an inscription on a tomb
stenography *n* shorthand writing

GREG
flock

aggregate *n* sum, mass, or collection
gregarious *adj* fond of the company of others

HEMO
blood

hematic *adj* pertaining to blood
hematose *adj* bloody
hemophilia *n* bleeding that cannot be controlled
hemorrhage *v* to bleed intensely

HOST, HOSP
host

hospice *n* a home for the sick and dying
hospitable *adj* receiving guests in a friendly, generous manner
hostel *n* a lodging place, especially for young travelers

HUME
lowly, earth

exhume *v* to unearth or disinter; disclose
humus *adj* dark, organically rich soil

inhume *v* to bury in the earth; inter
posthumous *adj* after the death

INT
within

intimate *adj* closely acquainted
intimation *n* indirect suggestion; hint
intrinsic *adj* essential to the nature of a thing

JAC, JEC
throw

abject *adj* sunk to a low condition; degraded; debased
conjecture *v* to form an opinion without sufficient proof or evidence; surmise
interject *v* to interrupt, come between, or intervene
jetsam *n* debris washed ashore from a ship; cargo thrown overboard to lighten a ship
jettison *v* to throw away a burden
trajectory *n* the curved path formed by an object in flight

JUD, JUR, JUS
right, law, swear

abjure *v* to reject, disavow, or renounce under oath
adjure *v* to bind or command solemnly, as under oath or threat of curse; to entreat earnestly
conjure *v* to entreat solemnly; to imagine or cause to appear
judicious *adj* using sound judgment
jurisdiction *n* authority to hear and decide a legal matter
jurist *n* a legal scholar or writer
perjure *v* to provide false testimony

JUNC, JOIN
join

adjunct *n* something added to (joined with) another thing

conjugal *adj* pertaining to the relationship between married persons

conjunct *n* association; combination

disjunct *adj* separated

enjoin *v* to order or forbid

junta *n* a group of political insiders

rejoinder *n* an answer to a reply

subjugate *v* to bring under the control of; to subdue

LAT
carry, bear

ablation *n* a carrying away

elate *v* to swell in spirit

oblation *n* a sacrificial offering

LECT, LEG, LIG
gather, choose, read

legible *adj* able to be read

legion *n* a great number; multitude

lexicon *n* a collection of words; dictionary

predilection *n* preference

prelect *v* to lecture or discourse

LEV
raise, light

alleviate *v* to make easier; to lighten a burden

levee *n* a raised river bank to prevent flooding

levity *n* lack of seriousness

levy *n* a tax or other mandatory payment

LIG
bind

allegiance *n* a group bound together by a common cause

liege *adj* bound to be faithful to a superior

ligature *n* anything that binds

obliged *v* indebted

LIQU
liquid

deliquesce *v* to melt away

liquescent *adj* becoming liquid

prolix *adj* long and wordy; to flow

LOC
a place

locus *n* place; locality

allocate *v* to set apart for a specific purpose

locomotion *n* act of moving (or power to move) from one place to another

LOQ
speak

colloquial *adj* informal, as in conversation or writing

colloquy *n* a mutual discussion of two or more persons

elocution *n* the art of public speaking

locution *n* style of speech

loquacious *adj* talkative

eloquent *adj* inclined to speak; articulate

obloquy *n* condemnation or verbal abuse, or the disgrace resulting therefrom

soliloquy *n* a point in a drama when a character reveals his thoughts to the audience

LUC
light, clear

elucidate *v* to make clear; to bring into the light

illustrious *adj* distinguished by greatness

lucent *adj* bright; shining

lucid *adj* clear; bright

luciferous *adj* affording light or means of insight

lucubrate *v* to work laboriously, especially at night (by artificial light)

luminary *n* a celebrity or dignitary; one who sheds light on a subject

luminous *adj* readily understood

pellucid *adj* easy to understand; allowing light through

LUD
deceive, play

allude *v* to refer to indirectly

collude *v* to conspire to commit a fraudulent act

delude *v* to deceive

postlude *n* a phrase played at the end of a musical piece

MAL
bad, evil

maladroit *adj* clumsy; awkward; inept

malady *n* any illness or disease

malaise *n* a vague feeling of anxiety or uneasiness

malapropism *n* humorous misuse of words

malcontent *n* a dissatisfied person

malediction *n* slander; curse

malefactor *n* an evil-doer; criminal

maleficent *adj* bringing or producing evil or disease

malevolent *adj* wishing bad or evil on others

malfeasance *n* misconduct, especially in public affairs

malice *n* ill will toward others

malign *v* to speak badly of another with the intent to harm

malignant *adj* extremely harmful or evil

malinger *v* to feign illness to avoid work

MAN
by hand, remain

immanent *adj* existing within the mind; inherent or indwelling

legerdemain *n* slight of hand; magic tricks; prestidigitation

manacles *n* handcuffs; shackles

manifest *adj* seen at hand; obvious; apparent

manumit *v* to release from slavery

remnant *n* anything left over

MATER, MATRI
mother

matriarch *n* the female ruler of a family

matriculate *v* to enroll at a college

matrilineal *adj* descended on the mother's side of the family

matron *n* an older married woman who has had children

MENT
mind

adamant *adj* determined (having made up one's mind)

mentality *n* intellectual character

dementia *n* a loss of mental abilities or powers

MERC
trade

mercantile *adj* pertaining to trade and commerce

mercenary *adj* for hire; motivated by money or other personal gain rather than by loyalty

mercurial *adj* volatile; changeable; fickle

MISS, MITT
send

emit *v* to send out

emissary *n* an agent sent on a specific mission

missive *n* a letter or note which can be sent by messenger

omissive *adj* leaving out; neglecting

pretermitted *adj* neglectfully omitted

remiss *adj* negligent in performance of one's duties

remit *v* to pay back or put back

MOD
manner, measure

commodious *adj* spacious, roomy

incommodious *adj* inconvenient

mode *n* manner

modicum *n* a small quantity

MON
warn

admonish *v* to strongly urge or caution

premonition *n* a forewarning

summon *v* to call together

MORT, MORI
death

morbid *adj* gloomy, as in dwelling on death; tenebrous

morbidity *n* death rate; incidence of disease

moribund *adj* dying or coming to an end

mortician *n* a funeral director

mortify *v* to punish oneself by self-denial; to embarrass or humiliate

mortuary *n* a place where the dead are held before burial or cremation

MULTI
many, much

multifaceted *adj* having many sides or aspects

multifarious *adj* having great diversity; having many different parts or elements

multiform *adj* having many different forms

multitude *n* a crowd; throng; great number

multiparous *adj* producing more than one offspring at a birth

MUN
gift

immune *adj* exempt from anything harmful

munificent *adj* very generous in giving

remunerate *v* to make payment for services

MUT
change

immutable *adj* not capable of change

mutate *v* to undergo a great change

transmute *v* to transform to another nature

NAT, NASC
born, natural

agnate *adj* referring to a relationship on the father's side of a family

cognate *adj* of the same or a similar nature or stock; having the same ancestor

denature *v* to take natural qualities from

innate *adj* from or existing at birth

naïve *adj* acting is if newly born; unsophisticated

nascent *adj* being born

natal *adj* pertaining to birth

renaissance *n* new birth

NAV, NAU
ship, sail

nausea *n* seasickness; stomach disorder; loathing

nautical *adj* pertaining to ships, sailing, or the sea

naval *adj* pertaining to ships

NEC, NEX
bind

annex *v* to add to, usually at the end

nexus *n* a connection, usually between people, ideas, or characteristics

NOC
hurt

innocuous *adj* harmless; benign

noxious *adj* harmful to health

nuisance *n* an annoying or troubling person or incidence

NOM
name

agnomen *n* a nickname

cognomen *n* a family (last) name; surname

denominate *v* to label or give a name to

ignominy *n* shame; dishonor

misnomer *n* the wrong name; incorrect designation

nomenclature *n* a system of names used in a particular field of study or activity

nominal *adj* in name only (not in fact)

NOT
know

annotate *v* to make explanatory notes

connote *v* to evoke an idea or emotion beyond the explicit meaning of the words used

notorious *adj* widely but unfavorably known

NOUN, NUNC
declare, announce

annunciate *v* to proclaim or promulgate

denounce *v* to accuse or inform against

enunciate *v* to pronounce clearly

renounce *v* to give up a right or opinion; retract; abdicate; repudiate

NOV, NEW
new

novation *n* a new contract or contractual term which replaces an existing one

novel *adj* new; unusual

novella *n* a short book, especially fiction
novice *n* one who is new to an endeavor
renovate *v* to make like new

OMNI
all

omnibus *n* a conveyance for all
omnifarious *adj* of all sort or varieties
omniscient *adj* all knowing
omnivorous *adj* eating everything

OSS, OSTEO
bone

osseous *adj* bony
ossuary *n* a deposit of bones; cemetery
osteopath *n* a person (physician) who
    treats diseases by manipulating bones

PAN
all, every

panacea *n* a cure-all for ills
pandemic *adj* pertaining to all people;
    universal; worldwide
panorama *n* a view of all directions

PAR, PEER
equal

disparage *v* to speak slightingly of
disparate *adj* not alike; dissimilar
par *n* average or normal status or value
parity *n* similarity in degree, amount, or
    quality between two things
peer *n* another person (or thing) of the same
    rank or status

PART
share (portion)

apportion *v* to divide into parts according
    to a plan

impart *v* to share with or bestow upon
    another a communication
parcel *v* to apportion in parts; also, a small
    package
parse *v* to break into parts, explaining or
    examining each part
partisan *adj* strongly favorable to and
    supportive of one side, especially a
    political party

PATER, PATR
father

compatriot *n* a fellow countryman
expatriate *n* one who renounces one's
    natural citizenship
paternal *adj* like a father
patron *n* a person (often wealthy) who
    supports a cause, endeavor, or person
patronize *v* to treat condescendingly; talk
    down to; look down on

PATH
feeling, disease

antipathy *n* hostile feeling; revulsion
apathy *n* lack of interest or feeling
empathy *n* understanding the feelings of
    another by experiencing them vicariously
pathological *adj* pertaining to disease;
    diseased
pathos *n* pity or compassion caused by
    something experienced or observed

PED, POD
foot (walking or progressing), child

expedient *adj* suitable for a particular
    purpose; practicable
expedite *v* to facilitate, quicken, or hasten
expeditious *adj* efficient and speedy
impede *v* to obstruct or hinder
impediment *n* a stumbling block; obstacle

pedagogy *n* the science of teaching methods

pedant *n* a teacher who overemphasizes rules and trivialities; a person who makes a display of learning

pedicure *n* care of the toenails

pedigree *n* a list of ancestry; family tree

pedagogy *n* the study of children

PEN
punishment

impenitent *adj* not regretful for offenses (sins) committed

penance *n* voluntary suffering for wrongdoing

penitence *n* regret for on offense committed

repent *v* to regret having done or not done some act

PEND, PENS, POND
hand, weigh

append *v* to add to; to supplement

compendium *n* an abridged form of a work containing its general principles

counterpoise *n* a weight that influences or offsets another

dispensation *n* a release from an obligation or burden

equipoise *n* equal distribution of weight; balance; equilibrium

impending *adj* looming; hanging over

pendant *n* a hanging object, especially jewelry

pendency *n* state of indecision or lack of finality

pendent *adj* hanging

pendulate *v* to swing; undulate

pendulous *adj* hanging freely; drooping

pensive *adj* thinking deeply (heavily)

ponderous *adj* bulky; very heavy; weighty

propensity *n* natural tendency, inclination, or bent

recompense *v* to compensate or make payment

stipend *n* an allowance or periodic payment for services

PHAN
show

diaphanous *adj* see-through, especially a fabric

epiphany *n* an appearance or apparition of a supernatural being

sycophant *n* one who seeks favoritism through flattering influential people

PHIL
love

audiophile *n* one who loves audio (musical) recordings and equipment

philanderer *n* a male flirt (engaging in brief affairs)

philanthropist *n* a lover of humanity; benefactor

philatelist *n* a stamp collector (lover of stamps)

philharmonic *adj* fond of music

philogeant *n* a lover of all good things

philologist *n* a scholar, student, or lover of languages

philomuse *n* a lover of poetry

PLA
please

complaisant *adj* desiring to please; gracious; affable

implacable *adj* not capable of being pleased or appeased

placate *v* to pacify, appease, or conciliate

placebo *n* a useless medicine used to gratify, soothe, or conciliate

placid *adj* serene; calm

PLE
full, plenty

complement *n* the full amount

expletive *n* something not needed

implement *v* to fulfill

plenary *adj* attended by all members (of a group)

plenitude *n* fullness; completeness

plethora *n* overabundance

replete *adj* having a plentiful supply; filled; abundant

PLI, PLE
fold

deploy *v* to spread out (unfold)

explicate *v* to make clear (unfold) the meaning of

exploit *v* to make use of for one's own advantage (also, an action or deed)

implicate *v* to entangle (enfold)

perplex *v* to twist or confuse

pliant *adj* easily folded, shaped, or influenced

plicate *adj* folded into pleats

ply *adj* layered; *v* to busy oneself with a task

replicate *v* to repeat; to fold as a leaf

suppliant *adj* pleading; entreating; beseeching

supplicate *v* to seek by earnest prayer; entreat; beseech; plead

POS, POT
able, powerful

plenipotentiary *adj* having full power or authority

posse *n* an armed band (group) having force and authority

potentate *n* one who possesses great power

prepotent *adj* having superior power of influence

puissant *adj* powerful, forceful—especially in poetry

PREC
pray, esteem, value

deprecate *v* to express strong disapproval or low esteem

imprecate *v* to invoke a curse; to pray or wish for misfortune upon another

precarious *adj* uncertain; dependent upon contingencies or circumstances

PREH
seize

apprehend *v* to seize or capture

comprehend *v* to understand

PRESS
press

imprimatur *n* sanction; approval (especially to print or publish)

oppress *v* to lie heavily upon; to keep down by force

repress *v* to put down; subdue; prevent natural development

reprimand *v* to scold or reprove severely

PROB, PROV
prove, like

approbation *n* approval
probate *v* in law, to prove the validity of a
  will
probative *adj* useful in proving
probity *n* integrity; honesty
reprobate *adj* vicious; unprincipled;
  depraved
reprove *v* to blame; censure

PROP
near

propinquity *n* nearness of relationship;
  affinity
propitiate *v* to win favor with; appease
proximate *adj* nearest (next to) in space or
  time
reproach *v* to rebuke, reprove, or blame

PROPR
one's own

appropriate *v* to acquire for oneself
expropriate *v* to take private land for
  public use
proprietary *adj* belonging exclusively to or
  owned exclusively by
propriety *n* proper or conforming behavior

PUG
fight

impugn *v* to challenge; contradict; refute;
  gainsay
oppugn *v* to reason or argue against; to
  dispute
pugilism *n* the art of hand-to-hand fighting;
  boxing
pugnacious *adj* quarrelsome

repugnant *adj* highly distasteful; inclined
  to oppose

PUNC, PUNG
point, prick

compunction *n* regret for wrong doing
  (twinge of conscience)
expunge *v* to delete; obliterate
poignant *adj* a piercing, pointed (as an idea
  or feeling)
punctate *adj* marked with points or dots
pungent *adj* sharp in taste or smell; acidic

PUR
cleanse

expurgate *v* to remove objectionable matter
purge *v* to cleanse by carrying (washing)
  away impurities

PUT
think, calculate

impute *adj* ascribe or attribute to another—
  especially, a fault
putative *adj* commonly thought; supposed;
  reputed
reputed *n* thought of; esteemed

QUES, QUIR
seek, gain

inquest *n* a formal (judicial) inquiry
inquisition *n* an official (legal or religious)
  investigation; inquest
perquisite *n* a benefit to which one is
  entitled by way of one's stature or position
query *v* to question or inquire
quest *n* the act of seeking
requisite *adj* inherently required or
  necessary

QUIE
quiet

acquiesce *v* to comply with or assent to passively, by one's lack of objection
coy *adj* pretending to be shy
quell *v* to suppress or quiet
quiescent *adj* calm; serene; peaceful
requiem *n* a musical service for the dead

RAP, RAV
sieze

rapture *n* great pleasure
ravage *v* to devastate
ravish *v* to seize by force; to carry away with emotion
surreptitious *adj* clandestine; done secretively

REG, RECT
rule

rectify *v* to make right
rectitude *n* conduct according to moral principles
regale *v* to entertain
regalia *n* the symbols and trappings of monarchy and nobility
regent *n* a ruler
regime *n* a system of government; the administration of a specific leader

RID, RIS
laugh

deride *v* to scorn or make fun of; laugh at in contempt (*n* derision)
ridicule *v* to make fun of; mock
risible *adj* laughable; ludicrous

ROG, ROGA
ask, beg

interrogate *v* to question
interrogatory *n* a formal (written) question
prerogative *n* privilege; superiority (above being questioned)

SACR, SECR
holy, sacred

consecrate *v* to declare to be sacred
desecrate *v* to commit sacrilege
sacrament *n* a solemn ceremonial oath
sacrilege *n* disrespect for or violation of sacred ideas or objects
sacrosanct *adj* very holy

SAL
healthy, safe

salubrious *adj* healthful
salutary *adj* promoting a beneficial purpose; wholesome
salve *v* to soothe; assuage

SAL, SULT, SIL
leap

assail *v* to leap upon violently
desultory *adj* passing randomly from one thing to another; aimless; rambling
dissilient *adj* bursting apart
exult *v* to rejoice greatly
resilient *adj* recovering quickly
salacious *adj* lustful; lecherous
salient *adj* standing out from the rest
transilient *adj* leaping from one thing to another

SANCT
holy

sanctify *v* to make holy
sanctimonious *adj* saintly; pretending to be holy; pious
sanction *v* to approve, authorize, or order

SANGUI
blood

consanguinity *n* relationship by blood
sanguine *adj* hopeful; confident; ardent
sanguineous *adj* containing blood; bloodthirsty

SAP, SIP
taste

insipid *adj* tasteless; dull (unexciting)
sapient *adj* having good taste; discerning
unsavory *adj* having an unpleasant taste or smell

SAT
enough

insatiable *adj* incapable of being fully satisfied
sate *or* **satiate** *v* to satisfy fully
saturate *v* to fill (soak) thoroughly

SCI
know

prescience *n* foreknowledge
unconscionable *adj* unscrupulous; characterized by a lack of conscience

SENS, SENT
feel

assent *v* to agree to
sententious *adj* pithy in expression; trite

sentient *adj* capable of perception; conscious
sentinel *or* sentry *n* a guard

SEQ, SEC
follow

obsequious *adj* excessively obedient or servile
sequacious *adj* following with smooth or logical regularity
ensue *v* to follow as a consequence
sequel *n* that which follows

SERV
serve

disservice *n* harm or injury
serf *n* an oppressed person; slave
servile *adj* slavelike
servitude *n* slavery

SES, SED, SID
sit

assiduous *adj* diligent; industrious
insidious *adj* wily; crafty; sly; treacherous
preside *v* to have control or authority
presidio *n* a military administrative fortification; garrison
sedate *adj* calm; serene
sedentary *adj* staying in one place; inactive
sedimentary *adj* settling to the bottom (especially, of a body of water)
sedulous *adj* diligent; persevering

SIGN
mark, sign, seal

ensign *n* a flag or banner
insignia *n* a mark or sign to identify or distinguish something

signatory *adj* having signed or joined in the signing of a document

signet *n* a sign or seal indicating authority

SIM, SEMB
like, resembling

assimilate *v* to make alike; incorporate; absorb

dissemble *v* to hide under false appearance

dissimulate *v* to pretend to be the opposite of

semblance *n* having the appearance of something else

similitude *n* resemblance

verisimilitude *adj* having the appearance of truth

SOLV
solve, loosen

absolve *v* to release from an obligation; to free from blame

dissolute *adj* loose in morals or behavior

insolvent *adj* bankrupt

resolute *adj* unwavering; determined

resolve *n* determination made, especially to solve a problem; *v* to determine to do something by will

solvent *n* any substance that dissolves

SON
sound, noise

assonance *n* similarity in sound (especially in vowels during speech)

consonance *n* pleasing, agreeable sound (especially music)

dissonant *adj* inharmonious

resonate *v* to prolong sound by vibration of ambient objects

resound *v* to reverberate

sonorous *adj* full, rich, and deep (sound)

SOPH
wisdom

sophist *n* one who reasons falsely; a teacher of philosophy

sophomoric *adj* immature

SPEC, SPECT, SPIC
see, look at

auspice *n* a prophetic sign; omen

auspicious *adj* having a favorable (successful) appearance

circumspect *adj* cautious; wary; watchful

perspicacious *adj* having clear judgment and understanding

perspicuous *adj* easily understood; clearly stated

prospectus *n* a brief description of a business plan or investment

specious *adj* appearing genuine but actually not; deceptive

specter *n* fear; an apparition or ghost

spectral *adj* ghostlike

SRIB, SCRIPT
write

ascribe *v* to attribute or refer to

conscript *v* to draft for military service

prescribe *v* to establish (by writing) a rule

proscribe *v* to forbid; prohibit

scrivener *n* a public or official writer; scribe

transcribe *v* to reduce spoken expression to writing

STA, STIT, SIST, STET
stand

desist *v* to cease; quit; stop

obstinate *adj* stubborn; standing against

stamina *n* endurance; power to withstand

stanchion *n* an upright support or prop
subsist *v* to stay alive by a specific means

STRI
bind

astringent *adj* causing to shrink or contract
stricture *n* a constraint; limitation
stringent *adj* strict

SUAD
sway

assuage *v* to pacify; lessen another's distress
dissuade *v* to turn another away from by providing convincing reasons; discourage

TACT, TANG, TIG, TAG, TING
touch

contagion *n* communicability (transmission) of a disease or idea
contiguous *adj* meeting or joining
contingent *adj* depending upon circumstances
tact *n* a sense for what is appropriate
tactile *adj* pertaining to the sense of touch
tangent *adj* touching (especially, a straight line touching a circle)
tangible *adj* capable of being felt, touched, or understood

TEMP
time, temper

extemporaneous *adj* improvised; without preparation; spontaneous; impromptu
intemperance *n* excess of any kind
temper *v* to make suitable for a purpose
temperance *n* moderation in behavior
tempest *n* a violent storm; tumult

TEN, TENT, TAIN, TINU
hold, hold together, belong to

appurtenant *adj* belonging to
continence *n* restraint; holding back one's passions and desires
impertinent *adj* inappropriate; rude; insolent
pertinacious *adj* exhibiting unyielding purpose; tenacious
pertinent *adj* relevant; to the point; appropriate
retentive *adj* having a good memory; able to retain or hold
tenable *adj* capable of being held together or defended
tenacious *adj* holding fast or firmly; unwavering
tenet *n* an opinion or principle which binds together a group of people; doctrine; dogma
tenure *n* the right to hold a position or office

TEND, TENS, TENT
stretch, strain

distend *v* to spread, enlarge, or expand
ostensible *adj* apparent; evident
ostentatious *adj* boastful; pretentious; showy
portend *v* to provide a warning or omen
tensile *adj* capable of being stretched

TERR
earth

disinter *v* to unearth
subterranean *adj* underground
terrestrial *adj* pertaining to the earth

TOR
twist, pain

contort *v* to twist out of shape; distort
extort *v* to wring from by force or threat
retort *n* a response to an argument
torque *n* a force that produces a twisting or rotating motion
torsion *n* twisting
tort *n* in law, a non-criminal wrongful act
tortuous *adj* twisting; curving

TRACT, TRAG
pull, draw

detract *v* to draw away from
intractable *adj* hard to handle; unmanageable
protracted *adj* drawn out; prolonged
tractile *adj* capable of being stretched
traction *n* pulling or hauling

TRUD
push, thrust

detrude *v* to thrust down
obtrusive *adj* imposing on; interfering

TUM, TUR
turmoil

perturbed *adj* thrown into disorder
turbid *adj* cloudy; confused
turbulent *adj* tumultuous; disorderly
turmoil *n* a disturbance; commotion; confusion

UND
wave, flow

abundant *v* to possess in great quantity
inundate *v* to deluge; overflow

redundant *adj* repetitious; superfluous
undulate *v* to move up and down or from one side to the other

VAG
wandering

vagary *n* odd or unexpected conduct; whim; caprice
vagrant *n* one who wanders the streets idly

VAL
strength, worth, valor

convalesce *v* to regain strength by resting
countervail *v* to use equal force against
prevail *v* to win or survive by virtue of one's strength
valiant *adj* brave; honorable
valor *n* bravery; courage

VEN
come

adventitious *adj* accidental; by chance
circumvent *v* to go around something
contravene *v* to oppose or violate an agreement or ruling
convene *v* to assemble; come together
intervene *v* to come between

VENG, VIND
avenge

avenge *v* to gain revenge by punishing the injuring party
vengeance *n* return of an injury for an injury
vindicate *v* to clear from criticism or blame by evidence
vindictive *adj* revengeful in spirit

VER
true

veracious *adj* truthful
veracity *n* truthfulness
verisimilar *adj* probable; having the appearance of truth
veritable *adj* genuine; truly

VERB
word

verbiage *n* wordiness
verbose *adj* wordy
verve *n* energy and enthusiasm (especially in expression)

VERS, VERT
turn

advert *v* to turn one's mind to
averse *adj* disliking; unwilling; turning away from
avert *v* to turn from; avoid
conversant *adj* understanding a subject fully
inadvertent *adj* accidentally
obverse *adj* turned toward the viewer
retroverted *adj* turned or tilted backwards
vertex *n* top, summit; apex
vortex *n* a whirling mass of water or air

VIA
way

convoy *n* an escort for protection
envoy *n* a representative of a government who transacts business with another government
obviate *v* to avoid by preventive measures; make unnecessary
pervious *adj* penetrable; permeable; open to influence
viaduct *n* an arched roadway

VIC
substitute, change

vicarious *adj* substituted for another; in place of
vicissitude *n* a change in fortune

VID, VIS
see

providence *n* divine guidance; luck; opportunity
visage *n* face; expression; countenance
vista *n* the view from a distance (especially of a landscape)

VINCE, VICT
conquer

evince *v* to show or convince in a clear manner
vanquish *v* to defeat or conquer; subdue
evincible *adj* capable of being conquered

VIV
life

convivial *adj* sociable; jovial
viable *adj* able to live or thrive
vivacious *adj* lively; energetic; spirited
vivarium *n* a place where plants or animals are kept alive by simulating their natural environment
vivify *v* to animate
viviparous *adj* bringing forth living young

VOC, VOK
call

avocation *n* minor occupation (calling); hobby
avow *v* to acknowledge; declare openly
convoke *v* to summon (call) together for an assembly or meeting

equivocate *v* to express an idea opinion indecisively or ambiguously

evocative *adj* causing to recall the past

evoke *v* to call up from the past

invoke *v* to call on (a divine being) for assistance or inspiration; plead; supplicate

provoke *v* to rouse to anger; arouse; irritate

vociferous *adj* crying out; clamorous

vouch *v* to affirm; to give evidence or testimony in support of

VOL
wish

benevolent *adj* well-wishing; kind

malevolent *adj* wishing evil on another person; ill-wishing

volition *n* exercise of the will

VULG
publish, people

divulge *v* to make public

promulgate *v* to publish or disseminate widely

vulgar *adj* common to the masses; unrefined

VULS
tear out

avulse *v* to pluck or pull off

convulsion *n* shaking from grief, rage, or laughter

divulsion *n* a tearing apart

revulsion *n* a violent reaction away from

Testworthy **Words** (The A–Z List)

If time is running out and you need to learn as many words as you can as quickly as possible, Chapter 7 is the place to do it. Here you'll find 285 of the most testworthy words, each one accompanied by its phonetic spelling, part of speech, brief definition, and helpful list of **similar words** (synonyms) and **contrary words** (antonyms).

Most of the words in Chapter 7 (including headwords, synonyms, and antonyms) appear elsewhere in the book in other contexts, so you will have plenty of opportunity to review all of the new words you are learning and fix them firmly in your memory. You can also use the **review quizzes** scattered throughout this chapter to see how well you're doing.

A–C

ABUT (uh BUT) *v.* to border upon; adjoin
similar: contiguous; tangent; adjacent; append; annex; nexus

ACUITY (uh KYOO ih tee) *n.* keenness; sharpness (as in perception
similar: perspicacity; astuteness; discernment; acumen

ADDLE (AD ul) *v.* to confuse, muddle, or bewilder, so as to annoy or irritate
similar: befuddle; perturb; obfuscate; confound; perplex; stupefy; pester
contrary: clarify; elucidate; explicate

ADEPT (uh DEPT) *adj.* skillful; competent
similar: proficient; able; adroit; deft
contrary: incompetent; loutish; inept

ADHERENT (ad HEER unt) *n.* follower; supporter; believer
similar: proselyte; disciple; apostle
contrary: antagonist; adversary; rival

AEGIS (EE jis) *n.* a shield or defense

ALLAY (uh LAY) *v.* to calm or pacify
similar: appease; assuage; abate; mitigate
contrary: aggravate; provoke; exacerbate; vex; affront; chafe; embitter; envenom

ANCILLARY (AN suh layr ee) *adj.* pertaining or connected to something but not part of it
similar: auxiliary; peripheral; marginal; tangential; ambient; extrinsic
contrary: primary; nuclear; chief; capital; cardinal; axial; definitive; incisive; fundamental; primary; ordinate; axiomatic

ANTAGONISTIC (an TAG uh nis tik) *adj.* opposed to; hostile
similar: contentious; combative; adverse; contrary; belligerent; pugnacious; bellicose
contrary: amiable; amicable; allied; sympathetic; congenial

APERTURE (AP er cher) *n.* an opening or gap (as in the aperture setting of a camera)
similar: orifice; breach; fissure; chasm

APLOMB (uh PLAHM) *n.* poise; composure
  similar: assurance; intrepidity; impassivity; unflappability; imperturbability
  contrary: intemperance; irascibility; petulance

APOTHEGM (APP uh them) *n.* a short, pithy, instructive saying
  similar: aphorism; epigram; maxim; adage; proverb; axiom

ASYLUM (uh SY lum) *n.* a refuge or sanctuary (especially, for criminals or the insane)
  similar: haven; sanitarium

AVARICE (AV er is) *n.* greed
  similar: cupidity; avidity; covetousness; parsimony
  contrary: philanthropy; charity; benevolence; munificence; beneficence; altruism

AWRY (uh RY) *adj.* twisted; gone wrong (as in plans that went awry)
  similar: amiss; astray; afield; askew; aslant; tortuous; serpentine; convoluted; vermicular
  contrary: true; assiduous; undeviating

BALK (BAWK) *v.* to stop short; refuse to continue
  similar: demur; spurn; shun; desist; halt; falter; stammer; suspend
  contrary: advance; proceed; persevere; persist; endure; pertinacious; dogged; indefatigable

BATE (BAYT) *v.* to moderate or restrain; hold back (as in bated breath)
  similar: impede; bridle; abate; repress; quell; quash; suppress; curb
  contrary: unfetter; emancipate; manumit; discharge; extricate

BAUBLE (BAW bul) *n.* a trinket
  similar: trifle; toy; triviality; memento; souvenir

BEHEMOTH (buh HEE mith) *n.* a huge creature
  similar: leviathan; mammoth; gargantuan; prodigious; titanic; colossal; vast
  contrary: dwarf; mannequin; pygmy; diminutive; bantam; lilliputian; minutia

BEREAVED (buh REEVED) *adj.* the state of having lost something cherished or valuable (as in the death of a family member)
  similar: bereft; deprived; denuded; forfeited

BILK (BILK) *v.* to deceive; defraud
  similar: dupe; swindle; beguile; delude; cozen; feign

BLAZON (BLAY zun) *v.* to proclaim or announce publicly or conspicuously
similar: herald; publicize; divulge; promulgate; publish; flaunt

BOISTEROUS (BOY ster us) *adj.* loud, rough, or violent
similar: clamorous; tumultuous; obstreperous; rambunctious; riotous; turbulent
contrary: sedate; staid; reconciled; subdued; placid; tranquil

BOVINE (BOH vyn) *adj.* cowlike; dull or inactive
similar: inert; loutish; slothful; torpid; indolent; languid; phlegmatic; listless
contrary: astir; exuberant; animated; vivacious; effervescent; ebullient

BRUSQUE (BRUSK) *adj.* abrupt or blunt in speech
similar: curt; bluff; crude; frank; boorish; sententious; terse
contrary: tactful; suave; glib

BUCOLIC (byoo KAHL ik) *adj.* rustic; pastoral
similar: idyllic; halcyon; provincial; agrarian; campestral; bucolic; georgic

BUNGLE (BUNG gul) *v.* to mishandle; botch up; make a bad mistake
similar: blunder; bollix; spoil; ruin; impair
contrary: ameliorate; rectify; finesse

CALIBER (KAL ih ber) *adj.* degree of quality, competence, or merit
similar: import; consequence; esteem; notoriety; gravity

CALLOUS (KAL us) *adj.* insensitive; unfeeling
similar: obdurate; indurate
contrary: humane; clement; beneficent; commiserating; benevolent

CANARD (kuh NARD) *n.* a rumor or false report
similar: hoax; gossip; hearsay; scandal; calumny

CANDID (CAN did) *adj.* sincere and forthright
similar: frank; ingenuous; guileless; earnest; fervent
contrary: hypocritical; sanctimonious; ingenuous; equivocal; mendacious; devious

CARDINAL (KAR dih nul) *adj.* chief; most important; primary
similar: capital; principal; pivotal; axial
contrary: subordinate; subsidiary; subservient; auxiliary; ancillary; negligible

CAUTERIZE (KAH ter yz) *v.* to burn with a hot iron or with fire, usually to cure or heal
    similar: sear; char; singe; scorch; brand; scald; parch

CAVIL (KAV ul) *v.* to raise irritating and trivial objections
    similar: quibble; carp; gripe; snivel; bewail

CLOY (KLOY) *v.* to weary by excess or overindulgence, especially of pleasure
    similar: glut; surfeit; satiate; superfluity; plethora

COMPORT (kum PORT) *v.* to behave; to conform oneself
    similar: comply; accord; acquiesce
    contrary: transgress; trespass; balk

CORNUCOPIA (kor nyoo KOH pee uh) *n.* abundance; plenty
    similar: plenitude; bounty; copiousness; profusion; affluence
    contrary: paucity; dearth; scarcity; want

COTERIE (KOH tuh ree) *n.* a close-knit group of people with common interests
    similar: clique; cadre; clan; cabal; retinue

Quiz Time (A–C)

Directions: Match each numbered word in the left column with its lettered definition in the right column. The answer key begins on page 237.

1.	addle	a.	behave or conform
2.	allay	b.	calm or pacify
3.	aperture	c.	confuse or bewilder
4.	aplomb	d.	gone wrong
5.	awry	e.	opening or gap
6.	bate	f.	poise or composure
7.	blazon	g.	proclaim publicly
8.	bucolic	h.	raise trivial objections
9.	cavil	i.	restrain or hold back
10.	cloy	j.	rustic or pastoral
11.	comport	k.	weary by overindulgence
12.	coterie	l.	clique

D–F

DAPPER (DAP er) *adj.* neat; trim
  similar: spruce; smart; natty; fastidious
  contrary: disheveled; unkempt; tousled; slovenly; rumpled; disarrayed; tatterdemalion

DEBONAIR (deh boh NAYR) *adj.* courteous; charming; having pleasant manners
  similar: dashing; ambrosial; rakish; genteel; gallant; urbane; amiable; complaisant
  contrary: impudent; impertinent; insolent; flippant; churlish; boorish; unceremonious

DEFT (DEFT) *adj.* proficient; skilled; competent
  similar: adroit; adept; dexterous
  contrary: maladroit; inept; gauche

DEPLETE (dee PLEET) *v.* to use up entirely; to empty
  similar: exhaust; dissipate; expend

DICTUM (DIK tum) *n.* an authoritative pronouncement, as from a judge
  similar: proclamation; edict; decree; order; behest; dictate; prescription; injunction; canon; mandate

DITHER (DIH ther) *n.* great excitement; agitation or trembling
  similar: commotion; frenzy; tumult; clamor; turbulence; ado; perturbation
  contrary: tranquillity; armistice

DOLT (DOLT) *n.* a stupid person
  similar: imbecile; simpleton; moron; ignoramus; dullard
  contrary: prodigy; genius; savant; virtuoso; sage; paragon

DOUR (DOW er) *adj.* sullen; gloomy
  similar: morose; somber; doleful; melancholy; lugubrious; saturnine
  contrary: blithe; jovial; jocund; insouciant; jaunty; roseate; sanguine

DROSS (DRAHS) *n.* waste matter; refuse
  similar: dregs; debris; rubble; jetsam; flotsam; excrement; remnant; vestige

EFFETE (eh FEET) *adj.* no longer able to bear young; worn out or exhausted.
  similar: sterile; infertile; barren
  contrary: fertile; fecund; prolific

EMACIATED (ee MAY shee ay tid) *adj.* withered, thin, or wasted
    similar: gaunt; haggard; degenerated; atrophied; wan; peaked; ashen; feeble; enervated
    contrary: robust; hardy; hale; brawny; stalwart

EMANATING (EM uh nay ting) *adj.* flowing from; issuing from
    similar: emitting; effusing; effluent; superfluent; prolix; prolific
    contrary: viscous; glutinous; mucilaginous

EMBROIL (em BROYL) *v.* to involve someone else in a dispute
    similar: entangle; enmesh; implicate; embattle; entrap
    contrary: extricate; exculpate; exonerate; absolve; dissociate; sunder

EMOLLIENT (ih MAHL ee unt) *n.* a softening ointment or other agent (*adj* having the ability to soften or relax living tissues)
    similar: unguent; salve; balm; liniment; cerate; unction; slacken; pliant; supple; malleable
    contrary: callous; frangible; congealable; calcifying; ossifying; petrifying; fossilizing

EMOLUMENT (ih MAWL yuh munt) *n.* salary or other compensation for employment
    similar: (earned) remuneration; stipend; honorarium; recompense
    contrary: (gifts) perquisite; gratuity; largess

EMULATE (EM uh nayt) *v.* to imitate in order to equal or surpass
    similar: model; mimic; simulate; ape; parrot; impersonate
    contrary (imitate to criticize or make fun of): mock; parody; satirize

ENTHRALL (en THRAWL) *v.* to captivate; hold under a spell; fascinate
    similar: mesmerize; bewitch; stupefy; enamor; enrapture; enchant; engross

EQUESTRIAN (eh KWES tree un) *n.* a rider on horseback (*adj* pertaining to horseback riding)
    similar: jockey; cavalry; dragoon
    contrary: pedestrian; afoot

ESPRIT (eh SPREE) *n.* sprightliness of spirit or wit
    similar: enthusiasm; vitality; morale; energy; verve; vim; vigor; zest; zeal; ebullience

EXEMPLARY (eg ZEMP luh ree) *adj.* outstanding; suitable as a model (either good or bad)
    similar: ideal; consummate; paragon; archetypal; quintessential; epitome; egregious; extant

EXHORT (eg ZORT) *v.* to urge by words; to caution or advise strongly
    similar: admonish; spur; incite; counsel; entreat; beseech; implore; induce

EXORBITANT (eg ZOR buh dent) *adj.* excessive; extravagant
    similar: inordinate; immoderate; plethoric; lavish; superfluous; turgid
    contrary: insufficient; wanting; bereft; depleted

EXTOL (ek STOHL) *v.* to praise
    similar: laud; commend; acclaim; hail; eulogize; panegyrize; esteem; venerate; adulate; revere
    contrary: inveigh; censure; fulminate

EXUBERANT (eg ZOO ber unt) *adj.* excited; enthusiastic
    similar: astir; animated; vivacious; effervescent; ebullient; reveling; frolicsome
    contrary: inert; loutish; slothful; torpid; indolent; languid; phlegmatic; listless

FACILITATE (fuh SIL uh tayt) *v.* to make easier (less difficult)
    similar: assist; expedite; further; succor; dispatch; precipitate
    contrary: impede; hamper; hinder; arrest

FATHOM (FATH um) *v.* to understand thoroughly; literally, to reach the bottom of something
    similar: discern; conceive; assimilate

FETID (FEH tid) *adj.* having an offensive smell
    similar: malodorous; putrid; noisome; rank; noxious; mephitic
    contrary: aromatic; odoriferous; redolent; fragrant

FETTER (FEH ter) *v.* to bind; chain
    similar: bridle; muzzle; lash; encumber; adjure; manacle; batten; gird; fob; indenture; enslave
    contrary: unfetter; emancipate; disencumber; extricate; exculpate; manumit

FILCH (FILCH) *v.* to steal
    similar: pilfer; purloin; misappropriate; abscond; peculate; embezzle

FLEDGLING (FLEJ leeng) *adj.* inexperienced (literally, a young bird)
similar: neophyte; novice; apprentice; proselyte; callow; green
contrary: seasoned; veteran

FLIPPANT (FLIP unt) *adj.* disrespectful; rude
similar: impertinent; impudent; insolent; audacious; impudent; churlish; unceremonious
contrary: debonair; chivalrous; duteous

FLOUT (FLOWT) *v.* to show disrespect
similar: mock; jeer; affront; snub; disdain; scorn; gibe
contrary: laud; hail; eulogize; panegyrize; venerate; defer

FLUX (FLUKS) *n.* a continuous moving on or passing by; constant succession or change
similar: instability; transmutation; metamorphosis; transfiguration; influx; efflux
contrary: stagnancy; stationary; inert; dormancy; stasis

FOIBLE (FOY bul) *n.* a small character weakness
similar: frailty; flaw

FOIST (FOYST) *v.* to force upon or impose upon fraudulently
similar: palm; swindle; dupe; chicane

Quiz Time (D–F)

Directions: Match each numbered word in the left column with its lettered definition in the right column. The answer key begins on page 237.

1.	debonair	a.	authoritative pronouncement
2.	deft	b.	bind or chain
3.	dictum	c.	captivate or fascinate
4.	dross	d.	courteous or charming
5.	effete	e.	disrespectful
6.	emollient	f.	no longer able to bear young
7.	enthrall	g.	proficient or skilled
8.	esprit	h.	small character weakness
9.	fathom	i.	softening agent
10.	fetter	j.	spirited
11.	flippant	k.	understand thoroughly
12.	foible	l.	waste matter

G–I

GAFFE (GAF) *n.* a social blunder
    similar: oversight; bungle; tactlessness; maladroitness; peccadillo

GALL (GAWL) *n.* bitterness; nerve (*v.* annoy)
    similar: effrontery; temerity; insolence; audacity; brashness; impertinence

GAMBIT (GAM bit) *n.* any move by which one seeks to gain an advantage; an opening move in chess in which a piece is sacrificed
    similar: stratagem; coven; machination; ruse; tactic; ploy; chicanery; arbitrage; subterfuge; artifice

GAMUT (GAM it) *n.* entire range
    similar: spectrum; breadth; scope; purview; panoply

GARISH (GAYR ish) *adj.* gaudy; overly showy
    similar: meretricious; ostentatious; tawdry; pretentious; florid; baroque; unbecoming
    contrary: seemly; unadorned; unobtrusive

GARNER (GAR ner) *v.* to gather; store up; collect; accumulate
    similar: glean; amass; hoard; cumulate; agglomerate; accrue; compile; anthologize
    contrary: distribute; issue; parcel; disseminate; dispense

GESTICULATE (juh STIK yoo layt) *v.* to gesture or motion
    similar: beckon; signal; wave

GLOWER (GLOW er) *v.* to scowl or frown
    similar: grimace; glare; smirk

GLUTTONOUS (GLUT un us) *adj.* excessive (immoderate) in engaging in an activity, especially in the partaking of food and strong drink
    similar: intemperate; immoderate; veracious; surfeit; cloy
    contrary: abstemious; abstinent; abstentious; moderate; temperate

GNOME (NOHM) *n.* dwarf
    similar: elf; mannequin; pygmy; lilliputian; bantam; sylph; goblin; gremlin
    contrary: leviathan; mammoth; colossus

GRANDIOSE (GRAN dee ohs) *adj.* magnificent; splendid; showy
similar: flamboyant; majestic; resplendent; ostentatious

GROVEL (GRAH vul) *v.* to behave in a servile fashion (literally, to crawl on the ground)
similar: cower; wallow; fawn
contrary: condescend; deign; patronize

GUISE (GYZ) *n.* appearance
similar: countenance; mien; demeanor; facade; semblance

HACKNEYED (HAK need) *adj.* commonplace; trite; overused
similar: banal; insipid; prosaic

HAP (HAP) *n.* chance or luck
similar: fortuitousness; serendipity; happenstance; coincidence

HARASS (huh RAS) *v.* to annoy by accosting or attacking repeatedly
similar: badger; harry; heckle; abrade; irk; chafe; vex; perturb

HARP (HARP) *v.* to dwell on a subject to the point of being tiresome or annoying
similar: brood; ruminate; sulk; muse; deliberate

HEBETIC (hih BET ik) *adj.* dull; fatigued (*n.* hebetude)
similar: lethargic; torpid; listless; phlegmatic; languid
contrary: vivacious; effervescent; ebullient; zealous; ardent; fervent; fervid

HEDONIST (HEE dun ist) *n.* a seeker of pleasure
similar: epicurean; debauchee; sensualist; libertine

HEEDLESS (HEED lis) *adj.* careless; unmindful
similar: remiss; negligent; oblivious; reckless; slack; lax
contrary: circumspect; wakeful; wary; rapt; vigilant; punctilious

HERALD (HAYR uld) *v.* to announce or foretell
similar: proclaim; divulge; blazon; promulgate; foreshadow; portend; presage

HERMETIC (her MEH tik) *adj.* sealed to be airtight; mysterious
similar: impervious; impermeable; inscrutable; caulked
contrary: pervious; permeable; porous; pregnable

HETERODOX (HEH ter oh dahks) *adj.* unconventional; unorthodox
   similar: eccentric; maverick; deviant; nonconforming; contrary; idiosyncratic; outlandish
   contrary: generic; cognate; doctrinal; sanctioned; kosher; homogeneous

HEW (HYOO) *v.* to cut into pieces with an ax or sword
   similar: hack; rent; lacerate; cleave; dissever

HOARY (HOR ee) *adj.* having white hair; very old
   similar: grizzled; ancient; ripened; antique; decrepit; doddering
   contrary: callow; nubile; fledgling; puerile; pubescent; juvenile; green

HORARY (HOR er ee) *adj.* occurring once an hour; hourly
   similar: iterative; quotidian; tertian

IMBUE (im BYOO) *v.* to inspire; to impregnate, or fill (especially with a quality or characteristic)
   similar: inculcate; instill; indoctrinate; permeate; fortify; admonish; inspirit

IMPALE (im PAYL) *v.* to pierce (as with a sword)
   similar: skewer; lance; skiver; crucify; spike

IMPASSE (IM pass) *n.* a predicament from which there is no escape; a path with no outlet
   similar: dilemma; quandary; straight; plight; mire

IMPIOUS (IMP yuss) *adj.* irreverent (*n* impiety)
   similar: sacrilegious; blasphemous; flippant; impudent
   contrary: reverent; pious; respectful; courteous

IMPROVIDENT (im PROV uh dent) *adj.* wasteful; neglectful
   similar: imprudent; negligent; remiss; heedless; prodigal; profligate; inadvertent
   contrary: prudent; provident; politic; mindful; punctilious

INCONGRUOUS (in KAHN groo us) *adj.* out of place; lacking in harmony (among parts)
   similar: inconsonant; inapt; unfitting; aberrant; anachronistic; enigmatic
   contrary: consonant; befitting; seemly; harmonious

INCULCATE (IN kul kayt) *v.* to teach persistently and earnestly
   similar: indoctrinate; admonish; ingrain; infix; brainwash

INDELIBLE (in DEL uh bul) *adj.* incapable of being erased or eradicated
   similar: permanent; ineffaceable; ineradicable; immutable
   contrary: eradicable; temporary; revocable; evanescent; temporal

INELUCTABLE (in uh LUK tuh bul) *adj.* inevitable; inescapable; irresistible
   similar: ineludible; inevasible; inexorable

INSCRUTABLE (in SKROO tuh bul) *adj.* impenetrable; not readily understood; mysterious
   similar: impervious; impermeable; hermetic; enigmatic; cryptic; abstruse; recondite
   contrary: pervious; permeable; porous; pregnable; fathomable; ascertainable

INVETERATE (in VEH ter ut) *adj.* deep-rooted; longstanding
   similar: habitual; entrenched; ensconced; ingrained; inbred; innate

IOTA (y OH tuh) *n.* a very small quantity
   similar: shred; trace; fleck; scintilla

Quiz Time (G–I)

Directions: Match each numbered word in the left column with its lettered definition in the right column. The answer key begins on page 237.

1.	gaffe	a.	airtight
2.	garish	b.	appearance
3.	garner	c.	commonplace or trite
4.	guise	d.	deep-rooted
5.	hackneyed	e.	gather or collect
6.	hedonist	f.	gaudy
7.	hermetic	g.	having white hair
8.	hoary	h.	incapable of being erased
9.	imbue	i.	inspire or fill
10.	impale	j.	pierce
11.	indelible	k.	seeker of pleasure
12.	inveterate	l.	social blunder

J–L

JADED (JAY did) *adj.* fatigued; exhausted; weary
  similar: enervated; spent; cloyed; depleted
  contrary: invigorated; revitalized; enlivened

JAUNT (JAWNT) *n.* a leisurely trip
  similar: excursion; stroll; amble; saunter; promenade

JAUNTY (JAWN tee) *adj.* carefree; lighthearted
  similar: insouciant; jocund; jocose; jovial; blithe
  contrary: dour; sullen; morose; somber; doleful; melancholy; lugubrious; saturnine

JEER (JEER) *v.* to deride, taunt, or ridicule
  similar: sneer; flout; gibe; mock; affront; scorn

JEOPARDY (JEH per dee) *n.* exposure to danger or treachery
  similar: peril; risk; vulnerability
  contrary: invulnerability; impregnability; sanctuary; asylum; refuge; haven

JOCOSE (joh KOHS) *adj.* given to joking; playful; lighthearted
  similar: jocular; jocund; waggish; jovial; facetious; blithe; trifling; buoyant; halcyon
  contrary: somber; demure; staid; sedate; stern; grim; lugubrious; pensive; saturnine

JOSTLE (JAH sul) *v.* to shove or bump
  similar: jar; collide; jolt; impact; nudge; propel

JUBILANT (JOO buh lunt) *adj.* characterized by great joy; rejoicing; joyful (especially due to a triumph or other joyous event)
  similar: elated; exuberant; exultant; reveling; frolicsome

JUNCTURE (JUNG cher) *n.* an intersection; a crisis
  similar: crossroads; concourse; junction; confluence; bifurcation; exigency; dilemma; quandary

JUT (JUT) *v.* to extend out; protrude
  similar: extrude; distend; bloat; bastion; cantilever

KALEIDOSCOPE (kuh LY duh skohp) *n.* anything characterized by dazzling variety, complexity, or change
    similar: variegation; matrix; array; mosaic; aurora; chameleon; protean; mutation

KINDLE (KIN dul) *v.* to spark, inspire, or fuel
    similar: incite; impel; foment; spur

KNEAD (NEED) *v.* to massage or mix (especially, bread dough)
    similar: amalgamate; alloy

KNELL (NEL) *n.* the sound of a bell rung to signal or signify something (as in death knell)
    similar: tocsin; summons; proclamation

KNOLL (NOHL) *n.* a small, grassy hill
    similar: hummock; hillock; promontory; kame

KNURLED (NERLD) *adj.* knotty; gnarled
    similar: contorted; serpentine

KRAFT (KRAFT) *n.* strong paper (usually brown in color) used for making bags and for wrapping

LACKEY (LAK ee) *n.* a servile follower; yes-man; hanger-on
    similar: acolyte; toady; minion; entourage; retinue

LETHARGIC (luh THAR jik) *adj.* sluggish or inactive; indifferent
    similar: torpid; listless; languid; phlegmatic; apathetic
    contrary: vivacious; effervescent; ebullient; zealous; ardent; fervent; fervid

LIBELOUS (LY buh lus) *adj.* defamatory; slanderous
    similar: derogatory; opprobrious; calumnious; maligning; vilifying
    contrary: laudatory; acclamatory; commendatory; eulogistic; adulatory; edifying

LIBIDINOUS (lih BIH duh nus) *adj.* lustful
    similar: licentious; prurient; lecherous; salacious; lascivious

LICIT (LIH sit) *adj.* legal; lawful; permitted
    similar: sanctioned; legitimate; mandated; decreed; warranted; empowered; ratified
    contrary: illicit; nefarious; spurious; interdicted; contraband; taboo

LINEAMENTS (LIN ee uh mins) *n.* features (especially, facial features)
  similar: visage; countenance; physiognomy; profile; guise

LIONIZE (LY uh nyz) *v.* to treat as a celebrity
  similar: exalt; revere; venerate; idolize; dote; esteem

LISSOME (LIH sum) *adj.* limber or pliable (see lithe, below)

LITHE (LYTH) *adj.* flexible; supple
  similar: pliable; pliant; lissome; compliant; resilient; malleable; ductile
  contrary: inelastic; frangible; intractable; refractory; implacable

LOITER (LOY ter) *v.* to linger or "hang around"
  similar: tarry; dally; sojourn; abide; dawdle; lag; loll
  contrary: dispatch; scurry; advance

LOPE (LOHP) *v.* to run slowly (especially, as a horse)
  similar: canter; jog; trot; saunter; amble
  contrary: gallop; sprint; scurry; hasten

LOUT (LOWT) *n.* a clumsy or stupid person
  similar: boor; oaf; maladroit; bungler

LUMBER (LUM ber) *v.* to move heavily or clumsily
  similar: trudge; plod; march; drudge

Quiz Time (J–L)

Directions: Match each numbered word in the left column with its lettered definition in the right column. The answer key begins on page 237.

1.	jaded	a.	carefree
2.	jaunty	b.	clumsy or stupid
3.	juncture	c.	dazzling variety
4.	kaleidoscope	d.	defamatory or slanderous
5.	knell	e.	exhausted
6.	knurled	f.	facial features
7.	lackey	g.	intersection
8.	libelous	h.	knotty
9.	lineaments	i.	limber or pliable
10.	lissome	j.	linger or hang around
11.	loiter	k.	servile follower
12.	lout	l.	sound of a bell rung as a signal

M–O

MAIM (MAYM) *v.* to mutilate or injury severely
  similar: mangle; deface; dismember

MANUMIT (man yuh MIT) *v.* to release from slavery or servitude; emancipate
  similar: liberate; discharge; unfetter; disencumber; exculpate; extricate; disenthrall
  contrary: enslave; indenture; fetter; bridle; muzzle; lash; encumber; manacle; adjure

MASOCHISM (MAS uh kiz um) *n.* intentional infliction of pain on oneself
  contrary: sadism

MENDACITY (men DAS ih tee) *n.* deceit; fraud (*adj.* mendacious)
  similar: chicanery; duplicity; disingenuousness; guile; artifice; sham; ruse
  contrary: candor; rectitude; probity; forthrightness; frankness; ingenuousness; guileless; earnestness

MEPHITIC (muh FIT ik) *adj.* offensive to the smell; noxious or poisonous
  similar: fetid; malodorous; putrid; noisome; rank; deleterious
  contrary: aromatic; odoriferous; redolent; fragrant; salubrious; salutary

METE (MEET) *v.* to measure; to distribute (as in mete out rations)
similar: allot; parcel; allocate; apportion; ration; divvy; dole; dispense; issue

METTLE (MET ul) *n.* character of a person
similar: constitution; spirit; composition; fabric

MIEN (MEEN) *n.* demeanor, appearance, or character
similar: air; comportment; mettle

MINION (MIN yun) *n.* a servile dependent; a servant or slave
similar: lackey; acolyte; proselyte; hireling; deputy; subordinate; peon; ensign

MISCONSTRUE (mis kun STROO) *v.* to misunderstand or misinterpret
similar: distort; pervert; err
contrary: discern; fathom; conceive; assimilate

MOLLIFY (MAH lih fy) *v.* to pacify, placate, or appease
similar: allay; ease; alleviate; assuage
contrary: vex; perturb; peeve; irk; chafe; abrade; exasperate

MOTILE (MOH tul) *adj.* capable of moving spontaneously
similar: ambulatory; mobile; transportable; migratory; transient
contrary: stationary; dormant; static; anchored; inert; sluggish; phlegmatic; entrenched; ingrained

MOTLEY (MAHT lee) *adj.* consisting of many colors; composed of many elements
similar: variegated; dappled; polychromatic; kaleidoscopic; psychedelic; prismatic; heterogeneous; sundry; commingled; multiform; manifold
contrary: monochromatic; homogenous; uniform; monolithic

MULCT (MULKT) *v.* to punish by fine or forfeiture; to deprive another of possession by fraud
similar: penalize; amerce; exact; sanction; confiscate; expropriate

MYRIAD (MEER ee ad) *n.* a great (large) number
similar: legion; multitude

NATTY (NAT ee) *adj.* neatly or smartly dressed
similar: dapper; chic; spruce; smart; foppish; fastidious
contrary: disheveled; slovenly; unkempt; tatterdemalion

NECROMANCY (NEK ruh mun see) *n.* magic that involves the dead
  similar: witchcraft; sorcery; sortilege; wizardry; thaumaturgy; shamanism; conjuration; occultism; alchemy; legerdemain

NEMESIS (NEM uh sis) *n.* an agent or act of punishment or retribution
  similar: vindication; vengeance; revenge; retaliation; recompense

NETTLE (NET ul) *v.* to annoy or irritate
  similar: vex; perturb; peeve; irk; chafe; abrade; exasperate
  contrary: allay; ease; alleviate; pacify; mollify; placate; assuage

NIGGLING (NIG leeng) *adj.* tending to dwell on minor or trivial points
  similar: picayune; pedantic; petty; carping; belaboring; quibbling; trifling

NONPLUS (non PLUS) *v.* to bring to a halt by confusion; perplex
  similar: stupefy; bewilder; confound; baffle; addle; befuddle
  contrary: clarify; elucidate; explicate

NOSTALGIC (nuh STAHL jik) *adj.* longing for the past
  similar: homesick; yearning; sentimental; mawkish; maudlin

NOXIOUS (NAHK shyus) *adj.* harmful to health; injurious
  similar: toxic; deleterious; baneful; virulent; pernicious; pestiferous; lethal; malignant
  contrary: salubrious; salutary; healthful; hygienic; tonic

NUBILE (NOO byl) *adj.* suitable for marriage (referring to a young woman), especially in physical development
  similar: eligible; maturated; ripe; precocious
  contrary: juvenile; pubescent; puerile

OBLIVION (uh BLIV ee un) *n.* the state of being forgotten (especially by the public)
  similar: vacuity; temporalness; obsolescence
  contrary: remembrance; amanuensis; reminiscence; nostalgia; memoir

OBSOLETE (ahb suh LEET) *adj.* out of date; no longer useful
  similar: outmoded; antiquated; archaic; anachronistic; vintage
  contrary: contemporary; prevailing; serviceable; utilitarian

OBTUSE (ahb TOOS) *adj.* slow to understand; insensitive (literally, blunt)
  similar: undiscerning; doltish; dull; dimwitted; moronic
  contrary: perspicacious; keen; astute; discerning

ODYSSEY (AH duh see) *n.* a long, eventful journey
similar: trek; peregrination; excursion; pilgrimage; junket; safari; transhumance; migration

OGLE (AW gul) *v.* to glance flirtatiously at
similar: eye; stare; leer; gape

ONUS (OH nus) *n.* burden or responsibility
similar: accountability; liability; culpability

OPULENCE (AHP yoo luns) *n.* wealth; luxury
similar: affluence; prosperity; privilege; indulgence; extravagance
contrary: destitution; pauperism; mendicancy; indigence

ORDINATE (OR dih nit) *adj.* fundamental; primary
similar: rudimentary; basal; inchoate; axiomatic; chief; capital; cardinal; axial; definitive; incisive
contrary: subordinate; subsidiary; subservient; auxiliary; ancillary

OUST (OWST) *v.* to force out or expel
similar: banish; evict; exile; ostracize; extradite

OVERT (oh VERT) *adj.* out in the open; not hidden
similar: perceptible; apparent; manifest; evident; palpable
contrary: covert; camouflaged; shrouded; veiled; clandestine; surreptitious

Quiz Time (M–O)

Directions: Match each numbered word in the left column with its lettered definition in the right column. The answer key begins on page 237.

1.	manumit	a.	annoy or irritate
2.	mendacity	b.	bring to a halt by confusion
3.	mephitic	c.	deceit or fraud
4.	mollify	d.	agent of punishment
5.	necromancy	e.	fundamental
6.	nemesis	f.	glance flirtatiously at
7.	nettle	g.	luxury
8.	nonplus	h.	magic involving the dead
9.	obtuse	i.	offensive to the smell
10.	ogle	j.	pacify or appease
11.	opulence	k.	release from slavery
12.	ordinate	l.	slow to understand

P–R

PALL (PAWL) *n.* something that covers over, especially in darkness or gloom; *v.* to become wearisome, tiresome, or unpleasant
> *similar:* shroud; cloy; surfeit; glut; oppress

PALLID (PAL id) *n.* pale or deficient in color (as from fear or ill health)
> *similar:* sallow; wan; ashen; anemic; waxen; blanched
> *contrary:* flushed; ruddy; rosy; cerise; rubicund; sanguine

PAN (PAN) *v.* to criticize harshly
> *similar:* censure; reprove; chastise; reprimand; reproach; remonstrate; inveigh; disapprobate; reprobate
> *contrary:* acclaim; extol; plaudit; laud; hail; adulate; commend; approbate; panegyrize; eulogize

PARLEY (PAR lee) *n.* a conference
> *similar:* council; intercourse; dialogue; rendezvous; tryst

PAROCHIAL (puh ROH kee ul) *adj.* narrow or limited in scope
   similar: provincial; insular; sectarian
   contrary: pandemic; universal; rife; epidemic

PERIPHERAL (per IF er ul) *adj.* pertaining to the outer region of something (as opposed to the core or center)
   similar: marginal; ambient; extraneous; extrinsic; auxiliary; ancillary
   contrary: nuclear; chief; capital; cardinal; axial; definitive; incisive; fundamental; primary; ordinate; axiomatic

PLATITUDE (PLAT ih tood) *n.* a trite remark; hackneyed statement
   similar: banality; truism; inanity; apothegm; maxim; adage; proverb; aphorism

POSEUR (poh ZYOOR) *n.* a person who pretends to be sophisticated or elegant in order to impress others
   similar: feigner; parvenu; upstart

PRATTLE (PRAT ul) *v.* to speak in a childish manner; babble
   similar: jabber; twaddle; chatter; drivel; gibberish

PUERILE (PYOOR yl) *adj.* pertaining to a child
   similar: callow; nubile; fledgling; pubescent; juvenile; green
   contrary: hoary; grizzled; ancient; ripened; antique; decrepit; doddering

PURLOIN (per LOYN) *v.* to steal or take dishonestly
   similar: pilfer; misappropriate; abscond; peculate; embezzle; foist

QUAFF (KWAHF) *v.* to drink with relish
   similar: guzzle; swig; imbibe; swill; ingurgitate; partake

QUAIL (KWAYL) *v.* to shrink with fear
   similar: cower; recoil; cringe; shudder; flinch; wince

QUAINT (KWAYNT) *adj.* unusual in a charming way
   similar: curious; peculiar; eccentric

QUALMS (KWAWLMS) *n.* misgivings; doubts
   similar: scruples; hesitance; skepticism; leeriness; wariness; reluctance; mistrust; trepidation; dread; circumspection

QUARRY (KWOR ee) *n.* a hunt or the object of a hunt; *v.* to extract stone from the earth's surface
 similar: pursuit; chase; prey; excavate

QUASH (KWAHSH) *v.* to put down or suppress
 similar: quell (see below)

QUAVER (KWAY ver) *v.* to shake tremulously
 similar: tremble; shiver; shudder; quiver

QUELL (KWEL) *v.* to put down or suppress
 similar: quash; subdue; squelch; allay; stifle; quench; vanquish
 contrary: spur; induce; promote; facilitate; provoke; goad; incite; foment; instigate

QUIBBLE (KWIH bul) *v.* to nitpick; to evade an issue by making irrelevant points
 similar: carp; cavil; gripe; elude; parry; muddle; obfuscate

QUIP (KWIP) *n.* a witty or sarcastic remark
 similar: mockery; insult; gibe; jeer; satire; banter; ridicule; derision

RABID (RAB id) *adj.* irritatingly extreme in opinion; raging violently
 similar: fanatic; frenzied; ultraistic; maniacal; fervent; fervid; ardent

RAIMENT (RAY munt) *n.* clothing; attire
 similar: vestments; garb; garments; apparel; habits; accouterments; ensemble; finery; regalia; trimmings; frippery

RAMPART (RAM part) *n.* a small mound of earth used defensively in battle
 similar: barrier; fortification; impediment; barricade; bar; blockade; bastion; escarpment; barbican; hummock; hillock

RAREFIED (RAYR ih fyd) *adj.* lofty; made less dense (as in rarefied gases)
 similar: exalted; esoteric; diffused; thinned; ethereal; vaporous

RECOURSE (REE kors) *n.* access to assistance in time of trouble
 similar: resort; aid; relief; succor; avail; remedy

REJUVENATE (ree JOO vuh nayt) *v.* to make fresh or young again
 similar: refresh; revitalize; reinvigorate; revive; reanimate; enliven; exhilarate; resuscitate

RELENT (re LENT) *v.* to surrender or give in
  similar: yield; capitulate; relinquish; cede; abdicate; succumb; acquiesce

RELIC (REL ik) *n.* a surviving memorial from the past
  similar: artifact; curio; vestige; remnant; bibelot; antique; memento

REPRIEVE (ruh PREEV) *v.* to delay punishment
  similar: suspend; defer; adjourn; pardon

REPRISAL (rih PRY zul) *n.* the infliction of an injury in return for an injury done
  similar: revenge; recompense; vengeance; vendetta

REQUITE (ruh QUYT) *v.* to repay; pay back
  similar: recompense; remunerate; reimburse; rebate; vindicate; avenge
  contrary: (be in) arrears; owe; withhold

RETRIBUTION (ret rih BYOO shun) *n.* vengeance
  similar: revenge; vindication; requital; recompense; retaliation

RIFT (RIFT) *n.* a break or opening
  similar: chasm; fissure; breach; crevice; cranny; cleft; aperture; orifice

RUFFIAN (RUF yun) *n.* a bully
  similar: scoundrel; miscreant; hooligan; thug

Quiz Time (P–R)

Directions: Match each numbered word in the left column with its lettered definition in the right column. The answer key begins on page 237.

1.	parley	a.	clothing
2.	parochial	b.	conference
3.	poseur	c.	make fresh or young again
4.	purloin	d.	misgivings or doubts
5.	quail	e.	narrow or limited in scope
6.	qualms	f.	opening
7.	quaver	g.	pay back
8.	quip	h.	pretending to be sophisticated
9.	raiment	i.	shake tremulously
10.	rejuvenate	j.	shrink with fear
11.	requite	k.	steal
12.	rift	l.	witty or sarcastic remark

S–U

SAGA (SAH guh) *n.* a myth or legend
  similar: tale; epic; fable; allegory; parable

SARTOR (SAR tor) *n. a* tailor
  similar: couturier

SCABBARD (SKAB erd) *n.* a case for a sword or other blade
  similar: sheath; quiver; holster

SCATHED (SKAYTHD) *adj.* harmed; injured
  similar: wounded; damaged; aggrieved; impaired

SCOTCH (SKAHCH) *v.* to injure so as to make harmless; to stamp out
  similar: foil; hinder; thwart; arrest; impede; forestall; preclude; interdict; sabotage; undermine; maim

SCOURGE (SKORJ) *v.* to whip (especially, as punishment)
similar: lash; switch; cane; chastise; castigate; discipline

SCRUPLE (SKROO pul) *n.* a moral or ethical consideration giving rise to hesitancy or doubt
similar: qualms; misgivings; demurral; conscience; unwillingness; leeriness; wariness; reluctance

SCURRILOUS (SKER uh lis) *adj.* obscene; indecent
similar: lewd; vulgar; uncouth; indecorous; lascivious; licentious; unsavory; libertine; bawdy; ribald
contrary: seemly; decorous; befitting; scrupulous; genteel; courtly

SEINE (SAYN) *n.* a type of fishing net
similar: snare; lure; trap

SHUN (SHUN) *v.* to stay away from; avoid
similar: eschew; avert; abstain; evade; elude; spurn; snub
contrary: embrace; enfold; welcome

SHUNT (SHUNT) *v.* to shove out of the way; turn aside
similar: reject; jettison; shed; discard

SPARTAN (SPAR tun) *adj.* characterized by a plain, simple lifestyle; undaunted and disciplined
similar: ascetic; severe; harsh; rigorous; unadorned; austere; stern
contrary: luxurious; opulent; lavish; elegant; indulgent; epicurean

SQUALID (SKWAH lid) *adj.* neglected, dirty, or poor (especially, living conditions)
similar: seedy; ramshackle; shabby
contrary: tidy; immaculate

STENTORIAN (sten TOR ee un) *adj.* extremely loud
similar: clamorous; boisterous; obstreperous; strident; plangent; tumultuous; forte; rambunctious; riotous; turbulent
contrary: quiescent; mute; tacit; placid; serene; sedate; staid; subdued; tranquil

SUBORN (suh BORN) *v.* to induce another in an unlawful manner; to persuade another to commit an unlawful act
similar: bribe; inveigle; entrap; coax; corrupt; deprave; beguile; seduce; entice; allure

SUNDRY (SUN dree) *adj.* various; diverse
  similar: variegated; myriad; multifarious

SVELTE (SVELT) *adj.* gracefully slender
  similar: lithe; willowy; lissome

SYBARITE (SIB uh ryt) *n.* a person devoted to luxury or pleasure
  similar: epicurean; voluptuary; hedonist; debauchee

TAPER (TAY per) *v.* to become narrower; *n.* a candle
  similar: cramp; contract; squeeze; compress; constrict; obelisk; pyramid; carafe
  contrary: distend; widen; splay; flare; flute

TEDIUM (TEE dee um) *n.* boredom; weariness
  similar: ennui; monotony; fatigue; pall; apathy; dullness; repetitiveness
  contrary: scintillation; exuberance; titillation; jubilation; ado; melodrama

TEPID (TEH pid) *adj.* luke warm (neither cold nor hot)
  similar: indifferent; apathetic; nonchalant; impassive; sedate

TETHER (TEH ther) *v.* to tie with a rope
  similar: leash; fetter; manacle; moor; berth; anchor

THRONG (THRAWNG) *n.* a large crowd
  similar: horde; swarm; host; multitude

TITHE (TYTH) *n.* a tax of one tenth (*v.* to give one tenth as a tax or donation)
  similar: levy; tariff; toll; duty; assessment

TOADY (TOH dee) *n.* a fawning flatter; a "yes-man"
  similar: acolyte; lackey; minion; entourage; retinue

TOCSIN (TAHK sin) *n.* an alarm, bell, or other signal
  similar: knell; portent; foretoken; omen

TRAVAIL (truh VAYL) *n.* laborious, arduous work
  similar: drudgery; toil; labor; moil

TRYST (TRIST) *n.* an appointment for a meeting (especially, a secretive meeting of lovers)
  similar: rendezvous; engagement; parley

TUTELAGE (TOO tuh lij) *n.* training under the guidance and protection of another
  similar: apprenticeship; guardianship; conservatorship; custody

TYRO (TY roh) *n.* a beginner
  similar: novice; neophyte; apprentice; amateur; rookie; greenhorn; proselyte

UNCANNY (un KAN ee) *adj.* mysterious; weird
  similar: eerie; bizarre; peculiar; inexplicable; aberrant; deviant; anomalous

UNCONSCIONABLE (un KAHN shun uh bul) *adj.* in violation of one's conscience
  similar: unscrupulous; corrupt; unethical; amoral; venal; sordid
  contrary: conscionable; just; equitable

UNGAINLY (un GAYN lee) *adj.* clumsy; awkward
  similar: inept; maladroit; oafish; gauche; bungling; loutish

UNGUENT (UN gwent) *n.* ointment
  similar: liniment; emollient; salve; balm; cerate; unction

UNREQUITED (un ruh KWY tid) *adj.* not reciprocated
  similar: unilateral; unrecompensed; delinquent; owing; due
  contrary: reciprocated; recompensed; remunerated; reimbursed; rebated; avenged;
    vindicated

UNWIELDY (un WEEL dee) *adj.* cumbersome or awkward
  similar: unmanageable; bulky; clumsy
  contrary: manageable; controllable; yielding; compliant; cooperative; acquiescent

UNWITTING (un WIT een) *adj.* unknowing; unaware; unintentional
  similar: ignorant; oblivious; inadvertent; involuntary
  contrary: witting; cognizant; deliberate; willful; voluntary; intentional

UPSTART (UP start) *n.* a person who has become arrogant as a result of a sudden
rise to a position of importance
  similar: parvenu; elitist; snob; opportunist

UTOPIA (yoo TOH pee uh) *n.* an imaginary place of political and social perfection
  similar: paradise; consummation; nirvana; millennium

UXORIOUS (uk SOR ee us) *adj.* overly devoted or submissive to one's wife
  similar: doting; fawning; indulgent

Quiz Time (S–U)

Directions: Match each numbered word in the left column with its lettered definition in the right column. The answer key begins on page 237.

1.	scabbard	a.	appointment for a meeting
2.	scourge	b.	awkward
3.	shunt	c.	case for a sword
4.	stentorian	d.	extreme violation of conscience
5.	sundry	e.	extremely loud
6.	tether	f.	large crowd
7.	throng	g.	shove out of the way
8.	tryst	h.	to tie with a rope
9.	tutelage	i.	to whip as punishment
10.	unconscionable	j.	training under guidance of another
11.	ungainly	k.	unknowing or unintentional
12.	unwitting	l.	various or diverse

V–Z

VAINGLORIOUS (vayn GLOR ee us) *adj.* excessively proud of one's accomplishments
> *similar:* vain; boastful; conceited; egotistical; haughty; pompous; arrogant
> *contrary:* retiring; unpretentious; unobtrusive; decorous

VANTAGE (VAN tij) *n.* an advantageous position or condition
> *similar:* benefit; boon; privilege

VAPID (VAP id) *adj.* lacking liveliness, spirit, or flavor
> *similar:* insipid; stale; banal; mundane; prosaic; phlegmatic; insouciant
> *contrary:* effervescent; ebullient; vivacious; savory

VARIEGATED (VAYR ee uh gay tid) *adj.* varied in appearance, especially in color
> *similar:* kaleidoscopic; polychromatic; dappled; motley; prismatic; mottled; mosaic; multifarious

VAUNT (VAWNT) *v.* to speak boastfully (vaingloriously) of
> *similar:* brag; flaunt; gloat; tout; brandish; publicize

VENTURESOME (VEN cher sum) *adj.* daring; hazardous
similar: venturous; audacious; intrepid; treacherous; perilous; jeopardous

VERGE (VERJ) *n.* edge; border
similar: threshold; brink; precipice; brim

VESPERTINE (VES per teen) *adj.* pertaining to or occurring during the evening
similar: crepuscular; nocturnal
contrary: diurnal

VICTUALS (VIK chyools) *n.* food; meals
similar: fare; comestibles; pabulum; pap; fodder; viand

VIE (VY) *v.* to compete
similar: contend; contest; rival; endeavor; clash; spar

VITRIOLIC (vit ree AH lik) *adj.* severely sarcastic or caustic
similar: scathing; sardonic; acerbic; mordant; trenchant; acrimonious; pungent

VOUCHSAFE (VOWCH sayf) *v.* to grant condescendingly; to guarantee
similar: bestow; endow; bequeath; ensure; pledge; warrant

WAFFLE (WAH ful) *v.* to straddle an issue or refuse to commit oneself to a position
similar: equivocate; waver

WAIF (WAYF) *n.* a person (especially a child) or animal without a home
similar: stray; orphan; urchin; rogue; foundling; ragamuffin; tatterdemalion

WARBLE (WOR bul) *v.* to sing in a birdlike manner
similar: cheep; twitter; coo; chirrup; whistle

WASTREL (WAY strul) *adj.* extremely or lavishly wasteful, especially with money
similar: prodigal; spendthrift; squanderer; profligate
contrary: frugal; penurious; sparing; provident; thrifty; parsimonious; miserly; illiberal

WEAN (WEEN) *v.* to break away from a dependency (especially, a baby's dependency on its mother)
similar: disengage; disentangle

WELTER (WEL ter) *v.* to roll, heave, or writhe
similar: flounder; wallow

WHEEDLE (WEE dul) *v.* to deceive or persuade by flattery
similar: cajole; coax; entice; inveigle; lure; seduce; beguile; hoax

WHIT (WIT) *n.* a tiny particle
similar: scintilla; bit; morsel; iota; shred; trace; fleck; minutia

WISTFUL (WIST ful) *adj.* characterized by a sad longing or yearning
similar: nostalgic; sentimental; melancholy; plaintive; lugubrious; pensive

WOE (WOH) *n.* misery; sorrow; grief
similar: affliction; distress; wretchedness; torment; melancholy
contrary: elation; mirth; glee

WRY (RY) *adj.* distorted, twisted, or devious (especially, a sense of humor)
similar: sly; insidious; crafty; foxy; vulpine; askew; awry; aslant; tortuous; serpentine; convoluted; vermicular

XANTHOUS (ZAN thus) *adj.* yellow or yellowish

XENOPHOBIA (zee nuh FOH bee uh) *n.* an unreasonable fear of strangers, foreigners, or anything foreign, strange, or different

XYLOID (ZY loyd) *adj.* resembling wood; woodlike
similar: ligneous

YELP (YELP) *v.* to cry sharply (as a dog)
similar: bark; shriek; yap; squeal; bellow

YIELD (YEELD) *v.* to surrender, give in, or submit
similar: relent; capitulate; defer; relinquish; cede; abdicate; succumb; acquiesce; comply; assent; accede
contrary: contravene; impede; thwart

YOKE (YOHK) *n.* a device for joining (linking) two things together; oppression, domination, or harnessing
similar: bridle; fetter; cinch; muzzle; halter

YOKEL (YOH kul) *n.* a country bumpkin
  similar: hayseed; boor; churl; rustic; peasant; curmudgeon
  contrary: urbanite; bourgeois

YORE (YOR) *n.* time past
  similar: ancient; antiquity; bygone; quondam; antecedent; anterior; erstwhile; antediluvian

ZENITHAL (ZEE nuh thul) *adj.* upright; erect
  similar: vertical; perpendicular; plumb

ZING (ZING) *n.* vitality; energy; animation
  similar: verve; vim; vigor; zest; zeal; esprit; gusto; ebullience

ZODIACAL (zoh dee AK ik) *adj.* pertaining to the heavens (especially, to an imaginary belt over which celestial bodies pass)
  similar: cosmic; astrologic; astronomic; universal; celestial; sidereal

ZONULE (ZOHN yul) *n.* a little zone (designated area)
  similar: band; belt

ZOOPHAGOUS (ZOO fih gus) *adj.* meat-eating
  similar: carnivorous; predatory

Quiz Time (V–Z)

Directions: Match each numbered word in the left column with its lettered definition in the right column. The answer key begins on page 237.

1.	vapid	a.	grant condescendingly
2.	variegated	b.	homeless
3.	vaunt	c.	lacking spirit or flavor
4.	vitriolic	d.	persuade by flattery
5.	vouchsafe	e.	sarcastic or caustic
6.	waif	f.	sing in a birdlike manner
7.	warble	g.	speak boastfully of
8.	wheedle	h.	time past
9.	whit	i.	tiny particle
10.	xanthous	j.	upright or erect
11.	yore	k.	varied in color
12.	zenithal	l.	yellowish

Quiz Time—Answers (A–Z)

Quiz (A–C)

1.	c	4.	f	7.	g	10.	k
2.	b	5.	d	8.	j	11.	a
3.	e	6.	i	9.	h	12.	l

Quiz (D–F)

1.	d	4.	l	7.	c	10.	b
2.	g	5.	f	8.	j	11.	e
3.	a	6.	i	9.	k	12.	h

Quiz (G–I)

1.	l	4.	b	7.	a	10.	j
2.	f	5.	c	8.	g	11.	h
3.	e	6.	k	9.	i	12.	d

Quiz (J–L)

1.	e	4.	c	7.	k	10.	i
2.	a	5.	l	8.	d	11.	j
3.	g	6.	h	9.	f	12.	b

Quiz (M–O)

1.	k	4.	j	7.	a	10.	f
2.	c	5.	h	8.	b	11.	g
3.	i	6.	d	9.	l	12.	e

Quiz (P–R)

1.	b	4.	k	7.	i	10.	c
2.	e	5.	j	8.	l	11.	g
3.	h	6.	d	9.	a	12.	f

Quiz (S–U)

1.	c	4.	e	7.	f	10.	d
2.	i	5.	l	8.	a	11.	b
3.	g	6.	h	9.	j	12.	k

Quiz (V–Z)

1.	c	4.	e	7.	f	10.	l
2.	k	5.	a	8.	d	11.	h
3.	g	6.	b	9.	i	12.	j

33 **Word Games**
for Smart Test-Takers

You'll need a pencil for Chapter 8, which provides a highly interactive approach to reviewing words from the other chapters in this book. You'll also encounter a few new words here. Each game in this chapter calls for you to either

- **match** a word with a descriptive word or phrase
- **pair** together synonyms and other related words
- divide a list of words into **groups** by definition

As you tackle these games, **your job is to look for the "best" match** among the available words in a list. In some cases, the best match may be pairs or groups of words that aren't *perfect* synonyms. That's because these are just the kinds of *imperfect* associations you will be asked to make on your test.

As you **check your responses** for the games, earmark those words that are still giving you trouble, then look them up in earlier chapters (using the index) as a final review for your exam.

Game 1: Respect Yourself

18 words about respect, honor, and praise (answers on page 260)

Determine which of the following five numbered words or phrases best describes each word in the list that follows. Write the number of your answer choice on the line to the left of each entry.

1. praise
2. an expression of praise
3. approval
4. an expression of approval
5. respect

___ accreditation	___ encomium	___ laudation
___ adulation	___ eulogy	___ obeisance
___ approbation	___ extol	___ panegyric
___ benediction	___ homage	___ ratification
___ deference	___ imprimatur	___ revere
___ doxology	___ kudos	___ sanction

Game 2: Rebel Razers and Rabble Rousers

11 words about destruction and rebellion (answers on page 261)

Determine which of the following three numbered phrases best describes each word in the list that follows. Write the number of your answer choice on the line to the left of each entry. *Note:* there is one oddball word that does not fit squarely into any of the three groups.

1. demolish
2. rebel
3. break or injure
• oddball

___ abrogate	___ incendiary	___ quisling
___ annihilate	___ lacerate	___ recreant
___ apostate	___ maim	___ rend
___ expunge	___ purloin	___ renegade

Game 3: Get a Job

18 words about occupations (answers on page 262)

Match each occupation in the lefthand column with the occupation in the righthand column that is most similar. Write the matching letter on the line to the left of each entry in the lefthand column.

___ actuary	a.	notary
___ apostle	b.	patron
___ bard	c.	storyteller
___ barrister	d.	clerk
___ concierge	e.	troubadour
___ conservator	f.	handyman
___ courtesan	g.	mercenary
___ curator	h.	sentinel
___ despot	i.	wine dealer
___ factotum	j.	farmer
___ impresario	k.	underwriter
___ incumbent	l.	courier
___ osteopath	m.	lawyer
___ purser	n.	chiropractor
___ raconteur	o.	fiduciary
___ scrivener	p.	candidate
___ vintner	q.	docent
___ yeoman	r.	potentate

Game 4: A Love-Hate Relationship

17 words about love and hate, like and dislike (answers on page 263)

For each word below, determine whether the word is closer in meaning to love (like) or hate (dislike), used either as a noun or a verb. Indicate your choice by writing "L" for "love" or "H" for "hate" on the line to the left of each word. *Note:* there is one oddball word that does not suggest either meaning.

- love (like)
- hate (dislike)
- oddball

___	abhor	___	delectation	___	penchant
___	abominate	___	execration	___	philogeant
___	amity	___	infatuation	___	pique
___	antipathy	___	loathe	___	predilection
___	bilk	___	odium	___	repugnant
___	captivate	___	narcissism	___	umbrage

Game 5: The Only Constant Is Change

10 words about the concept of change (answers on page 264)

Determine which of the four numbered words or phrases below best describes each word in the list that follows. Write the number of your answer choice on the line to the left of each entry. *Note:* there is one oddball word that does not fit squarely into any of the four groups.

1. change in behavior
2. change in form
3. substitution
4. constancy
- oddball

___	caprice	___	palimpsest	___	vagary
___	chameleon	___	succedaneum	___	vamp
___	fugacity	___	transmogrification	___	vicissitude
___	immutability	___	stasis		

Game 6: I Can See Clearly Now

17 words about the concept of clarity (answers on page 265)

Determine which of the five numbered words or phrases below best describes each word in the list that follows. Write the number of your answer choice on the line to the left of each entry. *Note:* there is one oddball word that does not belong in any of the five groups.

1. beyond understanding
2. to confuse
3. transparent
4. obvious or apparent
5. unclear or vague
• oddball

___ abstruse	___ hyaline	___ palpable
___ bewilder	___ limpid	___ patent
___ diaphanous	___ manifest	___ perspicacious
___ esoteric	___ muddle	___ recondite
___ fuliginous	___ nebulous	___ salient
___ hermetic	___ obfuscate	___ turbid

Game 7: Can I Take Your Order?

11 words about demands and requests (answers on page 265)

Determine whether each word in the following list is closer in meaning to demand (order) or request (plea), used either as a noun or a verb. Indicate your choice by writing "D" for "demand" or "R" for "request" on the line to the left of each word. *Note:* there is one oddball word that does not carry either meaning.

• demand or order
• request or plea
• oddball

___ adjuration	___ entreat	___ proscribe
___ beseech	___ impetration	___ repudiate
___ edict	___ implore	___ subpoena
___ enjoin	___ prescribe	___ supplicate

Game 8: Relatively Speaking
19 words about family relationships (answers on page 266)

Match each word in the lefthand column below to the word or phrase in the righthand column that best describes it. Write the matching letter on the line to the left of each entry in the lefthand column.

__ affinity	a.	a relative (family member)
__ agnation	b.	related by marriage
__ brood	c.	related by blood to a male ancestor
__ cognate	d.	one of the young of a beast
__ consanguineous	e.	multiple birth
__ fecundity	f.	pertaining to a child
__ filial	g.	pregnant
__ frugiferous	h.	ancestor
__ kin	i.	producing fruit
__ multiparous	j.	descendant
__ parturient	k.	father
__ patriarch	l.	related by blood
__ posterity	m.	offspring of a generation
__ procreate	n.	blood relationship on mother's side
__ progenitor	o.	a brother or sister
__ progeny	p.	to produce offspring
__ sibling	q.	giving birth to live young
__ viviparous	r.	young children of the same mother
__ whelp	s.	fertility

Game 9: It's All in the Altitude

13 words about highs and lows (answers on page 267)

For each word below, determine whether the word is closer in meaning to high or low. Indicate your choice by writing "H" for "high" or "L" for "low" on the line to the left of each word. *Note:* there is one oddball word that does not carry either meaning.

- high
- low
- oddball

___ abyss	___ excelsior	___ sublime
___ alluvial	___ fathom	___ supernal
___ apex	___ nadir	___ usury
___ appraise	___ pinnacle	___ zenith
___ benthal	___ scandent	

Game 10: There's No Place Like Home

17 words about homes, residences, and shelters (answers on page 267)

Determine which of the following four words or phrases best describes each word in the list that follows. Write the number of your answer choice on the line to the left of each entry. *Note:* there is one oddball word that does not belong squarely in any of the four groups.

1. home or permanent residence
2. temporary shelter
3. home for beasts
4. resident
- oddball

___ abode	___ denizen	___ nidus
___ berth	___ domicile	___ rookery
___ bivouac	___ herbarium	___ sojourner
___ cantonment	___ hostel	___ squatter
___ caravansary	___ hovel	___ yurt
___ columbary	___ lair	

Game 11: In the Mood

15 words about moods and dispositions (answers on page 268)

Determine which of the following three words or phrases best describes each word in the list that follows. Write the number of your answer choice on the line to the left of each entry. *Note:* there is one oddball word that does not belong squarely in any of the three groups.

1. cheerful
2. irritable
3. somber or gloomy
• oddball

___ acrimonious	___ irascible	___ pensive
___ bilious	___ jocular	___ petulant
___ buoyant	___ jocund	___ querulous
___ choleric	___ lugubrious	___ saturnine
___ demure	___ maudlin	
___ despondent	___ peevish	

Game 12: For Richer, for Poorer

18 words about wealth, poverty, and money (answers on page 269)

Divide the following list of 18 words into nine pairs of synonyms.

dowry	munificent	pilfer
emolument	parsimonious	profligate
impecunious	peculate	remuneration
largess	penurious	specie
lucre	penury	venal
mercenary	philanthropic	wastrel

Game 13: Good Versus Evil
16 words about morality (answers on page 270)

For each word below, determine whether the word is closer in meaning to righteous or depraved. Indicate your choice by writing "R" for "righteous" or "D" for "depraved" on the line to the left of each word. *Note:* there is one oddball word that does not suggest either meaning.

- righteous
- depraved
- oddball

__ altruistic	__ ignominious	__ opprobrious
__ beneficent	__ infamous	__ philanthropic
__ benevolent	__ licentious	__ pious
__ copious	__ magnanimous	__ reprobate
__ flagitious	__ nefarious	__ vile
__ heinous	__ odious	

Game 14: Let's Rock 'n Roll
12 words about motion (answers on page 270)

Determine which of the following three phrases best describes each of the words in the list that follows. Write the number of your answer choice on the line to the left of each entry. *Note:* there is one oddball word that does not belong in any of the three groups.

1. to swing or rock
2. to spin or rotate
3. to twitch or vibrate
- oddball

__ bandy	__ pirouette	__ vacillate
__ gyrate	__ quake	__ vellicate
__ librate	__ succuss	__ whirl
__ oscillate	__ turbinate	
__ perorate	__ undulate	

Game 15: It's about Time

14 words about times of the day and seasons of the year (answers on page 271)

Match each word in the lefthand column below to the word or phrase in the righthand column that best describes it. Write the matching letter on the line to the left of each entry in the lefthand column.

___ biennial		a.	summer
___ crepuscular		b.	hourly
___ diurnal		c.	daylight hours
___ estival		d.	spring
___ hibernal		e.	repeating
___ horary		f.	twilight
___ iterative		g.	morning
___ matutinal		h.	nighttime
___ nocturnal		i.	daily
___ perennial		j.	year-round
___ quotidian		k.	evening
___ tertian		l.	every third day
___ vernal		m.	every two years
___ vespertine		n.	winter

Game 16: The Cold Shoulder

10 words about interest and indifference (answers on page 271)

For each word below, determine whether the word is closer in meaning to passionate or indifferent. Indicate your choice by writing "P" for "passionate" or "I" for "indifferent" on the line to the left of each word. *Note:* there is one oddball word that does not suggest either meaning.

- passionate
- indifferent
- oddball

__ ardent	__ furtive	__ phlegmatic
__ avid	__ insouciant	__ procucurante
__ ebullient	__ nonchalant	__ smitten
__ fervent	__ perfunctory	

Game 17: Friend or Foe?

18 words about advocacy and opposition (answers on page 271)

Determine which of the following four words or phrases best describes each word in the list that follows. Write the number of your answer choice on the line to the left of each entry. *Note:* there are two oddball words that do not belong squarely in any of the four groups.

1. in favor of (pro)
2. opposed to (con)
3. biased (not indifferent)
4. indifferent or indecisive
- two oddballs

__ adherent	__ concomitant	__ predisposed
__ aficionado	__ espouser	__ recalcitrant
__ ambivalent	__ irresolute	__ stalwart
__ antagonistic	__ oppugning	__ tendentious
__ apposite	__ partisan	__ tepid
__ balking	__ phlegmatic	__ vacillating
__ bellicose	__ polemic	

Game 18: Indefinite Definitions

21 common words with uncommon meanings (answers on page 273)

Match each word in the lefthand column below to the word or phrase in the righthand column that best describes it. Write the matching letter on the line to the left of each entry in the lefthand column.

___ ape		a.	postpone
___ appropriate		b.	lessen vibration
___ crop		c.	tear
___ damp		d.	criticize
___ fault		e.	rind
___ fell		f.	dock
___ graft		g.	render harmless
___ list		h.	acquire
___ more		i.	ill-gotten gain
___ pan		j.	bare hill
___ rake		k.	custom
___ relief		l.	tilt
___ rent		m.	make suitable
___ scotch		n.	truncate
___ slip		o.	wasteful
___ spit		p.	raised
___ table		q.	straddle
___ tack		r.	mimic
___ temper		s.	skewer
___ waffle		t.	direction
___ zest		u.	fracture

Game 19: It's Quantity That Counts
11 words about numerical quantity (answers on page 273)

For each word below, determine whether the word is closer in meaning to many or few. Indicate your choice by writing "M" for "many" or "F" for "few" on the line to the left of each word. *Note:* there is one oddball word that does not suggest either meaning.

- many
- few
- oddball

__ dearth	__ legion	__ pleonasm
__ exiguous	__ maniple	__ profuse
__ galore	__ myriad	__ proscenium
__ innumerable	__ paucity	__ want

Game 20: The Fish That Got Away
14 words about size (answers on page 277)

Determine which of the following four words or phrases best describes each word in the list that follows. Write the number of your answer choice on the line to the left of each entry. *Note:* there is one oddball word that does not squarely belong in any of the four groups.

1. extremely large
2. large
3. small
4. extremely small
- oddball

__ capacious	__ exiguous	__ prodigious
__ commodious	__ infinitesimal	__ scintilla
__ corpulent	__ intumescent	__ sentient
__ diminutive	__ leviathan	__ tumid
__ epitome	__ modicum	__ turgid

Game 21: Pastimes and Passions
13 words about hobbies, avocations, and pastimes (answers on page 274)

Match each word in the lefthand column below to the word or phrase in the righthand column that is closest in meaning. Write the matching letter on the line to the left of each entry in the lefthand column.

___ debauchee	a.	apostate
___ demagogue	b.	scapegoat
___ dilettante	c.	savant
___ equestrian	d.	venal
___ iconoclast	e.	nemesis
___ incendiary	f.	proselytizer
___ kleptomaniac	g.	seditionist
___ martyr	h.	charlatan
___ mercenary	i.	peculator
___ mountebank	j.	courtesan
___ paramour	k.	aesthete
___ pundit	l.	jockey
___ vigilante	m.	epicure

Game 22: Sweaty Palms

14 words about fear, caution, and timidity (answers on page 276)

Determine which of the following four words or phrases best describes each word in the list that follows. Write the number of your answer choice on the line to the left of each entry. *Note:* there is one oddball word that does not belong in any of the four groups.

1. cautious or apprehensive
2. shy or reserved
3. pretended shyness
4. fearful or cowardly
• oddball

___ circumspect	___ diffident	___ solicitous
___ coquettish	___ garrulous	___ taciturn
___ coy	___ pudent	___ timorous
___ craven	___ pusillanimous	___ verecund
___ demure	___ reticent	___ wary

Game 23: Identical Twins

17 words about similarity and distinction (answers on page 273)

Divide the following list of 17 words into eight pairs of synonyms. *Note:* there is one oddball word that does not have a synonym.

aberration	commensuration	parity
accord	divergence	pasticcio
adumbration	effigy	rapport
cartoon	germane	semblence
coalesce	implicate	travesty
collateral	multifarious	

Game 24: Getting into Shape

15 words about physical shape (answers on page 278)

Match each word in the lefthand column below to the word or phrase in the righthand column that best describes it. Write the matching letter on the line to the left of each entry in the lefthand column.

___ acerate	a. heart-shaped
___ annular	b. club-shaped
___ aquiline	c. twisted
___ cardioid	d. abruptly angled
___ clavate	e. shrub-shaped
___ concave	f. needle-shaped
___ cuneiform	g. egg-shaped
___ dendriform	h. indented
___ geniculate	i. convex
___ gibbous	j. crescent-shaped
___ helix	k. wand-shaped
___ lunular	l. spiraling curve
___ ovoid	m. ring-shaped
___ tortuous	n. wedge-shaped
___ virgate	o. curved

Game 25: Talking Trilogies
16 words about spoken and written expression (answers on page 278)

Divide this list of words into five groups of three synonyms each. *Note:* there is one oddball word that is distinct in meaning from all of the other words on the list.

aphoristic	laconic	sententious
bombastic	loquacious	succinct
declamatory	magniloquent	terse
elocutionary	oratorical	turgid
garrulous	pithy	
glib	prolix	

Game 26: The Blame Game
19 words about disapproval, criticism, and punishment (answers on page 279)

Determine which of the following four words or phrases best describes each word in the list that follows. Write the number of your answer choice on the line to the left of each entry. *Note:* there is one oddball word that does not belong in any of the four groups.

1. to free from blame
2. to disapprove, criticize, or blame
3. to criticize or condemn abusively
4. to punish or discipline
•   oddball

___ absolve	___ excoriate	___ ostracize
___ acquit	___ exculpate	___ reprimand
___ castigate	___ execrate	___ reproach
___ censure	___ exonerate	___ reprove
___ chastise	___ fulminate	___ vindicate
___ deprecate	___ indict	___ vituperate
___ eschew	___ inveigh	

Game 27: Dam Is Not a Four-Letter Word

17 three-letter words (answers on page 280)

Match each word in the lefthand column below to the word in the righthand column that is nearest in meaning. Write the matching letter on the line to the left of each entry in the lefthand column.

___ apt	a.	cantilever
___ coy	b.	ballade
___ ebb	c.	abjure
___ err	d.	mezzanine
___ ewe	e.	tribulation
___ hap	f.	serendipity
___ hew	g.	gaffe
___ jut	h.	aspiration
___ ken	i.	purview
___ nib	j.	apposite
___ ode	k.	tortuous
___ pan	l.	laminated
___ ply	m.	rival
___ vie	n.	censor
___ woe	o.	fauna
___ wry	p.	demure
___ yen	q.	rend

Game 28: The Need for Speed
12 words about speed (answers on page 282)

For each word below, determine whether the word suggests quickness or slowness. Indicate your choice by writing "F" for "fast" or "S" for "slow" on the line to the left of each word. *Note:* there is one oddball word that does not suggest either one.

- fast
- slow
- oddball

__ adagio	__ dispatch	__ mercurial
__ apace	__ hermetic	__ perfunctory
__ celerity	__ languid	__ torpor
__ courser	__ largo	
__ dilatory	__ lethargy	

Game 29: Muscle Beach
19 words about strength and weakness (answers on page 282)

For each word below, determine whether the word suggests strength or weakness. Indicate your choice by writing "S" for "strength" or "W" for "weakness" on the line to the left of each word. *Note:* there is one oddball word that does not suggest either one.

- strength
- weakness
- oddball

__ asthenic	__ evanid	__ pith
__ atony	__ eviscerate	__ prepollent
__ debility	__ flaccid	__ prepotent
__ decrepit	__ geld	__ puissant
__ dint	__ impregnable	__ sinewy
__ emasculate	__ languor	__ stalwart
__ enervation	__ lassitude	

Game 30: Outstanding in Their Fields

14 more words about occupations (answers on page 283)

Match each word in the lefthand column with the word or phrase in the righthand column that best describes it. Write the matching letter on the line to the left of each entry in the lefthand column.

___ herpetology		a.	fish
___ husbandry		b.	clothing
___ ichthyology		c.	classification
___ masonry		d.	mediation
___ necromancy		e.	bricks
___ ombudsman		f.	birds
___ ornithology		g.	animal skins
___ pathology		h.	magic
___ pedagogy		i.	students
___ philately		j.	stamps
___ sartorial		k.	classic texts
___ scholiast		l.	reptiles
___ taxidermy		m.	domesticated animals
___ taxonomy		n.	disease

Game 31: I Cogitate, Therefore I Am

12 words about existence (answers on page 284)

Determine which of the following four words or phrases best describes each word in the list that follows. Write the number of your answer choice on the line to the left of each entry. *Note:* there is one oddball word that does not squarely belong in any of the four groups.

1. existing
2. newly existing
3. enduring or everlasting
4. temporary; not lasting
• oddball

__ aoristic	__ neonate	__ temporal
__ evanescent	__ perdurable	__ transient
__ extant	__ perennial	__ transitory
__ inchoate	__ protracted	
__ incipient	__ tangible	

Game 32: Less is More...More or Less

11 words about adding, reducing, and completeness (answers on page 284)

Determine which of the following four words or phrases best describes each word in the list that follows. Write the number of your answer choice on the line to the left of each entry. *Note:* there is one oddball word that does not belong in any of the four groups.

1. to fill or complete
2. to supplement or add
3. to lessen or reduce
• oddball

__ abate	__ ascititious	__ defalcate
__ acquiesce	__ attenuate	__ effectuate
__ aggrandize	__ augment	__ mitigate
__ append	__ consummate	__ sate

Game 33: Arm Twisting

14 words about human volition (answers on page 285)

Divide this list of words into seven pairs of synonyms. *Note:* there is one oddball word for which there is no synonym in this list.

alacrity	expostulate	refractory
caprice	extemporaneous	remonstrate
contumacious	impromptu	tenacious
ductile	obstreperous	tractable
ebullience	pertinacious	whim

Answers and Definitions

Game 1

1. praise

adulation excessive praise, often beyond that which is deserved
extol to praise
kudos praise; honor; glory
laudation praise or commendation

2. an expression of praise

benediction a recitation of praise (to god)
doxology a hymn of praise (to god)
encomium a formal expression of high praise
eulogy an oration in praise of a deceased person
panegyric an oration or writing in praise or commendation of a person or thing

3. approval

approbation approval; commendation
sanction to approve; in law, punishment or reward

4. an expression of approval

accreditation recognition as acceptable; approval and bringing into trust or favor
imprimatur an official license, approval, or sanction, especially to be published or printed
ratification official approval; sanction

5. respect

deference respect or courtesy shown; yielding to another's judgment, opinion, etc.
homage respect or reverence
obeisance a physical demonstration of respect (e.g., bowing or saluting)
revere to admire or respect greatly

Game 2

1. demolish

abrogate to put an end to, do away with, or set aside
annihilate to destroy completely
expunge to blot out, rub out, or obliterate

2. rebel

apostate a person who abandons a faith or cause
incendiary a person who willfully stirs up strife
quisling a traitor who collaborates with the enemy
recreant a traitor or apostate; coward
renegade a person who abandons a party or movement and defects to the other side; a traitor

3. break or injure

lacerate to tear jaggedly; to wound or hurt deeply
maim to deprive of some part of the body by wounding
rend to tear violently

oddball

purloin to steal or take dishonestly

Game 3

actuary a specialist or expert on statistics, especially in the area of insurance
underwriter a person whose job is to access, select and reject risks, usually for the purpose of determining insurability and insurance rates
(k)

apostle a person sent on a mission to deliver a special message; missionary
courier a messenger or deliverer carrying important or urgent messages or parcels
(l)

bard a prominent poet or other writer (of the renaissance period)
troubadour a poet-musician of the medieval period
(e)

barrister a counselor-at-law; attorney; lawyer
(m)

concierge a person who has charge of a building's entrance; doorkeeper; custodian or head porter
sentinel a sentry or guard
(h)

conservator one who is authorized to handle the property and/or personal affairs of another who is incapable of doing so for himself or herself
fiduciary one charged with the legal responsibility for administering and/or managing another's assets
(o)

courtesan a woman who prostitutes herself for hire; a prostitute
mercenary a person for hire, motivated primarily by money rather than loyalty
(g)

curator a person in charge of the artwork in a museum
docent a tour guide at a museum
(q)

despot a ruler having absolute power; tyrant; dictator
potentate a monarch, dictator, or similar person possessing great political power
(r)

factotum a handyman; one who performs various jobs
(f)

impresario a manager, promoter, or sponsor for performing artists
patron a person who supports a cause, endeavor, or person (e.g., a patron of the arts)
(b)

incumbent the holder of an office, especially a political office
candidate one who seeks an office, usually through election or appointment
(q)

osteopath a person (physician) who treats diseases by manipulating muscles and bones
chiropractor a medical practitioner who treats diseases by manipulation of body joints, especially the spine
(n)

purser a clerk on a passenger ship in charge of safekeeping money and possessions of crew and passengers
(d)

raconteur a skillful teller of stories and anecdotes
(c)

scrivener a professional or public copyist, scribe, or notary
notary a person officially authorized to authenticate legal documents (contracts, deeds, etc.)
(a)

vintner a purveyor or producer of wines
(i)

yeoman the owner of a small estate; a middle-class farmer
(j)

Game 4

love (like)

amity friendship
captivate to capture the affection of; to attract
delectation delight; enjoyment
infatuation foolish love
narcissism excessive love of oneself
penchant inclination; decided taste; bias
philogeant a lover of all good things
predilection a predisposition to prefer, like, or choose

hate (dislike)

abhor to detest or loathe; to shudder from
abominate to hate to the greatest degree
antipathy aversion; strong dislike
execration an expression of extreme and violent hatred; act of cursing or utter detestation
loathe to dislike greatly; detest
odium hatred; dislike
pique resentment at being slighted; a fit of displeasure
umbrage offense or resentment

oddball

bilk to deceive; defraud

Game 5

1. change in behavior

caprice sudden, whimsical, or unpredictable change
chameleon a lizardlike reptile noted for its color changes according to its temperament or to blend in with its environment
vagary odd or unexpected conduct; whim; caprice

2. change in form

transmogrification to change into a different shape; transform
vamp any piece added to an old thing to give it a new appearance; repair; patch

3. substitution

palimpsest a parchment written upon twice, the second writing replacing the first
succedaneum someone or something that replaces another; a substitute

4. constancy

immutability inability to change or vary
stasis equilibrium or inactivity caused by equality of opposing forces

oddball

fugacity volatility; uncertainty; instability

Game 6

1. beyond understanding

abstruse difficult to understand; esoteric
esoteric understood only by a select few with special knowledge
recondite difficult to understand; esoteric

2. to confuse

bewilder to confuse; befuddle
muddle to confuse or make unclear
obfuscate to confuse; make unclear or muddled

3. transparent

diaphanous sheer; almost transparent
hyaline glassy; transparent
limpid clear; transparent

4. obvious or apparent

manifest readily perceived or understood; evident; obvious
palpable readily or easily seen or perceived
patent evident; obvious
salient conspicuous; prominent; notable

5. unclear or vague

fuliginous smoky; sooty
nebulous hazy; vague; cloudy
turbid murky; unclear; muddled; confused

oddball

perspicacious discerning; having keen perception or judgment

Game 7

demand

enjoin to command or order someone to do something; to prescribe with authority
edict a decree or official command or order

prescribe to lay down as a rule or order to be followed
proscribe to prohibit; forbid
subpoena a court order compelling a witness to provide information or to be present at a court hearing

request

adjuration an earnest appeal; solemn urging
beseech to beg or plead urgently
entreat to request earnestly; beseech; implore
impetration a petition or request
implore to plead or beg; beseech
supplicate to request or petition humbly and earnestly

oddball

repudiate to deny or reject utterly

Game 8

affinity kinship based on marriage; fondness, attraction, or bond **(b)**
agnation blood relationship by a line of males only **(c)**
brood young children of the same mother, especially if nearly of the same age **(r)**
cognate blood relationship on the mother's side; also, of the same or a similar nature or stock **(n)**
consanguineous related by blood **(l)**
fecundity capacity to germinate or produce fruit; fertility **(s)**
filial pertaining to a child (son or daughter) **(f)**
frugiferous producing fruit; fruitful **(i)**
kin a relative (family member) **(a)**
multiparous producing more than one offspring at a birth **(e)**
parturient producing or about to produce young; fruitful **(g)**
patriarch father **(k)**
posterity all offspring (descendants) of a common ancestor or of a generation; succeeding generations; future times **(m)**
procreate to produce offspring **(p)**
progenitor ancestor; forefather; ascendant **(h)**
progeny descendants; offspring **(j)**
sibling a brother or sister **(o)**
viviparous giving birth to live young rather than laying eggs **(q)**
whelp one of the young of a dog or other beast; to bring forth or give birth to **(d)**

Game 9

high

apex peak; summit; pinnacle
excelsior loftier; still higher; ever upward
pinnacle apex; highest point
scandent climbing, especially plants that climb either by twining or with tendrils
sublime lifted up; lofty; elevated by joy
supernal being in a higher place or region; relating or belonging to things above; celestial; heavenly
usury an excessively high or illegal rate of interest
zenith the point on the celestial sphere directly overhead

low

abyss a great depth (e.g., of a gorge or ocean)
alluvial pertaining to sediment deposits, usually at the bottom of a body of water
benthal pertaining to the deepest zone or region of the ocean
fathom to reach the bottom of something; to understand thoroughly
nadir the point on the celestial sphere directly below the observer (the lowest point)

oddball

appraise to determine the market value of any property

Game 10

1. home or permanent residence

abode residence; dwelling; habitation
berth a place on a ship to reside or to sleep
domicile a place of permanent residence
hovel a small, poor cottage; hut

2. temporary shelter

bivouac an encampment for the night without tents or covering
cantonment temporary shelter, place of rest, or quarters for an army
caravansary a large unfurnished building where caravans rest at night

hostel an inn for travelers
yurt a circular, portable dwelling (used primarily in central Asia)

3. home for beasts

columbary dovecote; pigeon house
lair a resting place, especially for wild beasts
nidus nest; repository for the eggs; breeding place
rookery a breeding place of gregarious birds; a dilapidated building with many rooms and occupants

4. resident

denizen dweller or inhabitant of a country or region; an adopted or naturalized (non-native) citizen
sojourner one who dwells or lives in a place as a temporary resident or stranger
squatter one who settles upon land without a title in the property and without express consent of the owner

oddball

herbarium a collection of dried or preserved plants

Game 11

1. cheerful

buoyant light-hearted; vivacious; cheerful; also, tending to rise or float
jocular not serious; joking; facetious; jesting
jocund merry; cheerful; lively; sportive

2. irritable

acrimonious caustic, bitter, or stinging in behavior or speech
bilious ill-tempered; choleric; passionate; peevish
choleric characterized by anger; irascible
irascible easily provoked to anger
peevish cross, ill-tempered; fretful
petulant showing sudden irritation over minor annoyances; ill-humored
querulous characterized by complaining or whining; fretful

3. somber or gloomy

demure serious, grave, or staid; affectedly decorous or serious
despondent low-spirited; depressed
lugubrious mournful or sorrowful, especially ridiculously or feignedly so
pensive thoughtful; reflective; sober or sad
saturnine characterized by a gloomy temperament

oddball

maudlin excessively sentimental; easily moved to tears; also, drunk or given to drunkenness

Game 12

dowry money or property given by the bride's family to the bridegroom at marriage
largess a generous bestowal of gifts

emolument salary or other compensation for employment
remuneration payment for services

impecunious lacking money; penniless; indigent
penury poverty

lucre monetary gain; money
specie money in the form of coins

mercenary available for hire
venal capable of being bought or obtained for money or other consideration; mercenary

munificent very generous
philanthropic charitable (giving to charity)

parsimonious sparing in expenditure of money; frugal to excess
penurious excessively sparing in the use of money; stingy; miserly

peculate to steal or misuse public money entrusted to one's care
pilfer to steal repeatedly

profligate extravagant; recklessly wasteful
wastrel extremely or lavishly wasteful, especially with money

Game 13

righteous

altruistic concerned with the needs of others; generous
beneficent benevolent: kind-hearted
benevolent kind-hearted; generous
magnanimous noble or elevated in mind; generous
philanthropic charitable
pious devout

depraved

flagitious shamefully wicked; heinous; villainous
heinous reprehensible; abominable; odious
ignominious shameful; dishonorable; disgraceful
infamous notorious in disgrace or dishonor
licentious wantonly offensive; lawless; immoral; lewd; lascivious
nefarious depraved; wicked
odious offensive; disgusting; detestable; repugnant
opprobrious disgraceful; dishonorable; infamous; ignominious
reprobate vicious; unprincipled; depraved
vile morally base or evil

oddball

copious abundant; plentiful

Game 14

1. to swing or rock

bandy to beat to and fro; toss about
oscillate to move backward and forward; swing or sway; vary or fluctuate between fixed limits
undulate to cause to move backward and forward, or up and down in waves
vacillate to move one way and the other; reel back and forth; waver

2. to spin or rotate

gyrate to revolve around a central point; move spirally about an axis
pirouette to whirl or turn on one's toes

turbinate whirling, in the manner of a top
whirl to rotate or spin swiftly

3. to twitch or vibrate

librate to vibrate before resting in equilibrium
quake to tremble or shake
succuss to shake forcibly
vellicate to twitch or cause to twitch convulsively or spasmodically

oddball

perorate to make a speech

Game 15

biennial occurring (blossoming, sprouting) every two years **(m)**
crepuscular pertaining to twilight **(f)**
diurnal referring to or occurring during the daylight hours **(c)**
estival pertaining to summer **(a)**
hibernal relating to winter **(n)**
horary occurring once an hour; hourly **(b)**
iterative repeating **(e)**
matutinal pertaining to or functioning in the morning **(g)**
nocturnal pertaining to the darkness or to organisms active or functional at night **(h)**
perennial continuing through the year; perpetual; a plant that lives for two or more years **(j)**
quotidian occurring or returning daily; everyday (commonplace) **(i)**
tertian occurring every third day **(l)**
vernal relating to the spring **(d)**
vespertine pertaining to or occurring during the evening **(k)**

Game 16

passionate

ardent hot or burning, especially as to passions
avid eager; intensely desirous; greedy
ebullient excited; enthusiastic; animated
fervent passionate; ardent
smitten struck or affected with passion (e.g., love, fear, hatred)

indifferent

insouciant indifferent; unconcerned; without a care; carefree
nonchalant indifferent; careless; cool
perfunctory performed without care
phlegmatic not easily excited to action or passion; sluggish or heavy
procucurante unconcerned; nonchalant; indifferent

oddball

furtive sneaky; surreptitious; secretive

Game 17

1. in favor of (pro)

adherent follower; supporter; believer
aficionado a devoted follower
espouser one who advocates, promotes, or argue for
polemic a person who argues for or advocates a particular position (*adj* polemical)
stalwart a staunch supporter

2. opposed to (con)

antagonistic opposed to; hostile
balking stubbornly resisting; refusing to continue
bellicose inclined to argue or fight; hostile
oppugning reasoning or arguing against
recalcitrant stubbornly defiant

3. biased (not indifferent)

partisan advocating or favoring the views of one party
predisposed inclined beforehand
tendentious biased; advancing a point of view

4. indifferent or indecisive

ambivalent having conflicting emotions; wavering
irresolute unable to decide (make up one's mind)
phlegmatic apathetic; sluggish; unemotional; cool

tepid luke warm (neither cold nor hot)
vacillating moving one way, then the other; wavering

oddballs

apposite appropriate; suitable; apt; fitting
concomitant associated with; accompanying; connected

Game 18

ape to imitate, mimic, or impersonate **(r)**
appropriate to acquire for oneself **(h)**
crop to trim off or truncate **(n)**
damp to lessen a vibration **(b)**
fault a fracture in the earth's crust **(u)**
fell a bare, uncultivated rocky hill or mountain; to cut down (a tree) **(j)**
graft money or property gained through political corruption **(i)**
list to tilt from side to side **(l)**
more a custom or folkway considered essential to the welfare of a particular society **(k)**
pan to criticize harshly **(d)**
rake a wasteful person; a wicked or licentious person **(o)**
relief raised; projecting from a background surface **(p)**
rent a tear, split, or rupture **(c)**
scotch to injure so as to make harmless; to stamp out **(g)**
slip a water channel between piers where boats dock **(f)**
spit a pointed skewer to hold meat over coals or fire **(s)**
table to set aside temporarily; postpone **(a)**
tack the direction a vessel takes in relation to the wind **(t)**
temper to make suitable for a purpose **(m)**
waffle to straddle an issue or refuse to commit oneself to a position **(q)**
zest the outside rind of any citrus fruit which contains the essential oils used for flavoring **(e)**

Game 19

many

galore plentiful; in abundance
innumerable countless many
legion a great number; multitude

myriad a great number or variety
pleonasm redundancy of language in speaking or writing; the use of more words than are necessary to express the idea
profuse abundant; lavish

few

dearth lack of abundance; scarcity; poverty; paucity
exiguous scanty; meager; small; thin (in size or quantity)
maniple a handful; any small company of soldiers
paucity fewness; smallness of number; scarcity; exiguity; insufficiency
want scarcity; dearth

oddball

proscenium the front part of a stage, marked off at top by an arch

Game 20

1. extremely large

corpulent excessive fat; fleshy; obese
leviathan a large, great whale
prodigious extraordinary in bulk, extent, or quantity; marvelous or wonderful

2. large

capacious roomy; spacious
commodious spacious; roomy
intumescent swollen or enlarged, especially from heat
tumid swollen; inflated or pompous
turgid distended, swollen, or bloated beyond a natural state

3. small

epitome a compact or condensed representation of anything; brief summary
exiguous scanty; meager; small; thin (in size or quantity)
modicum a small quantity

4. extremely small

diminutive very small; tiny
infinitesimal infinitely or unquantifiably small
scintilla smallest particle; spark; iota

oddball

sentient having the power of one's senses

Game 21

debauchee a seeker of sensual pleasure
epicure a person dedicated philosophically to the pursuit of pleasure
(m)

demagogue a charismatic leader who persuades by appealing to emotions
proselytizer a person who attempts to convert others to his or her own belief system
(f)

dilettante a person who dabbles in the arts for amusement
aesthete a person who is concerned with or appreciates aesthetics—e.g., the fine arts
(k)

equestrian a rider on horseback
jockey one who rides horses in races
(l)

iconoclast a person who attacks cherished beliefs or traditions
apostate one who defects from or abandons one's faith, church, or principles
(a)

incendiary a person who maliciously starts fires to destructive fires; a person who inflames or incites others to quarrel and discontent
seditionist a person who incites others to rebel against the government or to resist lawful authority
(g)

kleptomaniac a person who has a compulsive desire to steal
peculator one who steals or misuses money or property entrusted to one's care
(i)

martyr a person who is persecuted for defending his or her religious principles
scapegoat a person forced to take the blame for the mistakes of others
(b)

mercenary for hire; motivated by a desire for money or personal gain
venal able to be bribed or bought; corruptible
(d)

mountebank a fraud; pretender; con artist
charlatan a fraud; quack; con artist
(h)

paramour an illicit lover
courtesan a prostitute, especially a mistress of a man of wealth or nobility
(j)

pundit an expert or authority
savant a learned person or scholar
(c)

vigilante one who takes justice into one's own hands
nemesis an agent or act of punishment or retribution
(e)

Game 22

1. cautious or apprehensive

circumspect cautious; wary; watchful
solicitous showing anxiety, uneasiness of mind, or concern (especially for the future well-being of others)
wary cautious; guarded; careful

2. shy or reserved

diffident lacking in self-confidence; timid; shy
pudent modest; bashful
reticent reserved; disposed to be silent
taciturn reserved in speech; inclined to be silent
verecund bashful; modest

3. pretended shyness

coquettish affectedly shy and modest, designed to attract
coy affectedly shy and modest
demure coyly (affectedly) shy and modest; reserved

4. fearful or cowardly

craven cowardly
pusillanimous lacking courage; characterized by a cowardly spirit
timorous fearful; timid

oddball

garrulous talkative; loquacious; inclined to speak

Game 23

aberration a deviation from what is normal, common, or morally right
divergence a deviation from a common point; branching

accord agreement or consensus
rapport a mutual understanding, accord, or sympathy that promotes communication

adumbration a faint sketch, outline, or shadow; an imperfect portrayal or representation
cartoon a preliminary sketch (drawing) or outline

coalesce to grow together, as similar parts; unite by natural affinity or attraction
implicate to bring into connection with; involve; interweave

collateral related to, but not strictly a part of, the main thing or matter under consideration
germane akin; closely allied; appropriate or fitting; relevant

commensuration equivalence in measure, degree, or extent
parity equality or equivalence; close correspondence

effigy an image, likeness, or representation of a person
semblence likeness or resemblance, either actual or apparent; similitude

pasticcio a work of art imitating directly the work of another artist (or of multiple artists)
travesty a ridiculous translation or imitation of a work

oddball

multifarious having great diversity or variety; made up of many differing parts

Game 24

acerate needle-shaped **(f)**
annular forming a ring; ringed; ring-shaped **(m)**
aquiline curving; hooked; prominent, like the beak of an eagle **(o)**
cardioid heart-shaped **(a)**
clavate club-shaped, growing gradually thicker toward the top **(b)**
concave hollow and curved; cupped; indented **(h)**
cuneiform wedge-shaped **(n)**
dendriform resembling a tree or shrub in structure **(e)**
geniculate bent abruptly at an angle, like the knee when bent **(d)**
gibbous shaped like the moon between its half-moon and the full-moon phases; convex **(i)**
helix a non-planar spiraling curve such as that formed by the thread of an ordinary screw **(l)**
lunular crescent-shaped (having the form of the new moon) **(j)**
ovoid egg-shaped **(g)**
tortuous twisted **(c)**
virgate wand-shaped; straight and slender **(k)**

Game 25

group 1

laconic brief and to the point; terse
succinct brief and to the point; concise; terse
terse to the point; concise; brief

group 2

aphoristic given to expressing oneself in aphorisms (short, pithy maxims or proverbs)
pithy given to expression in short, terse maxims and aphorisms
sententious pithy and terse in expression; trite; moralizing

group 3

bombastic pompous, high-sounding, as in speech or writing
magniloquent bombastic, pompous, or grandiose in talk or speech
turgid inflated, overblown, pompous (speech or talk)

group 4

declamatory speaking or writing purely for oratorical, persuasive, and rhetorical effect
elocutionary pertaining to the art of public speaking
oratorical pertaining to oratory—the art of formal speech

group 5

garrulous excessively talkative
loquacious talkative
prolix given to longwinded, lengthy speech or writing

oddball

glib expressing oneself fluently but with lack of thought, restraint, or sincerity

Game 26

1. to free from blame

absolve to free from blame; release from an obligation
acquit to clear from blame or fault, especially for a crime
exculpate to free from blame
exonerate to clear from blame
vindicate to clear from blame, accusation, or suspicion

2. to disapprove, criticize, or blame

censure to severely criticize or find fault with
deprecate to express disapproval of
indict to charge with a crime or accuse of wrongdoing
reprimand to formally scold, reprove, or rebuke
reproach to find fault with, blame, or scold
reprove to blame; rebuke; censure

3. to condemn or criticize abusively

excoriate to denounce or berate severely; to remove the skin from
execrate to curse or condemn; express abhorrence for
fulminate to denounce or condemn vehemently; to explode or erupt violently
inveigh to denounce or condemn
vituperate to censure harshly and abusively

4. to punish or discipline

castigate to punish, chastise, or criticize severely
ostracize to banish, exile, or exclude by general consent
chastise to discipline or restrain in order to correct or avoid unwanted (usually immoral) behavior

oddball

eschew to avoid or abstain from

Game 27

apt suitable; fitting
apposite appropriate; suitable; apt; fitting
(j)

coy pretending to be shy
demure coyly (affectedly) shy and modest; reserved or staid
(p)

ebb to recede or fall back (as the tide)
abjure to reject, disavow, or renounce under oath
(c)

err to make an error or mistake
gaffe a social blunder
(g)

ewe a female sheep
fauna animal life found in any particular region
(o)

hap chance or luck
serendipity accidental good fortune or luck
(f)

hew to cut into pieces with an ax or sword
rend to tear into pieces
(q)

jut to extend out; protrude
cantilever to project out from a vertical support
(a)

ken scope of knowledge
purview scope or range (of operation or understanding)
(i)

nib any projecting piece or part
mezzanine a low, extensive balcony above the ground floor of a building
(d)

ode a lyric poem marked by exalted feeling
ballade an instrumental piece, usually long, that is lyrical and romantic in style
(b)

pan to criticize harshly
censor to criticize
(n)

ply layered
laminated formed in layers
(l)

vie to compete
rival to try to equal or surpass; to compete with
(m)

woe misery; sorrow; grief
tribulation a great suffering, distress, or trouble
(e)

wry distorted, twisted, or devious (especially a sense of humor)
tortuous twisting; curving; winding; not direct or straight
(k)

yen yearning; longing
aspiration strong desire; longing
(h)

Game 28

quickness

apace at a quick pace; fast; speedily
celerity quickness; swiftness
courser a swift or spirited horse; a type of bird noted for its speed in running
dispatch to send off quickly and speedily
mercurial having the qualities the mythological god Mercury: swiftness; sprightliness; volatility
perfunctory performed in a careless or mechanical manner (usually quickly)

slowness

adagio in music, slowly, leisurely, and gracefully
dilatory prone to defer action; delaying; procrastinating; slow or sluggish
languid weak; weary; slow in progress
largo in music, very slow, solemn, and grave
lethargy abnormal drowsiness; lack of energy
torpor sluggishness; stupor

oddball

hermetic sealed to be airtight; mysterious

Game 29

strength

dint force; power
impregnable incapable of being subdued; unconquerable
pith the vital or essential part; concentrated force; vigor; strength
prepollent superior in power; predominant; prevalent
prepotent having superior power or influence
puissant powerful; strong; mighty; forcible (especially, a ruler or a nation)

sinewy well braced; strong; firm; tough
stalwart brave; bold; strong; daring; vehement

weakness

asthenic causing weakness; debilitating
atony lack of tone; weakness of the bodily system or organ
debility state of being weak; weakness; feebleness; languor
decrepit frail and feeble, especially due to age
emasculate deprive of virile, masculine power; castrate
enervation the act of weakening (reducing strength)
evanid liable to vanish or disappear; faint; weak; evanescent
flaccid soft and weak; flabby; lack of firmness and stiffness
geld castrate; emasculate; deprive of anything essential
languor feebleness; weakness; faintness; weariness
lassitude weariness; debility

oddball

eviscerate disembowel; remove the entrails or organs from; gut

Game 30

herpetology the study of reptiles **(l)**
husbandry exploitation of domesticated animals for consumption, load carrying, etc.**(m)**
ichthyology the study of fish **(a)**
masonry stonework or brickwork **(e)**
necromancy magic that involves the dead; witchcraft; sorcery **(h)**
ombudsman an intermediary between a citizen and the government who investigates complaints by citizens **(d)**
ornithology the study of birds **(f)**
pathology the study of the processes and causes of disease **(n)**
pedagogy the art or science of teaching **(i)**
philately the field of stamp collecting **(j)**
sartorial pertaining to tailors or tailoring (clothing) **(b)**
scholiast an ancient commentator or annotator of classic texts **(k)**
taxidermy preparing, stuffing, and displaying animal skins **(g)**
taxonomy the science or technique of classification (of animals, plants, etc.) **(c)**

Game 31

1. existing

extant still existing; not destroyed or lost; outstanding
tangible real or actual, as opposed to imagined

2. newly existing

inchoate recently begun or commenced; new in existence
incipient beginning to exist or to become manifest; commencing; initial
neonate newborn

3. enduring or everlasting

perdurable permanent; everlasting
perennial lasting for a long time
protracted prolonged; continued; extended

4. temporary; not lasting

evanescent fleeting; temporary; ephemeral
temporal pertaining to time, the present life, or this world (as opposed to an eternal spiritual life)
transient of short duration; not permanent; not lasting or durable
transitory passing ("in transit"); not permanent; existing only for a time

oddball

aoristic anxious or concerned about uncertain future events

Game 32

to fill or complete

consummate to complete or make perfect
effectuate to cause to happen; effect
sate to satisfy completely

to supplement or add

aggrandize to make greater, more powerful, or richer
append to add or attach to; annex
augment to make greater in size or extent

to lessen or reduce

abate to bring down or reduce in number or degree; lessen; diminish
attenuate to make slender or less dense; make less complex; weaken
defalcate to diminish, abate, or reduce in size
mitigate to lessen or reduce in severity or harshness

oddball

acquiesce to comply with or assent to passively, by one's lack of objection or opposition

Game 33

alacrity cheerful readiness or willingness
ebullience enthusiasm

caprice a sudden whimsical change or start in feeling, opinion, or action; temporary eccentricity
whim a sudden change or start of the mind; temporary eccentricity

contumacious obstinate; stubborn; disobedient; unyielding
refractory stubborn; unmanageable; disobedient; unruly

ductile easily led; complying; yielding to motives, persuasion, or instruction
tractable capable of being easily led, taught, or managed

expostulate to reason earnestly with a person about improper conduct, urging him or her to make redress or to desist
remonstrate to present and urge reasons against a course of action

extemporaneous acting without special preparation, especially in speaking
impromptu improvised; without previous study or preparation

pertinacious adhering persistently, resolutely, and obstinately to any plan or purpose
tenacious stubbornly persistent, purposeful; irresolute

oddball

obstreperous noisy; boisterous; clamorous

INDEX
—Main Entries